The Administrative Behavior
of Federal Bureau Chiefs

HERBERT KAUFMAN

The Administrative Behavior
of Federal Bureau Chiefs

THE BROOKINGS INSTITUTION
Washington, D.C.

THE BROOKINGS INSTITUTION is an independent organization devoted to nonpartisan research, education, and publication in economics, government, foreign policy, and the social sciences generally. Its principal purposes are to aid in the development of sound public policies and to promote public understanding of issues of national importance.

The Institution was founded on December 8, 1927, to merge the activities of the Institute for Government Research, founded in 1916, the Institute of Economics, founded in 1922, and the Robert Brookings Graduate School of Economics and Government, founded in 1924.

The Board of Trustees is responsible for the general administration of the Institution, while the immediate direction of the policies, program, and staff is vested in the President, assisted by an advisory committee of the officers and staff. The by-laws of the Institution state: "It is the function of the Trustees to make possible the conduct of scientific research, and publication, under the most favorable conditions, and to safeguard the independence of the research staff in the pursuit of their studies and in the publication of the results of such studies. It is not a part of their function to determine, control, or influence the conduct of particular investigations or the conclusions reached."

The President bears final responsibility for the decision to publish a manuscript as a Brookings book. In reaching his judgment on the competence, accuracy, and objectivity of each study, the President is advised by the director of the appropriate research program and weighs the views of a panel of expert outside readers who report to him in confidence on the quality of the work. Publication of a work signifies that it is deemed a competent treatment worthy of public consideration but does not imply endorsement of conclusions or recommendations.

The Institution maintains its position of neutrality on issues of public policy in order to safeguard the intellectual freedom of the staff. Hence interpretations or conclusions in Brookings publications should be understood to be solely those of the authors and should not be attributed to the Institution, to its trustees, officers, or other staff members, or to the organizations that support its research.

Foreword

PROFESSIONAL observers of the federal government have long taken virtually for granted the independence and great power of the heads of major bureaus in the executive departments. To many, their influence seemed too obvious to require examination. But Herbert Kaufman, suspecting that the belief might be based on a few conspicuous examples or on deduction rather than on the weight of empirical evidence, decided to observe the administrative behavior of six bureau chiefs in selected departments to try to find out whether the commonly accepted image applied to them.

He does not suggest that the six he studied were typical of all bureau chiefs in the federal government. But, he reasoned, if half a dozen "specimens" other than the most familiar and commonly cited ones led to different conclusions about the character of bureau chiefs' work and the part the chiefs play in the governmental system, some of our traditional precepts would have to be corrected. And even if the research only confirmed the traditional precepts, a close examination of the chiefs in action would provide a more complete portrait of the day-to-day activities of these government executives than was previously available.

He studied them for more than a year. This book sets forth his findings and conclusions. In some respects, they corroborate conventional lore of executive behavior, but in others they raise questions about the way we think of federal administrators, the federal administrative system and, indeed, large organizations generally. Because this book is aimed at an audience not intimately familiar with the administrative world of Washington, some parts of it will doubtless seem elementary and obvious to old Washington hands. But even they, I believe, will find instructive the panoramic vista of the job of the bureau chief, and will be intrigued and perhaps challenged by the inferences and speculations based on that perspective.

Herbert Kaufman's research was supported in part by a grant from the National Science Foundation. The views expressed here are the author's alone. They should not be ascribed to the National Science Foundation or to the trustees, officers, or other staff members of the Brookings Institution.

BRUCE K. MACLAURY
President

April 1981
Washington, D.C.

An Expression of Gratitude

I NEEDED the help of many people to conduct this study, but to none am I more indebted than to the seven bureau chiefs, identified in appendix C, whose cooperation was the sine qua non of the research. They were more generous, patient, understanding, and instructive than I had dared hope, and I am pleased to record publicly the depth of my appreciation.

Their generosity was rivaled by that of their staffs. People at all levels in the bureaus went out of their way to provide information and insights necessary for the study. Similarly, congressional staffers gave of their time and knowledge to help with the work. There are too many such debts to permit me to record them individually, but I want all my benefactors to know how grateful I am.

Without the exceptional ability and industry of Carmen J. Dupree, my assistant in 1978–79, the project would not have gotten off the ground, and I cannot imagine how I would have completed it without the help of Jill Ehrenreich, my assistant in 1979–80. They made a great contribution to this book, and I happily acknowledge my debt to them.

Five people read and commented on the manuscript, pointing the way to improvements and saving me from a number of errors. For this assistance, my thanks to my colleagues Martha Derthick and Paul Quirk, to Robert M. Ball and Robert C. Wood, and to one anonymous reader.

I also thank Elizabeth H. Cross, who edited the manuscript; Florence Robinson, who made the index; and David Morse, a virtuoso of word-processing, who kept track of the endless revisions and corrections of the manuscript, producing clean, legible copy from the mounds of paper I dumped on his desk.

The late Wallace S. Sayre, my friend and mentor for many years and a brilliant and original student of bureaus and bureau chiefs, contributed more to this book (and to much of my other work) than I can say. It was the late Arthur W. Macmahon, however, who first introduced me to the subject, and I was influenced also by Herbert A. Simon, especially through his *Administrative Behavior*. All three men are innocent of any implication in the form and content of this volume, but I doubt that the study would ever have been conducted had it not been for the stimulus and guidance they and their work provided.

H. K.

Contents

The Administrative Behavior
of Federal Bureau Chiefs

The Bureaus and Their Chiefs at the Time of This Study

ANIMAL AND PLANT HEALTH INSPECTION SERVICE (APHIS)
Francis J. Mulhern, administrator

CUSTOMS SERVICE
Robert E. Chasen, commissioner

FOOD AND DRUG ADMINISTRATION (FDA)
Donald Kennedy, commissioner

FOREST SERVICE*
John R. McGuire, chief
R. Max Peterson, chief

INTERNAL REVENUE SERVICE (IRS)
Jerome Kurtz, commissioner

SOCIAL SECURITY ADMINISTRATION (SSA)
Stanford G. Ross, commissioner

For profiles of the bureaus and their chiefs, see appendixes B and C.
* McGuire was replaced by Peterson during the year covered by this study.

CHAPTER ONE

Toward Filling a Gap

SEASONED observers of the Washington scene would probably come up with different lists if they were asked to identify the positions of leadership in the federal government. The criteria of leadership are ambiguous.

Nevertheless, I suspect that the chiefs of the major bureaus of the executive departments would be included in most of the lists. Although only a few bureau chiefs have ever attained wide popular recognition, people familiar with the workings of the government tend to ascribe to all of them a great deal of influence on governmental decisions and operations.

Despite their presumed importance, they have not been extensively studied. The odd disjunction between the power attributed to them and the dearth of information about them is what gave rise to this study.

SPARSELY STUDIED WIELDERS OF POWER

That they are important has seemed so obvious to some scholars as to require no proof. In their classic study of federal administrators (including, but not limited to, bureau chiefs) in 1939, Arthur W. Macmahon and John D. Millett declared, "The importance of the bureaus and the critical position of their heads in the line of command need no demonstration."[1]

I suspect that many observers of the governmental scene would repeat that sentiment today. Indeed, one chief—the late J. Edgar

1. *Federal Administrators: A Biographical Approach to the Problem of Departmental Management* (Columbia University Press, 1939), p. 307.

Hoover, director of the Justice Department's Federal Bureau of Investigation for almost half a century—became a household word throughout the country, if not the world. The significance of such officials is, by this standard, self-evident.

Of course, hardly any of the other scores of bureau chiefs in the federal government ever matched the widespread recognition achieved by Director Hoover or equaled his length of service in one position. Nevertheless, even if he is regarded as an aberration, authorities on public administration still seem to believe in the importance of this office.

Some of them implicitly derive its importance from the position and potential power of bureau chiefs as heads of organizations. For example, Macmahon and Millett remarked, "In the past, the relative absence of central managerial organs, together with the heterogeneous content of the departments, has made the bureaus often so autonomous that they have almost seemed the real departments."[2] A task force of the first Hoover Commission commented that "the bureau chief is in a formidable position to disregard a department head if he chooses to do so."[3] Leonard D. White, a pioneer in the study of public administration, reserved an entire section of the fourth edition of his long-lived textbook for the "tradition of bureau autonomy."[4] Francis E. Rourke, a leading student of bureaucratic power in America, said in 1969, "It is possible for an administrative agency to establish a position of virtually complete autonomy within the executive branch."[5] Another authority, when studying the U.S. Forest Service, in 1975 took it for granted that "to some degree, of course, all large bureaus, particularly those with highly specialized missions, enjoy considerable autonomy from the departments of which they are part."[6] Harold Seidman, long a high officer in the old Bureau of the Budget, noted in his 1980 analysis of the government, "Without the loyalty,

2. Ibid.

3. U.S. Commission on Organization of the Executive Branch of the Government, Task Force on Departmental Management, *Departmental Management in Federal Administration*, prepared for the commission (Government Printing Office, 1949), pp. 33–34; quotation from p. 34.

4. *Introduction to the Study of Public Administration*, 4th ed. (Macmillan, 1955), p. 78.

5. *Bureaucracy, Politics, and Public Policy*, 2d ed. (Little, Brown, 1976), p. 65.

6. Glen O. Robinson, *The Forest Service: A Study in Public Land Management* (Johns Hopkins University Press, 1975), p. 22.

or at least neutrality, of their principal bureau chiefs, [secretaries] can be little more than highly ornamental figureheads."[7] Or as one commentator on the transition to Ronald Reagan put it, "Watch the bureaus, not the cabinet. . . . The new administration's real tone will be determined less by those at the top than by the second line."[8] If these assertions, spanning a generation, are accurate, it stands to reason that bureau chiefs are figures to be reckoned with.

Some experts in governmental administration simply proclaim flatly, on the basis of their personal knowledge, that bureau chiefs are independent power centers. One bureau chief said, "We don't need the Department. We are perfectly able and willing to take care of ourselves."[9] An expert in administration wrote that "department heads may be said to be faced with a chronic state of mutiny in their bureaus."[10] And Richard E. Neustadt, in his assessment of the presidential office, put it this way:

Like our governmental structure as a whole, the executive establishment consists of separated institutions sharing powers. The President heads one of these; Cabinet officers, agency administrators, and military commanders head others. Below the department level, virtually independent bureau chiefs head many more.[11]

With so many students of government administration assuming, implying, or asserting the power and independence of bureau chiefs in the federal system, you might think the chiefs would have been examined in great detail over the years. But the published literature on them is far less extensive than expected. And studies based on direct observation of their behavior are rare.[12] This book and the research it records are an effort to fill at least part of a curious gap.

7. *Politics, Position, and Power: The Dynamics of Federal Organization*, 3d ed. (Oxford University Press, 1980), pp. 135–36; quotation from p. 136.

8. Philip M. Boffey, "The Editorial Notebook," *New York Times*, December 8, 1980.

9. Charles McKinley, "Federal Administrative Pathology and the Separation of Powers," *Public Administration Review*, vol. 11 (Winter 1951), p. 22.

10. Marver H. Bernstein, *The Job of the Federal Executive* (Brookings Institution, 1958), p. 84, citing Herbert Emmerich.

11. *Presidential Power: The Politics of Leadership*, 2d ed. (Wiley, 1976), p. 107.

12. In addition to the books by Macmahon and Millett (*Federal Administrators*) and by Bernstein (*Job of the Federal Executive*), a good many studies of federal bureau chiefs and other high administrative officers, based on interviews and documentary sources rather than direct observation, have appeared. Prominent among them are the works, fully cited in the Bibliography at the end of this volume, by Corson (1952), Corson and Paul (1966), David and Pollock (1957), Free-

METHOD OF INQUIRY

What I set out to do was observe for a year a number of bureau chiefs as they did their jobs. By watching them at work—literally spending whole days looking over their shoulders—at various times during the annual cycle of their activities, I planned to piece together a detailed, comprehensive, operational image of their job and of their place in the political system. I wanted to take as little on faith as possible; my objective was to see for myself what they did.

Setting the Size of the Sample

So I undertook to secure the cooperation of six federal bureau chiefs—six because that was the point at which two considerations intersected. On the one hand, while I could have achieved greater depth of coverage with one or two, the possibility of being misled by chance selection of a single aberrant case would be greater with so few examples than with a larger group. On the other hand, I feared that, if I spread myself too thin, my command of the data would be impaired. Six agencies seemed to me as many as I could handle adequately, and a large enough set to avoid the risk of being led astray by one markedly deviant choice.

Moreover, the contrasts and comparisons possible with six cases much exceed what can be done with even five, let alone fewer.

Six thus yielded an appealing balance of manageability and flexibility. I was prepared to reduce the sample size if that number proved to be more than I could handle. I was also ready to expand it if the research unearthed elements that could not be properly dealt with in the smaller group. Neither change turned out to be necessary; the original estimate turned out to be just the right size for the sample.

---

man (1955), Heclo (1977), Lau, Newman, and Broedling (1980), Lewis (1980), Maass (1951), McGeary (1960), Mann (1964), Morgan (1965), Pressman and Wildavsky (1973), Saxon (n.d.), Smith (1960), Stanley, Mann, and Doig (1967), Terrell (1969), Warner, Van Riper, Martin, and Collins (1963). But there have been some published studies based on observation or experience, including Downs (1967), Pinchot (1947), and Wilson (1978). See also the unpublished study by Sproull (1977). Business executives' behavior has been extensively examined; for an admirable review of the literature, see Henry Mintzberg, *The Nature of Managerial Work* (Harper and Row, 1973), especially apps. A and C.

The agreement of all those I approached initially to serve as subjects in the study is testimony to the extraordinary openness of the administrative system and the interest of its leaders in furthering research; although some limits and safeguards had to be established, especially to assure complete compliance with laws governing privacy and confidentiality, which restricted what I could see and hear, the consent of the selected chiefs to admit me to their inner councils and to discuss their work with me was generously granted. For them, my presence was sometimes a bother and a distraction, but they tolerated it all the same and helped me when I needed background to follow what was going on. My access was not total, but it was ample. It was supplemented by my attendance at their public appearances in the Washington area and by other sources of information.

Defining "Bureau"

Getting the cooperation of the subjects was easier than deciding what officials should be considered bureau chiefs. "Bureau" is a cloudy designation. I could not rely on official names as a criterion. Some of the agencies that bore this title, such as the Bureau of Land Management, the FBI, and the Bureau of the Census, were major components of cabinet departments. Others, like the Bureau of Occupational and Adult Education and the Bureau of Education for the Handicapped in the Office of Education of the Education Division of the late Department of Health, Education, and Welfare, were subdivisions of departmental components. Some, like the Bureau of the Mint, were clearly line organizations; others, like the Bureau of Personnel Management Evaluation in the old Civil Service Commission, were purely staff. The Bureau of Reclamation built and operated public works projects, the Bureau of Outdoor Recreation mostly gave grants to the states and their subdivisions, the Bureau of Labor Statistics collected, analyzed, and published economic data, and the Bureau of Foods in the Food and Drug Administration regulated and oversaw important segments of the economy. They varied in size, budget, and public visibility, as well as character of mission and place in the hierarchy. "Bureau" in the title of a federal agency revealed nothing more about the status or character of the organization than that it was not a cabinet department.

By the same token, agencies with different titles often occupied very similar positions in the hierarchy. For example, the U.S. Geological Survey, the Ocean Mining Administration, and the National Park Service were all sister units of the Bureau of Mines and the Bureau of Indian Affairs in the Department of the Interior. The Department of Health, Education, and Welfare at the time I was contemplating this study included the Office of Human Development Services, the Public Health Service, the Health Care Financing Administration, and the Education Division, among other components. The Department of Transportation strongly favored "administration" as the name of its principal line divisions (six of eight were so titled), but Agriculture leaned toward "service" as the preferred choice.

Such inconsistencies troubled the first Hoover Commission in 1949, which recommended that the nomenclature in the departments be standardized throughout the government.[13] But it never was. Diversity still reigned as I embarked on this project, and official names could not be used to identify bureaus.

I therefore adopted my own criteria for use in this project. They were not wholly arbitrary; on the contrary, they were formulated to define a universe of agencies that I believed most students of public administration would readily agree deserved to be called bureaus. The criteria were so stringent that they probably excluded some agencies many people would have regarded as bureaus, but I was reasonably sure that any agency included would be almost universally considered a bureau. To reduce the diversity of the universe to manageable proportions, I restricted eligibility for inclusion to components of all but one of the domestic civil departments existing in 1978. The Departments of State and Defense were eliminated because their international involvements and orientation and the unique elements of the armed services set them apart. The Department of Energy was omitted because it had been established only a short time earlier; its structures and relationships were still extremely fluid and would have added many more uncertainties to an already difficult and novel undertaking. The so-called independent agencies and commissions, located outside cabinet departments, would also have introduced a wide variety of additional factors. Even within the domestic depart-

13. Commission on Organization of the Executive Branch of the Government, *General Management of the Executive Branch,* a report to the Congress (GPO, 1949), pp. 30, 41.

ments, the number of differences was great enough to compel caution in generalization. I feared that if I widened the circle still further the diversity would be too much to handle.

Within the departments, to qualify for designation as a bureau, organizations had to satisfy four specifications. First, they had to be the departmental subdivisions closest to the secretaries that were not headed by assistant secretaries or other ranks of secretary. Second, they had to be line rather than staff agencies. Third, they had to be functional, not territorial, subdivisions of the departments (that is, regional offices were not treated as bureaus). Fourth, at least 10 percent of their total membership had to be serving in field stations outside the headquarters city.

Choosing the Sample

In 1978 a total of seventy-nine agencies met all these requirements; see appendix A for the list. The six in this study, thumbnail descriptions of which appear in appendix B, were picked from this group of seventy-nine. They were: in the Treasury Department, the Internal Revenue Service and the U.S. Customs Service; in the Department of Health, Education, and Welfare, the Food and Drug Administration and the Social Security Administration; in the Department of Agriculture, the U.S. Forest Service and the Animal and Plant Health Inspection Service.

The chiefs of the first four were called "commissioner"; "chief of the Forest Service" was the official designation of that agency's leader; and the head of the Animal and Plant Health Inspection Service was an "administrator." They were the "specimens" for this inquiry. (Actually, seven individuals were included in the sample because my observation of the Forest Service continued after the retirement of the chief who had been in office when the study began. Short biographies of all seven appear in appendix C.)

In selecting these specific cases, I particularly sought contrasts and similarities in features of the bureaus and their environments that I thought might affect the behavior of their chiefs. In each of three departments (so as to "control" crudely for departmental influences), I sought a pair of bureaus that differed in age, size, budget, and mission. And I tried to include chiefs appointed in different ways and with different lengths of service. I figured that the choices dictated by these criteria would give me as broad and yet controlled a range of factors and consequences as I could handle.

Things fell quickly into place. I decided to include the Forest Service because I had previously examined its field officers in great detail and was therefore familiar with much of its history and operations.[14] I went after the Internal Revenue Service because I wanted to see if the chief of a massive bureau was different from other chiefs. The Social Security Administration was included because I needed a second massive bureau to check out my findings on the IRS. (The two "chiefships" were different, however, in that the internal revenue commissioner was traditionally responsible for tax administration but not for tax policy, which was handled by the assistant secretary of the treasury for tax policy, while the social security commissioner historically had both policy and administration.) These selections committed me to the Departments of Agriculture, Treasury, and Health, Education, and Welfare. All I had to do then was pick the companion agencies in these departments.

To balance each of the three initial choices, I looked for much smaller bureaus for pairing. To go with the Forest Service (which was the largest component of the Department of Agriculture even though it was about half the size of the IRS and the SSA), I chose the Animal and Plant Health Inspection Service, which had fewer than 13 percent as many employees. In Treasury, my first choice for pairing was the Bureau of Alcohol, Tobacco, and Firearms, with fewer than 5 percent as many workers as the IRS. In HEW, the Food and Drug Administration, with about 10 percent as many employees as the SSA, was the companion agency. Before the study could get under way, however, the chief of the Bureau of Alcohol, Tobacco, and Firearms retired. Since the SSA was headed by an acting chief at the time, I feared the results of my inquiry might be skewed if two of the six agencies were in this predicament; one would be acceptable and even desirable, but not a full third of the sample. So I turned to the Customs Service, whose commissioner was a recent appointee and seemed likely to remain in place throughout the study, and whose work force consisted of about 16 percent as many employees as the IRS. A few months later, the acting commissioner of social security was replaced by a regular appointee, and the roster was complete.

14. Herbert Kaufman, *The Forest Ranger: A Study in Administrative Behavior* (Johns Hopkins Press, 1960).

When the observations commenced in 1978, the length of service of the specimen chiefs in their respective bureaus was not distributed as evenly as I might have hoped, perhaps because a change of administration had taken place the previous year. Three of them (the commissioners of internal revenue, customs, and food and drugs) had been in office only a little over a year, having been appointed in the spring of 1977. The social security commissioner did not take office until the observation was actually under way. Two, on the other hand (the chief of the Forest Service and the administrator of APHIS), were in their sixth year as chiefs. So the spread was not ideal. Still, it did furnish a range of experience for comparative purposes.

In other respects, the choice of chiefs yielded a wider spread. Two (the SSA and the IRS) were presidentially appointed and confirmed by the Senate; two (Customs and the FDA) were noncareer executive assignments; two (the Forest Service and APHIS) were career service appointments. (The last four were secretarial appointments, and the last two were approved by the Civil Service Commission.)

If you trace them back to their origins, two of the agencies (the IRS and Customs) were over a century old; two (the FDA and the Forest Service) had some seventy years of existence behind them; one (the SSA) was past forty; one (APHIS) had been a separate organization for only about six years. Or if you go back only to the point where they took on their present characteristics, the IRS would be dated from 1913, when the income tax, sanctioned by a constitutional amendment, was adopted, and Customs and the FDA from 1927, when they were formally organized as bureaus; by this standard at the time of the fieldwork in this study, two of the agencies (the IRS and the Forest Service) were over sixty, two (Customs and the FDA) were fifty-one; one (the SSA) was forty-three; and one (APHIS) was six. The distribution was reasonably broad.

Three of the bureaus (the SSA, the IRS, and the Forest Service) in fiscal year 1978 had administrative expense budgets of $1.2 billion or more. The other three (Customs, the FDA, APHIS) had corresponding budgets of $600 million or less. Two (the IRS and Customs) were primarily collectors of revenues. One (the SSA) was principally a disburser of funds. Two were engaged in regulation—one (the FDA) primarily to protect the health of people, the other (APHIS) to protect the health of food crops and livestock. One (the Forest Service) was the manager of vast tracts of natural resources owned by the government. (But each performed subsidiary functions resembling the primary activities of bureaus in other categories. For example, Customs policed borders for narcotics interdiction, the IRS cooperated with strike forces against organized crime, the regulatory agencies policed the activities under their jurisdiction to detect and abate violations of law, and the Forest Service policed the national forests to discourage and end infractions of statutes and regulations. At the same time, the Forest Service was a major collector of funds for the government, bringing in $700 million from the sale of timber and from fees for permits of all kinds. No agency did just one thing.) Three of the bureaus (the Forest Service, the IRS, and Customs) had been established by statute; one (the SSA) by statute and presidential reorganization; and two (APHIS and the FDA) by secretarial order.

The willingness of all the chiefs thus selected at the start of the study to participate in the research is rather remarkable in the annals of government bureaucracies. Every one of them agreed when approached, the only refusal coming from the successor to one of the subjects when he took office in the closing months of the study. Their ready cooperation was at odds with the reputation of high-level bureau officials for secretiveness, sensitivity, and suspicion, especially since they were not promised a chance to veto the report on the findings. (Instead, I pledged that they would see the manuscript before anybody else was allowed to read it and that, if irreconcilable differences arose between them and me, their objections would be reported at the point of protest, as fully as they wished, alongside my position. But there were no protests, and their comments were confined to correcting factual errors and pointing up substantive omissions.) The standing of the Brookings Institution undoubtedly played a large part in winning their confidence. Nevertheless, the relative ease of access to the inner workings of the federal administrative establishment must be extraordinary compared with the officiousness and defensiveness of administrative officers and agencies in most parts of the world. I was lucky to enjoy the cooperation of so distinguished a group that conformed so closely to my a priori specifications.

Conducting the Research

The observation started in late 1978 and went on for approximately a year. I covered all the chiefs simultaneously, moving from one to another all through the observation period so as to see all of them in all phases of their annual administrative cycle. My data did not lend themselves to literal matching of the subjects to isolate individual variables, nor were they amenable to statistical analysis. For one thing, with such a small number of chiefs, even though they were selected to constitute a balanced set, imitations of laboratory rigor would have been misplaced. Anyway, the data collected were not of the kind validly subject to such treatment.

Much of the information was impressionistic and much of the evidence anecdotal. The core of it came from thirty-one full days when I observed the chiefs, sitting in their offices as they went about their routines, scanning the materials crossing their desks, sitting in on most of their meetings, listening to their telephone calls, sometimes joining them for lunch, often discussing what was going on when they had a break in their activities. I or my research assistant spent another seven days in their outer offices tracking the flow of traffic and communications to learn who and what were diverted from the inner sanctums. Extensive notes were taken on all these sessions, which were spread over some fourteen months to sample all phases of the agencies' annual cycles.[15]

I also attended hearings or press conferences at which the chiefs appeared and usually chatted with them afterward about what had gone on. In several instances I attended the staff debriefings of the chiefs following their appearances.

Underpinning the direct observation of the chiefs in action was a review of documentary sources of information and over five dozen interviews with people in the agencies and with congressional staff members. I familiarized myself with relevant statutes and regulations, with departmental controls, with bureau reports and other publications, with the major secondary literature on the bureaus, and with all recent official reports on them. My research assistant collected and analyzed the chiefs' appointment calendars for at least several months at different parts of the year, and we kept a running file of clippings on all six bureaus during the life of the study. We read also the hearings and reports of the legislative, oversight, and appropriations committees that we were unable to attend; these covered two fiscal years.

15. See pp. 124–26, below.

So the descriptions and inferences reported in this study emerged from deep immersion in the administrative lives of the bureaus and their chiefs. Still, they are essentially impressions, formed without benefit of quantitative treatments of data or formal analysis. The careful selection of bureaus for the sample was intended to assure wide exposure to potentially contradictory experiences, not to produce a statistically validated set of propositions.

Some social scientists do not regard work of this kind as science. On the other hand, it is akin to the techniques of cultural anthropologists, who have long been aware that holistic observation, despite its shortcomings, yields insights and information other approaches cannot produce.[16] Indeed, the benefits of this mode of research have recently been winning renewed favor among students of organizations, achieving methodological recognition under the title "unstructured observation" from leading scholars[17] and inspiring an entire issue of the *Administrative Science Quarterly*[18] on the virtues and advantages of "qualitative methodology." All social science entails large elements of personal judgment on the part of researchers; consequently, the contribution of every approach, including the less as well as the more rigorous, is needed to build understanding of the phenomena we seek to describe and explain.

Just because my methodology was admittedly impressionistic in large degree, however, I did not abandon all efforts to maintain objectivity. When my observation began to convince me that the chiefs were not as freewheeling and self-directing as prevailing doctrines portray them, I made it a point to watch for contrary evidence to offset the natural inclination to score points by challenging conventional wisdom. I also sent the first drafts of chapters to the chiefs for comments as soon as the drafts were written, believing that they would tend to see their roles in a light different from my perceptions, thus forcing me to take a second look at my impressions. Also, fearing that all the chiefs might have assented to items about which they had reservations because each thought the items were valid for the others,

16. See David G. Mandelbaum, "Anthropology: Cultural," in David L. Sills, ed., *International Encyclopedia of the Social Sciences* (Macmillan and Free Press, 1968), vol. 1, pp. 313–17.

17. See the remarks and citations by Mintzberg, *Nature of Managerial Work*, pp. 226–27, where he acknowledges the method's weaknesses but points out, on pp. 221–29, that every other method also has failings.

18. Vol. 24 (December 1979).

I eagerly accepted the suggestion by one of them that they all be brought together in a seminar to review the whole manuscript as revised on the basis of their individual comments. On October 27, 1980, five of the seven listed in appendix C met at the Brookings Institution (Donald Kennedy and Robert E. Chasen were unable to attend) and compared reactions and interpretations. Finally, the manuscript was reviewed by informed readers who were not bashful about questioning the plausibility of the evidence produced or challenging the inferences drawn from that evidence. These measures to preserve objectivity could not eliminate the impressionistic elements from the findings. But they meant that the findings were not reached casually or decided arbitrarily or without supporting evidence.

TWO CAUTIONARY NOTES

The Limitations of the Data

The data presented here should be used cautiously because they do have certain limitations. The first is that the presence of the researcher unquestionably affected the behavior of the subjects. A leading student of executive behavior has held that the effects were inconsequential in his research,[19] and certainly the pressure of the chiefs' work often absorbed them to the point where they were apparently oblivious to everything but the matter before them. On the other hand, they often interrupted what they were doing to explain or discuss what I was watching and hearing, and we sometimes got into more general conversations about their jobs and their agencies. Furthermore, when I followed them into meetings, they usually introduced me and gave a brief explanation of what I was doing. One of them even said he found himself working harder to try to impress me, and speculated that greater openness in administration might lead to improved performance. Because there were so many other constraints on what they did, I doubt that my observation grossly distorted their behavior. But I certainly was not the proverbial fly on the wall that so many observers would like to be when they study human behavior.

19. Mintzberg, *Nature of Managerial Work*, pp. 269–70.

Second, I was not able to observe 100 percent of the chiefs' activities. For example, I lacked the money to accompany them on trips away from Washington (averaging perhaps 15 to 20 percent of their time, but running over 35 percent in one case), so I got my information on their travels from what they told me, from their official reports, from the comments of their staffs, and from occasional observation of planning for forthcoming journeys. Also, I was asked to wait outside on a few occasions when a chief thought my presence would inhibit a delicate conversation with a visitor; I was usually filled in afterward on what had taken place, but I did not see these encounters for myself. In the case of the IRS, because of privacy requirements, observation had to be confined to days when no matters concerning individual taxpayers were on the agenda, and no such items were ever discussed or even identified. So my data were not without gaps or hearsay.

Third, the year or so of my observation may not have been typical of most years in Washington—if any year can be. Two of the three secretaries encompassed by the study were dismissed by the president before the two-thirds mark of his first term. The shadow of Watergate hung over the government still, and the power of the president was far from its peak. Inflation and unemployment were on the rise. Conceivably, much of what I saw could have been the peculiar product of the times.

Fourth, even if the times were not unusual, a single year in the life of a bureau chief might not suffice to yield a rounded view of the position. Incumbents learn on the job, so their later years of service may not be the same as the early years. Relationships inside and outside the agency, uncertain and fluid at the outset, probably become more stable and predictable with the passage of time. Commitments are made, pledges are given, obligations are called in, expectations are formed. At the same time, fatigue may set in. The effects of such tendencies would hardly be discernible in one year, and broad cycles in the administrative life of bureau chiefs would certainly take longer to detect.

Furthermore, any given year might miss the occasional crises, dramatic changes of policy, and upheavals in the history of a bureau that create opportunities for great accomplishments by administrators or even force them to act on a grand scale. This could give a false impression of administrative passivity. By the same token, if the year should catch a number of such turbulent events, it could give a false impression that leaders were continually engaged with crises. Actually, in this research, I encountered both turbulence and tranquillity, and my judgments are based on consideration of the contrasting conditions. Nevertheless, I must remind the reader that a year provides only a glimpse of reality.

Still, for all the limitations of the data, I believe they are instructive. Because the patterns emerged so clearly despite the differences among the agencies and among the individuals studied, it seems likely that they constitute the basic attributes of the position of bureau chief in the federal executive departments. I am confident that the major outlines will stand up under the test of further studies. I hope they will be put to this test.

The Character of the Adduced Evidence

To maintain the confidentiality of sources of information as prominent and distinctive as the chiefs in this study, I was often obliged to resort to extremely vague language when describing examples of the behavior on which my findings and conclusions are based. This lack of specificity makes some of the illustrations sound contrived and even synthetic. When I say that I heard one of the chiefs resisting pressure from a sister agency, the reader wants to know which chief, which sister agency, what sort of pressure, over what sort of issue. And when I report that one of the chiefs negotiated carefully with some of his top subordinates to block a move by other subordinates at an upcoming meeting, it is only natural to wonder in which of the bureaus this maneuvering took place, with whom, and why. Suppressing the detail not only robs the narrative of color and concreteness; it arouses doubt about authenticity.

Nonetheless, to avoid any possibility of abusing the access I was granted and to reduce the chances that third parties—other members of the bureaus, other government officials, other visitors in the chiefs' offices when I happened to be present—might feel offended or injured by disclosure of things said privately, and perhaps tentatively, I decided to keep the illustrations anonymous as long as they were not part of the public record. All of them, however, are actual events or actions. I did not devise hypothetical examples to make a point. Each case is linked directly to my field notes, which were taken at length during the periods of observation or, in the case of interviews, written immediately after each conversation. The linkage is documented, not merely remembered; a set of footnotes that do not appear in this volume because they would violate the anonymity of the sources is part of the project files. These footnotes were gathered not only to enable me to rediscover, if ever I must, the origin and the full substance of the examples I gave, but also to compel me to go back to my notes instead of depending on my memory for the facts. Occasionally, in the course of discussion, I offer some surmise and conjecture; such reflections are clearly indicated. Where I present illustrations, no matter how generally or obscurely phrased, they are all things I saw and heard.

In the last analysis, I believe, my decision to protect the anonymity of my sources will make it easier rather than more difficult to test the validity of my findings and conclusions. For it will help preserve the climate of trust and cooperation that persuaded my subjects to open themselves to the kind of scrutiny on which this inquiry depended. I hope other researchers will therefore be able to conduct similar studies. Even if they, too, do not publish all the details of what they see and hear, the accuracy of what I have reported here will be supported or challenged as their observations converge on or diverge from my own. For that reason, I will not be dismayed if this volume provokes healthy skepticism but will welcome it as a stimulus and a prelude to further research.

PLAN OF THE BOOK

The substantive portions of this report are divided into two parts. One presents the findings, the other the inferences and speculations proceeding from the findings. The presentation moves from particulars about the chiefs as a group and about their bureaus to analysis of their places in the governmental system, and thence to the implications of this analysis for administrative practice and theory. For me, at least, it was not without its surprises.

CHAPTER TWO

Variations on a Theme

BECAUSE all the chiefs included in this study occupied comparable organizational positions in the executive branch, one might expect them to resemble each other closely. On the other hand, because there were so many differences between their bureaus and between them, one might anticipate wide variation in their administrative behavior.

As it turned out, the similarities in their administrative behavior were striking. Although their styles and methods were not identical, the differences may fairly be described as variations on a theme rather than as different themes. That is, they had so much in common that each could easily empathize with any or all of the others. They faced common problems, devised similar strategies, had like experiences. Brought together, they understood one another at once. It would be an exaggeration to say that they could have been rotated among their agencies and instantly have taken over from one another. But had that been done, they all would have felt familiar in their new positions as a result of their service in their old ones. They would have reached for the levers to which they were accustomed, and they would have found many of those levers, working in much the same way, in their new surroundings.

Their activities, regardless of all the differences between them, fell into four categories: (1) deciding things, (2) receiving and reviewing intelligence about the state of their own organizations and of the external environment, (3) representing their bureaus to the external environment, and (4) motivating their work forces. The lines between the categories are not sharply defined; rather, the classes overlap, and a single act may partake of several. Nevertheless, the distinctions are helpful in understanding the job of the bureau chiefs.

17

DECIDING THINGS

Executives are usually portrayed as decisionmakers, and the six bureau chiefs certainly did make decisions. But making decisions, in a narrow sense, did not occupy much of their time. A decision is "made," after all, at the instant when consideration of alternative possible courses of action ceases because one of the possibilities is authoritatively adopted and the chain of actions dictated by that alternative begins. It takes no longer than is required to say yes or no, to check this box or that one on a form, or to declare one course of action selected and all others rejected.

Of course, if decisionmaking is defined to include everything from the identification of a need or opportunity for choice to establishing the behavior that will implement the choice, it is a long and often tortuous process. Weeks, months, or even years can elapse from the first suggestion that alternatives should be considered and the scanning and evaluation of options to the elimination of options from consideration, the selection of the sole survivor, and the introduction of practices required by the selection. Broadly conceived, decisionmaking is a vast category.

The term is employed here in its narrower meaning—not because the narrower definition is better than the broader one, but because it is more useful for the purposes of this analysis.[1] The chiefs participated only intermittently and with various degrees of intensity in the larger process (which was the usual way of exercising initiative), depending on their delegations of authority, other demands on their time, and how concerned they were about the matter being deliber-

1. One of the chiefs could not accept the narrower definition of decisionmaking even though he appreciated the reasons for it. He argued that some of the deliberation treated here as simply another form of intelligence receipt and review was actually so directly and specifically tied to particular items for choice on the chiefs' agendas that it should be identified as part of the making of decisions. By that standard, he estimated, much more of the chiefs' time would be allocated to decisionmaking than is reported in this study—as much, he estimated from his own experience, as 15 percent.

Try as I would, however, I could not subdivide the receipt and review of intelligence into subcategories based on my observations. In one sense, all information was collected and analyzed as a foundation for decision. But as I explain in the next section of this chapter, it had other uses as well. I could not confidently distinguish the uses. Therefore I held fast to my initial position even though I recognize that many people will not agree with it.

ated. They often started the process, and their interventions, even when brief, influenced its course. And they frequently brought deliberations and disputes to an end by announcing their judgment; such exercises of authority were their distinctive contribution to the process. So their role in it was important. Nevertheless, the process, once launched for a given issue, ran more or less autonomously to the point of resolution; subordinates did most of what was necessary to bring it to that point. That is why the chiefs' distinctive part in "making" the decision is treated here in the narrow sense, and what is commonly included in the broad definition appears here as part of the *preparation* for decision, discussed later on. And that is why I state that *making* decisions claimed little of the chiefs' attention.

Another reason the chiefs spent comparatively little time on decisionmaking is that they did not make large numbers of significant organizational decisions. Everybody, of course, makes scores of choices of a minor kind each day—what to wear, what to eat, which chore to tackle first, whether to go bowling or to the movies, which newspaper to buy, and so on. Bureau chiefs had their share of organizational equivalents, such as approving arrangements of their own offices, dealing with potholes in headquarters driveways, and sanctioning visual aids supporting their testimony and public appearances. But these did not consume much of the chiefs' time or energy. I am speaking of decisions that affect large numbers of people or profoundly affect the lives and well-being of even a few, that arouse people with influence, that involve large amounts of money, or that can shake the bureaus' reputations and security and effectiveness. There is no sharp line separating significant from trivial matters; they shade into each other. Nevertheless, even if one used a very liberal standard of significance, I am confident that he would find that the chiefs did not pour out important decisions in a steady stream. Days sometimes went by without any choice of this kind emerging from their offices, and it was an unusual week when any of them could be said to have made as many as half a dozen. The Hollywood image of executives firing off critical decisions in machine-gun fashion is far removed from the reality of executive life as I saw it. Consequently, the chiefs were able to spend more time on other elements of their jobs.

That is not to say, however, that few important decisions were made anywhere in their organizations. In all the bureaus, numerous decisions emerged from the interactions of subordinates at all levels, in the field as well as in headquarters, that would have to be regarded as important by even a stringent definition of significance. Just because a decision is not made by a chief does not mean that it is trivial. Many of the lower-level decisions were technical in character—the management of computers, the procedures for chemical analysis, the assessment of import duties on specific shipments, the detection of disease threats to farm animals, or the methods of preventing fires in national forests. Others were essentially policy matters—the program emphases in a region, degrees of tolerance of minor violations, the trade-off between obeying top-management directives and observing occupational or local standards when they conflicted with each other, the initial disposition of claims and inquiries by individuals and groups. Judgments of these kinds came out of the six bureaus every week, and some of them affected powerful political interests, large segments of the public, and the standing and accomplishments of the agencies. Yet only a small fraction of them were issued or even reviewed by the chiefs themselves. It could not be otherwise if the chiefs were to have time for other duties and if the decisions were to be made in timely and informed fashion.

What came to a chief for decision and what was left to others was determined by a subtle interplay between explicit delegations of authority and the personal relations between the chiefs and their subordinates. All the bureaus inserted in their administrative manuals (and several bureaus inserted in their published regulations as well) descriptions of the areas and functions for which specified officers were responsible, thereby identifying who was permitted to sign what. In the Forest Service, top officers routinely anticipated impending major decisions and worked out a special division of responsibility for each set. No matter how extensive these signature rules were, however, there were always borderline cases. Sometimes they involved two coordinate units, in which case the heads of both units would sign. Often there were uncertainties about whether someone at a lower level could sign; in such instances, the usual practice was to get the higher authority's signature in order to put the firmest possible foundation under the issuance, especially if the issuance entailed any controversy. People did not seem to agonize over the ambiguous situations, but they could not always explain fully how they decided whether to handle things themselves or pass them on to their bosses for signature; "you just know" was a common answer. Within a few months after a new chief took over, it seemed to be a reflex action, apparently satisfactory to the subordinates and the chiefs alike. Yet the way in which this problem was resolved helped determine the character of the chiefs' leadership. If great numbers of matters were referred to them for decision, other vital parts of their jobs would have been neglected and backlogs of matters awaiting decision would have accumulated. Neglect of external relations, inattention to the work force, or disregard of intelligence about the state of the bureaus and of their environments could have damaged the welfare and morale of the agencies. At the same time, big backlogs would have provoked complaints and criticism from clients, from other agencies whose own actions were delayed, and from frustrated subordinates, and caused outrage in Congress and the upper reaches of the executive branch. So there were strong incentives to install fine-mesh screens around the chiefs to hold down the number of things they decided personally.

On the other hand, if hardly anything came to them for decision, they could have been reduced to ciphers in the lives of their organizations. When subordinates decide everything, superiors become figureheads despite their other functions. They lose credibility as spokesmen and leaders, and the flow of intelligence to them dries up as their sources discover their impotence.

This dilemma could theoretically have led to hasty review and routine approval of all the issues submitted to the chiefs, thus avoiding the buildup of backlogs while nominally preventing isolation of the leaders. None of the chiefs resorted to this technique, however—for obvious reasons. Uncritical acceptance of everything from below would have emptied their roles of influence as surely as receiving nothing; no subordinate would have taken their preferences into account when proposing actions if all subordinates knew in advance that whatever was proposed would automatically prevail.

So they had to strike a balance—and keep adjusting practices to maintain it. Competing tendencies pushed decisionmaking both upward and downward; now one would have to be checked and now the other. Thrusting decisions upward were such factors as risk-aversion on the part of subordinates, top-management anxiety about the judgment or reliability of subordinates, recognition by subordinates that their chiefs had objectives or could see consequences not readily perceived at lower administrative levels, respect for the knowledge and wisdom of the chiefs, the inability of subordinates themselves to re-solve differences of opinion about a matter at issue, the quest for uniformity of policy throughout the country, and the need for common administrative practices to permit ready movement of personnel from station to station and to assure the compatibility of computer programs at all locations throughout each agency. Pulling decisions downward were the specialized knowledge of subordinates about their fields of expertise or their geographical areas, their commitment to the programs in their charge and their resulting impatience with restraints and delays from above, the undeniable organizational benefits of speedy action that come from encouraging subordinates to act on their own, and the advantages of innovation gained by encouraging experimentation and inventiveness in the field. A tug-of-war therefore went on constantly.

Under these conditions, despite the explicitness of the formal signature rules in all the agencies, practices were often fluid and asymmetrical and not always logical. That is why the chiefs' decisions dealt with a mixture of subjects of varied importance, ranging from the trivial ones mentioned earlier to major ones like approving the selection of a regional commissioner, the standards for evaluating the performance of senior civil servants, the strategy for handling a delicate interagency conflict or a sensitive congressional request or a difficult inquiry by a journalist, the choice of a contractor to conduct a study, the identification of cases to press as part of an enforcement campaign, the composition of a team to visit a foreign country to gather data for a pending action, or the rank order of program priorities in a budget presentation. Events, intuition, and mutual accommodation, no less than planning and management, determined what came to them. Consequently, the patterns in the agencies were not identical. For example, Customs Commissioner Robert Chasen and Food and Drug Commissioner Donald Kennedy came from outside the government to bureaus staffed by career personnel and depended on top-level career officers to keep internal routines running smoothly. Even Internal Revenue Commissioner Jerome Kurtz, whose specialization as a tax laywer before accepting the leadership of the IRS made him extremely knowledgeable about that organization, found he had to rely heavily on his ranking career officials to manage internal administrative processes; they knew the people, the procedures, the details of management, and he, beset with substantive problems of tax collection and with external-relations duties, was not inclined to second-guess them. Yet Social Security Commissioner Stanford Ross, who also came to his post from outside the government, found himself drawn into problems of internal administration from the start—partly, he thought, because so much of the business of the SSA consisted of administrative operations, partly because various of his predecessors had been immersed in these matters and the tradition of involvement thrust itself upon him, and partly because he saw so many serious problems in internal management. Similarly, Administrator Francis Mulhern of the Animal and Plant Health Inspection Service and Forest Service Chiefs John McGuire and Max Peterson—all career officials who came up through the ranks of their respective agencies—were intimately familiar with and accustomed to handling internal management, and they continued to do so when they became the leaders of their organizations. The chiefs did not all take the same path in their efforts to avoid the extremes of overload and isolation.

On the other hand, practices apparently did tend to converge; common demands, expectations, and formal requirements shaped the institutional roles. The career chiefs were, as one of them put it, "weaned away" from their early preoccupation with internal administration. And Commissioner Ross sought deliberately to reorganize his top staff so he *could* leave more internal matters to his aides. But Commissioner Kurtz found he could not avoid investing hours of his own time in such details as the elimination of 200 of the 86,000 jobs in the IRS despite his confidence in his staff's ability to handle internal operations. Thus, though the tension between the antipodal dangers of overwhelming the head of the organization and secluding him were resolved a little differently in each case, all the resolutions turned out to be variations on a common theme rather than unique strategies. However special the individual circumstances, all the agencies and all the chiefs gravitated toward balances of similar kinds.[2]

There were few signs that the chiefs were either overloaded or iso-

2. My research was not extended or detailed enough to detect long-range tendencies toward centralization or decentralization. A plausible cycle would be initial reliance by each chief on practices developed by his predecessor, a period of centralization as soon as a new chief felt familiar enough with his organization to institute procedures with which he was more comfortable, and a trend toward decentralization after he had installed a few of his own people in key posts and developed confidence in other subordinates. But this is only hypothetical.

lated. The distribution of decisions among organizational levels, as set by the balance between the upward and downward pressures, apparently was acceptable to the chiefs, the other members of their organizations, and the people they served or regulated. I encountered no complaints or controversies directly or indirectly indicating dissatisfaction. The near-equilibrium of opposing tendencies kept decisionmaking levels within generally tolerated ranges.

So the chiefs spent less time deciding what to decide than they did on substantive decisions. Yet if you were to drop in on them at random, making decisions in the narrow sense is not what you would be most likely to find them doing. Chances are that such a visit would discover them engaged in one of the other three categories of activity, especially the reception and review of intelligence.

RECEIVING AND REVIEWING INFORMATION

In *The Lonely Crowd*, David Riesman's description of "other-directed" people conjured up images of individuals with figurative, supersensitive antennae coming out of their heads to alert them to what other people were thinking.[3] In the case of the six bureau chiefs, an even more outlandish metaphor might be appropriate. They could be pictured as having not only elaborate receptors but radar and sonar transmitters constantly sweeping 360 degrees to call their attention by return signals to things they might otherwise have missed. The return signals would come in a variety of forms and through a host of channels—formal and informal, planned and chance, confidential and public, direct and roundabout, simultaneous and serial. The metaphor is fitting because, in all six bureaus in this study, information about what was going on inside the organizations and in the organizational surround was received continually in headquarters.

The Purposes of Organizational Intelligence

Unlike Riesman's "other-directed" people, the purpose of this information collection was not so much to conform to prevailing attitudes and beliefs as to provide ample notice of approaching hazards

3. David Riesman, *The Lonely Crowd* (Yale University Press, 1950), p. 22.

and opportunities and to help the chiefs prepare for impending decisions. But it was not only future-oriented; the information was also gathered to tell them what they had done and how well they had done it. Unquestionably, the data were intended to permit leaders to exercise as much influence over the course of events—over the torrent of activities into which they were plunged—as they could exert. Yet I suspect the information would have been collected even if they believed they could exert no influence, because it helped them orient themselves. Many people find it uncomfortable not to know where they are, how they got there, and where they are going even if they cannot do much about the trajectory. To answer these questions, a steady flow of information is essential.

Much more arrived at headquarters, considered as a collectivity, than any of the chiefs themselves could examine in even the most perfunctory way.[4] What came to them personally were totals, summaries, and narratives assembled or computed or drawn from raw data. Indeed, little of what arrived at headquarters had ever been solicited by the chiefs personally. Most streams of information had originated in earlier administrations, often in response to an edict from Congress (frequently, but not invariably, embodied in legislation), a demand from a governmentwide staff agency of the executive branch, or a request from a previous chief or one of his aides.[5] They continued because they were still formally required, because they proved useful to at least some influential people, and because the usefulness of continuing activities is seldom questioned. So the chiefs were only vaguely aware of the many streams of raw information, and they were deeply interested in only some of them.

Nevertheless, much of the information they did get was extracted and digested from these streams, without which the digests and totals could not have been prepared. Specialists in headquarters monitored and processed them, furnishing the chiefs with the gist of each body of material. Like all of us, the chiefs were the beneficiaries of processes and data they themselves had not ordered or mastered. The flow of intelligence about conditions inside and outside the bureaus

4. This finding is consistent with the findings in my earlier study of nine federal bureaus; see Herbert Kaufman, *Administrative Feedback: Monitoring Subordinates' Behavior* (Brookings Institution, 1973), pp. 53–60.

5. Herbert Kaufman, *Red Tape: Its Origins, Uses, and Abuses* (Brookings Institution, 1977), pp. 13–15; Kaufman, *Administrative Feedback*, p. 56.

presented them with the same kind of dilemma that deciding what to decide did. If the chiefs had tried to scrutinize everything, they would have been overwhelmed and would therefore have learned nothing. If they had been zealous about avoiding inundation, they could have deprived themselves of information helpful in identifying hazards and opportunities and in making decisions. As with decision rules, a balance had to be struck.

In this case the balance was achieved with few hard-and-fast formal orders. It was done almost entirely on an informal basis. Each chief and the people around him developed an understanding of what the chief wanted, and most of it was handled routinely and automatically. From time to time, for a specific situation, a chief would call for a report on an investigation or a series of meetings; occasionally he would indicate that he preferred not to see certain reports or to attend certain meetings. So the flows were adjusted intermittently. For the most part, though, they were governed by rules that had become habitual for everybody, and the data streamed in. And they kept the chiefs busy.

SCANNING FOR POTENTIAL EMBARRASSMENT. One of the major reasons the chiefs sought to maintain a flow of intelligence to themselves was uneasiness about being caught in embarrassing situations. In particular, they did not want to be exposed as ignorant of events or conditions within or outside their bureaus that were known to others and that influential people thought they should have known about. Washington is a city that trades in information, especially in "inside dope," and a leader discovered to be uninformed about something salient to his position or organization is apparently considered not only deficient or ineffective, but possibly as losing influence, access, and control. A reputation for weakness, whether deserved or not, often leads to actual weakness as people inside and outside an organization defer less and less to the victim, thereby reinforcing the reputation and diminishing deference further. The chiefs kept their intelligence scanners in motion constantly to reduce this danger.

Of course, nobody expects administrators to be apprised of every detail affecting their organizations; it would be regarded as a misuse of their time if they allowed themselves to be immersed in trivia. But there is no clear line between what superiors or colleagues or subordinates or members of Congress or the press or interest groups or the public will hold to be trivial and what they will regard as something the administrators should have known. Since the psychological distress and the political costs of exposed ignorance can be most painful, the six chiefs tended to prefer getting too much information to getting too little. With an excess, they could disregard the insignificant but have confidence that they had not been deprived of anything important; with an insufficiency, they might not discover the deficiencies until too late.

So none of them were caught off base during my study. But the grounds for their precautions were illustrated vividly when the head of a bureau in the Department of Justice was derided for his inability to answer questions for the Subcommittee on Immigration, Refugees, and International Law of the House Appropriations Committee at the time this study was in progress. According to one reporter, he was "reduced to nervous mumbling" after being unable to answer a number of factual questions about his agency's operations, prompting the committee chairwoman to score the agency for being "totally out of our control" and "out of touch with the 20th century," and provoking another committee member to complain that the situation was "just damned sad." The commissioner subsequently told a reporter that he had not received the questions in advance of the hearing, which is the way such testimony is usually handled.[6] That is exactly the sort of embarrassment a good organizational intelligence system is supposed to avert. And that is why my six chiefs and their aides preferred a surfeit of information to a dearth. This was a way to keep themselves abreast of the latest developments, to anticipate probable queries from any quarter, and to be familiar enough with every aspect of their programs to be able to answer questions for which they had not specifically prepared. It took a great deal of the chiefs' time, but they obviously considered the investment worthwhile.

I doubt that the journalists, members of Congress, and others who quizzed the chiefs took perverse and malicious pleasure in holding administrators up to ridicule, although it might seem that way to a casual observer. Rather, they probably considered it a moral obligation and sound strategy to probe for weak spots in the administrative establishment. They obviously did worry about the need to keep bureaucracies under control, and searching inquiries and public exposure were among the most effective means to this end. Turning the

6. Warren Brown, *Washington Post,* March 16, 1979.

spotlight on bureaucratic failings also got good publicity for the critics. Moreover, such demonstrations of their power helped them maintain their respective institutions' places in the political system; proof that they knew or could find out what was going on, and could punish through their control of publicity as well as through other means, reminded members of the executive branch that legislators, journalists, and private groups were not to be slighted. Humiliating administrators was thus not so much an exercise in sadism as a by-product of pursuing other goals. The chiefs therefore accepted aggressive questioning as a fact of life and a legitimate function of nonbureaucratic participants in the governmental process, and one even seemed to enjoy the give-and-take. In any event, the practice certainly gave them an incentive to get all the intelligence they could about everything having any bearing on their bureaus.

Another purpose served by the reception and review of intelligence was deterrence of noncompliance and wrongdoing by subordinates. This is not to say that the chiefs saw their subordinates as deliberately disobedient or corrupt. But the inescapable ambiguities of instructions and general policies as applied to specific cases, the misinterpretation of leaders' intentions and wishes, the day-to-day tension of dealing directly with the public, the pressure of local interests on bureau personnel administratively and perhaps geographically distant from headquarters, and the temptation presented to employees by government property and public funds temporarily under their control, all combined to cause inequitable variations in executing the law, occasional impatience with clients, and the possibility of dishonesty. Intelligence about the actual behavior of field employees permits clarification of directives and guidelines from the chiefs, which reduces one source of difficulty. Also, if employees know that their conduct is under surveillance, they are apt to try harder to comply with orders and to resist temptation. Organizationally prescribed administrative feedback was therefore extensive in all six bureaus. A body of data about field behavior accumulated continuously in their respective Washington offices.[7]

The chiefs saw little of it. For the most part, they relied on specialists on their staffs to keep track of activities at lower levels. Indeed, the division of labor in even the smallest of the bureaus produced such a grid of crosscutting jurisdictions that the specialists checked

7. See also Kaufman, *Administrative Feedback*, pp. 5-11, 24-41, 49-50.

on and restrained each other in both headquarters and field.[8] With budgeting, auditing, personnel, legal, enforcement, procurement, buildings management, civil rights, data processing, management analysis, and other overhead services, as well as specialized line functions and territorial offices, all having to cooperate to get anything done, deviant behavior in any component was likely to surface sooner or later. The controls were more or less automatic; the chiefs were not at them constantly. Most of this intelligence did not actually cross their desks.

But when something wrong was detected, even if the failing was not large or widespread, the chiefs expected to be notified at once. This requirement symbolized the importance the leaders attached to compliance and integrity and provided them with opportunities to dramatize their concern. Equally important, it enabled them to be aware of problems and launch corrective actions before outside agencies—the General Accounting Office, the Office of Management and Budget, the Office of Personnel Management, congressional investigators, the press, or others—uncovered them to the embarrassment of the chiefs. During this study, for example, a Forest Service survey of its own time and attendance reports turned up payments of claims for overtime work by four employees who had never worked the hours reported.[9] The cases were referred to a U.S. attorney for prosecution. The action served notice that such conduct would be discovered and would result in severe penalties. It also spared the chief of the service the surprise and humiliation of having others reveal it.

Still another reason for the importance attached by the chiefs to receiving an abundance of information was their quest for multiple sources of intelligence about the internal workings of their bureaus and the bureaus' environments. They needed these to probe or challenge their subordinates' views, to ask the right questions, and to assess the accuracy of reports and recommendations given them by those who worked for them. Multiple intelligence sources multiplied the chiefs' workload but reduced the chances that the chiefs would become prisoners of their staffs.

The avoidance of embarrassment was thus a powerful incentive

8. For a fuller discussion of this point, see Herbert Kaufman, *The Limits of Organizational Change* (University of Alabama Press, 1971), pp. 31–36.

9. U.S. Forest Service, "The Friday Newsletter," no. 32, August 11, 1978, and no. 45, November 10, 1978; Bailey Morris, "Forest Service Employees Probed in Embezzlement," *Washington Star*, August 15, 1978.

for the chiefs to allocate much of their time and energy to the receipt and review of intelligence. But the need to prepare for decisions was even stronger.

PREPARING FOR DECISIONS. Although the making of decisions, as that phrase was defined earlier in this chapter, took little of the chiefs' time, getting ready to make the choices that the chiefs took upon themselves or had thrust upon them occupied substantial portions of their days. A great deal of the intelligence they reviewed was to help them in this task.

Once a matter was placed on a chief's agenda for decision, whether on his initiative (not an everyday occurrence but by no means unknown) or by his acquiescence or even contrary to what he would have liked, a process of trying to answer a series of questions followed. Decisionmakers usually wanted to know what options were open, what consequences could be expected from each option, what the costs and benefits of each set of consequences were likely to be, and, in the light of the different effects and the different probabilities attached to them, which course of action was indicated.

The chiefs themselves did not have all the information required to answer these questions; most of it was prepared by their immediate staffs and other subordinates. The work consisted of five elements: data collection, analysis of collected data, formulation of alternative courses of action, evaluation of the alternatives, and discussion of the options with the chiefs. The chiefs then decided the issues on the basis of this information. That is, they set the process of preparation in motion by agreeing or proposing that a matter be readied for decision, and they brought the process to a close by choosing one option and rejecting all the others.

These exercises of authority by the chiefs are what many people consider the distinguishing characteristic of executives. Through their ability to introduce items into the organizational agenda for eventual decision, or at least to admit items at the request of others, and to defer or delete items, to terminate research and discussion of the items by calling for final presentation of the arguments for and against each option, and to discard all options but one, the chiefs could influence what their work forces did, what their bureaus recommended or proposed to other participants in policy formation, and how the agencies responded to various challenges and pressures. This is the operational meaning of displaying initiative and providing leadership, which is probably the main reason that this aspect of their job gets extensive attention from students of organizations and heavy emphasis from practicing executives.

But it gets attention and emphasis also because it claims executive time. Although the chiefs themselves were not deeply involved in the labor of gathering and sifting and arraying the information required for decision, these activities of their subordinates generated progress reports and conferences that engaged their energies, compelling them to evaluate evidence and arguments and to judge whether things could proceed to resolution or needed still more data. Moreover, although screening mechanisms controlled the volume of issues that came to them for decision, a great variety of subjects—general policy choices, specific programmatic alternatives, budget matters, personnel issues, legal problems, procedural options, possibilities of reorganization, jurisdictional controversies, external-relations difficulties, and others—were among those that got through; confronting each was therefore in many ways a separate learning process. Even though others did the detailed work, getting ready for decisionmaking kept the chiefs busy.

Nonetheless, it was only one of their functions and only one of the purposes for which they received and reviewed information.

APPRAISING PERFORMANCE. They sought information to determine not only what was happening and what choices lay before them, but also how well they and their agencies were doing. They were always asking how close the performance of the bureaus came to the targets set by law and by administrative decisions. As far as possible, they wanted quantitative measures of the distance between achievements and stated organizational goals. A great deal of the intelligence passing before them was gathered to answer their questions about these distances.

The chiefs relied on these indicators of quality of performance in all their activities. The indicators helped them evaluate the soundness of past decisions and assess the need for corrective action. They were criteria for the division of the chiefs' time among the innumerable tasks facing them. They provided both answers to critics and a basis for claiming credit. They furnished grounds for distinguishing between high achievers and poor performers in the work forces. Every choice and every judgment the chiefs had to make ultimately came down to these estimates of what was on course and what was not.

If they had had no other incentives to gather and review intelligence about the state and performance of their bureaus, just the requirements for making such choices and judgments would have forced them to institute such a system.

I have the impression, however, that two additional motives drove them to collect intelligence of this kind: their curiosity and their pride. They wanted, for their own satisfaction and orientation, to know how well their bureaus were doing under their stewardship. And they wanted that sense of direction and progress that passengers on a ship demand as the vessel plows through seemingly unchanging seas. So the bureau chiefs spent substantial portions of their time examining and pondering data about the output of their bureaus and the differences between what was actually done and the goals.

This was not a purely mechanical task. Often there were disagreements and controversies about the targets themselves. And even when the targets were not challenged, it was not always easy to decide how close an agency had come to them. If the Forest Service, for example, managed to reach its timber sales goal but achieved only 80 percent of its grazing and 60 percent of its wildlife objectives in a given year, would that have been as good as attaining 80 percent of all three goals? If the Social Security Administration reduced overpayments of benefits by 20 percent by tightening screening procedures so drastically that delays of proper payments to those eligible increased 15 percent, was it doing its job better? If the Food and Drug Administration banned a food preservative entailing some risk of cancer and thereby markedly increased the dangers of food poisoning by deadly botulin, would that move the agency closer to or away from its goals? If the Internal Revenue Service cut in half the amount of time a taxpayer had to wait for help in filling out a tax return, was that an improvement if it was accompanied by a higher error rate in the advice and assistance given? No amount of information would automatically have answered these questions; they were matters of judgment.

The judgments could not be made, however, without information. The chiefs therefore continually asked for evidence of how well the bureaus were doing and inquired how performance could be improved. In this way, they were responsible for the continuation, if not the initiation, of much of the intelligence that converged on them. To the flows generated by the other purposes of intelligence reception and review, this one added a substantial stream of its own. The combined effect of all three was to occupy substantial fractions of the chiefs' time and attention.

Modes of Intelligence-Gathering

There are only three ways of gathering the kind of information required for the foregoing purposes. One is direct observation. Another is talking with people who have the information. The third is reading sources that contain the information.

The chiefs used all three methods. Conferring distinctly took the most time, reading came next, and direct observation was third. Chances are that the quantitative yields of intelligence from the methods were in the same order. But the effects are harder to assess; direct observation, for example, leavened the decisions and actions taken at headquarters with awareness of the problems of people in field offices, so its impact reached far beyond the amount of time allocated to it by the chiefs. All three methods, therefore, were probably of equal value to the chiefs in the long run despite the differences in the hours each absorbed, and any executive deprived of any one of them would undoubtedly have felt—and been—handicapped.

CONFERRING. None of the bureau chiefs had much time to themselves in the course of a day. I observed them only in headquarters,[10] of course, where I estimate that at least 60 percent of their time—as much as three-quarters in some periods with the average above two-thirds—was spent in the company of other people or on the telephone.[11] But from what I could glean of their schedules when traveling, the percentages were even higher in the field; only the intervals of intercity transportation seemed to afford them any respite from personal interaction with others, providing opportunities for reflec-

10. They spent an average of 80 to 85 percent of their time in headquarters, although one chief dropped as low as 65 percent, during the year of observation.

11. This estimate, independently arrived at, is in the same range as the findings of John J. Corson and R. Shale Paul in *Men Near the Top* (Johns Hopkins Press, 1966), p. 49, and of Henry Mintzberg, *The Nature of Managerial Work* (Harper and Row, 1973), p. 38. It is slightly lower than the figures developed by Lee S. Sproull, "Managerial Attention in New Education Programs: A Micro-Behavioral Study of Program Implementation" (Ph.D. dissertation, Stanford University, 1977), pp. 27, 55. See also Sune Carlson, *Executive Behaviour: A Study of the Work Load and the Working Methods of Managing Directors* (Stockholm: Strombergs, 1951), pp. 71–74.

tion, taking stock, and planning. Their lives were full of listening and talking, in that order.

Many of their personal contacts had nothing to do with gathering intelligence; as is brought out later, the chiefs were often *sources* of information for other officials and employees of the government and for the public, and they also met with others to perform their other two functions—to conduct their external relations and to motivate and direct their work forces. But surely the majority of the time they expended on personal contacts was for their own education, enlightenment, and information. It was by this means that they got most of their insight into their own organizations and the organizational environment.

The aspects of their personal contacts that took place in Washington and that I was able to observe were principally with subordinates in their bureaus and mostly, though by no means exclusively, with the headquarters staff. These took the form of recurrent meetings, impromptu calls on the chiefs, and special briefings.

There was no common pattern to the recurrent information meetings. Two of the chiefs met daily with selected members of their headquarters staffs. Most had general staff meetings once a week. One scheduled them every two weeks. The commissioner of food and drugs met separately with the top staff of each of his major line components once a week; hardly a day went by when he was in town without an hour or so having been automatically set aside for such a gathering. Regional officials were brought together from two to four times a year. Three or four times a year, the top headquarters officers assembled with the chiefs to formulate budget requests and to prepare budget presentations to congressional appropriations subcommittees. Thus in addition to impromptu meetings or field visits, no high-ranking headquarters officer was likely to go more than a matter of days without a regularly scheduled meeting with his chief, and no high-ranking regional official more than a few months. Recurrent meetings formed the frameworks of the chiefs' personal contacts in their bureaus.

The frameworks were fleshed out by the impromptu calls on the chiefs by people inside and outside the bureaus. The vast majority of those who called in person were members of the headquarters staffs, squeezing in a few minutes between scheduled meetings or taking advantage of openings in the chiefs' schedules to converse at greater length. Usually they came in to get clearance for something they wanted to do but about which they had some doubts. Often they dropped in with information about something pending that they thought their bosses should be prepared for, especially if the situations entailed any possibility of wide publicity. Routinely, headquarters officials who had been in the field for any reason were apt to stop by to describe informally what they had observed. Sometimes aides just wanted to sound out the chiefs' attitudes on various matters to guide their own thinking. In the course of a day, therefore, headquarters staffers dropped in intermittently from the start to the close of business. And when a chief was about to leave on an extended field trip—of a week or more, say—which was always announced in advance in the agencies, the traffic just before his departure grew particularly intense as his aides and lieutenants tried to complete business that would otherwise have had to wait until his return.

Outsiders were far less likely to appear without appointments. However, personal friends, former employees, professional associates, and occasionally people referred by congressmen or friends would be received without advance arrangements if there was time. And while much of the conversation in such instances had little to do with the work of the bureau, the visitors almost always brought news of people, events, and attitudes of general interest and potential usefulness to the host.

But outsiders reached the chiefs mainly through the telephone. The instruments of the chiefs' secretaries rang all day long, and the secretaries were exceedingly deft in deflecting calls to other offices when the items did not demand the personal attention of the chiefs. They would also get information from callers instead of putting them through so that the items could be placed before the chiefs in an orderly and convenient fashion. On the other hand, they were equally skillful in making sure that nobody who should have access to their chiefs was denied entry or unduly delayed. Calls from members of Congress, White House staff, top officers of the departments, leaders of clientele or professional groups, journalists whose inquiries could not be better and more appropriately handled elsewhere in the bureaus, and leaders of other government agencies, for example, were in this category. Within the bureaus, calls from ranking field officials also were accorded this receptive treatment, but most field officers dealt more frequently with specialists at headquarters than with the chiefs. A large part of the chiefs' telephone time was thus taken up by calls from outside their bureaus.

Some callers rang up the chiefs for the express purpose of imparting intelligence. Administrative superiors and congressional offices, for instance, occasionally suggested how matters of concern to them might be handled. For the most part, however, callers wanted something from the chiefs—a favor, perhaps, a word of advice, or a bit of information. Yet such requests were useful; they alerted the chiefs to what was happening in the environment and even in their own organizations; for the purposes of organizational intelligence, what is asked can be as instructive as what is declared. The calls were therefore a benefit as well as a demand and a cost, and while many of them were accepted simply to avoid alienating the callers, the chiefs also had a positive incentive to receive them.

As a result of all these impromptu claims on their time, a day that might begin with only a couple of things scheduled for a chief would fill up as it wore on. Their days in their offices were therefore episodic, disjointed, fragmented.[12] In a single morning, they often had to deal with half a dozen or more diverse topics. Their focus of attention shifted frequently; to an observer, their working time sometimes looked like a series of interruptions. Even without the impromptu demands on them, they often had enough on their schedules to lend their activities a disconnected air. The impromptu demands greatly intensified the fragmentation, and the energies of the chiefs were scattered. At the same time, they were able to inject themselves into many facets of the bureaus' operations, and had thrust upon them a good deal of intelligence about those operations that they might otherwise have failed to notice or receive.

Less regular than the recurrent meetings (which took place whether or not specific choices had to be made or specific actions had to be taken) but less spontaneous than the impromptu calls were the special briefings of the chiefs—heavily compressed, ad hoc cram courses and rehearsals set up whenever circumstances made it opportune or necessary to get them ready for decisions or for personal appearances. The briefings varied from intensely concentrated digests of material on narrow subjects to wide-ranging discussions of philosophy, policy, and alternative strategies and tactics for achieving chosen ends. They

12. See Mintzberg, *Nature of Managerial Work,* pp. 31–35; and Sproull, "Managerial Attention," pp. 27, 55–58.

constituted the largest single category of staff meetings—not because there were innumerable decisions or appearances to make, but because many preparatory efforts turned out to require more than one meeting.

Although most of the work of preparing for decisions by the chiefs was not done by the chiefs themselves but by their subordinates, and although the amount of time the chiefs spent preparing for decision was but a fraction of the total time invested by their organizations in this activity, and although they did not render major decisions in rapid-fire fashion, there were usually several matters in various stages of consideration that required many briefings and took a good deal of the chiefs' time. The chiefs took pains to prevent pre-decision briefings from taking an excessive amount of their time; the delegations of authority and the briefing rules described earlier served this end. Also, in matters the chiefs did not regard as of major importance, they sometimes encouraged their subordinates to agree among themselves on a course of action, which the chiefs would then review and either ratify or return for further work. In matters that deeply interested them, they would ask their staffs for informal progress reports from time to time, occasionally dropping in on the staff deliberative proceedings when they could find the time. Now and then they scheduled interim briefings to make sure staff discussions were heading in directions acceptable to them, sometimes striking options from the agenda or inserting or reinstating possibilities rejected or overlooked by the staff. When the staff work was complete, they would call decision meetings—gatherings for the express purpose of arriving at final choices in the form of formal action documents. In these ways, they strove to exercise influence over the preparations for decisions without allowing them to absorb all their time. They apparently had to keep their guard up constantly because some subordinates were eager to plead for favorite causes at length and frequently, and some were reluctant to take a single step without leadership guidance and involvement all along the line of the preparations. Despite their precautions, however, special briefings for decision and decision meetings still composed a significant part of the chiefs' workload and a major source of the intelligence they received.

So did ad hoc briefings for congressional testimony, for participation in their superiors' preparations for decisions, and for public appearances. Briefings for these activities had two goals. One was to equip the chiefs to make the best possible case for the positions they were about to set forth. The other was to avoid the embarrassment, described earlier, that can beset a leader who is not ready to engage in presentations, negotiations, or responses to sharp questioning. The staffs always wanted more of the chiefs' time to prepare them than they could get. They therefore condensed information, organized it, indexed it, and coded it so that the chiefs could find whatever they needed in a short time under pressure and skim through it systematically in their last-minute reviews before the spotlight was turned on them. Staff members sometimes arranged mock sessions of the forums in which the chiefs had to appear, with staffers playing the parts of some of the inquisitors the chiefs would face. They took pride in the ability of their chiefs to absorb large volumes of material quickly, but as their confidence in their leaders grew, the temptation to pack in still more also grew. The chiefs therefore had to restrain their efforts at exhaustiveness and persuade them that some risks had to be taken if the briefings were not to devour too much of the chiefs' time. All the same, the intelligence that came to the chiefs this way was plentiful.

Since so much of the information they received was furnished by, and filtered through, their subordinates, the chiefs were theoretically in jeopardy of becoming instruments of their own work forces, manipulated by those who controlled the data. The danger was not very great in practice, however. In the first place, their staffs were seldom unanimous on important issues, and the differences of opinion and perception among them commonly rose to the top. In the second place, the chiefs' external-relations functions, described below, opened lines of communication and intelligence outside the hierarchies they headed and exposed them to perceptions, values, facts, and interpretations quite different from those taken for granted within their bureaus. In the third place, they customarily questioned their subordinates searchingly about the data, assumptions, analysis, inferences, and proposals they produced. It was not unusual for a chief unpersuaded by the conclusions reached by his staff, uneasy about the basis of the conclusions, or simply convinced that a second look at the preparatory work would strengthen it to return staff products for additional research and deliberation. Chiefs rarely substituted their personal judgment for their staffs' work. (The logic of this practice was that the chiefs lacked the time and expertise to get into the details of every issue, but they could judge when a proposal was consistent with their policies, feasible, and politically sound.) Although they had to rely heavily on their subordinates for most of their intelligence, they took measures to preserve a measure of independence for themselves.

Some forms of briefing that I had thought would reinforce their autonomy by furnishing large quantities of independent information, but that would also use up much of their time, did neither. Briefings associated with inspections or audits routinely conducted in all government agencies were one such surprise for me. The chiefs seldom received anything more than written summaries of the routine reports, leaving the details to appropriate specialists on their staffs. Only when warning lights went on, signaling an immediate or emergent problem, would the chiefs get a personal briefing on the situation. And if the issue was deemed serious enough to warrant formal investigation, the results were ordinarily presented in personal meetings. Consequently, only a small part of the intelligence received by the chiefs came through briefings of this kind, and only a small part of their time was devoted to them.

The same may be said of hearings (which are, after all, a form of briefing) held by the bureaus. Private parties, government employees, and state and local governments affected by agency decisions have rights of appeal. But the lines of appeal in the IRS, the SSA, and Customs bypassed the chiefs, going instead to special courts and then the regular courts. Appeals from decisions of the Animal and Plant Health Inspection Service ran directly to the Department of Agriculture. Only in the Forest Service and the FDA were the bureau chiefs squarely in the appeals channels. Even in these cases, however, formal appellate proceedings before the chiefs were not an everyday occurrence. In none of the bureaus, therefore, was this form of personal contact a major source of information or a major preoccupation of the chiefs.

Public hearings preceding the issuance of regulations (and, in the case of the FDA, connected with meetings of advisory committees, bodies consisting mostly of outsiders with a special interest in or knowledge of the bureau's work) gave people a chance to place their views before the leadership of the bureaus and therefore were probably a little more instructive than appellate proceedings because they tapped the opinions of the concerned public. But the chiefs did not preside over all these hearings, nor did they always stay for the full length of the discussions. Though exposure to the intensity of feeling sometimes shook them, it is doubtful that they often heard anything they could not have anticipated.

Nevertheless, if all forms of the chiefs' personal contact and discourse, especially with their own staffs, are taken as a whole, this channel provided more of the intelligence acquired by the chiefs and took more of their time than any other channel. That is not to denigrate the mounds of written matter that crossed their desks in a never-ending parade. They had extremely heavy reading loads, allocated a great deal of their time to reading, and depended on it for a substantial fraction of their information. Their in-baskets, certainly, were rarely empty.

READING. Most of the material that came across their desks was passed upward by their own organizations, and most of that was information supplied by immediate subordinates about their own activities, submitted in the form of memorandums, reports, or duplicates of their correspondence with others. Much of the chiefs' reading time was thus occupied by communications on internal operations of the bureaus' leadership corps furnished after the fact. The chiefs were, as I described earlier, thus protected against potentially embarrassing gaps in their knowledge, were equipped to call attention to unnecessary and undesirable contradictions and inconsistencies within their bureaus, and were reassured that responsibilities assigned to members of their staffs had been carried out. At the same time, the subordinates established that they were not trying to evade or undercut their bosses, and their reported actions, if not promptly reversed, could be regarded as having been approved by their superiors in case anything untoward ensued.

Another large category of internal materials for the eyes of the chiefs consisted of documents for signature or approval, or as background for decision or public appearances. Most of the letters and memorandums signed by the chiefs were drafted by others in the chiefs' names; the signatories merely wrote their names in the appropriate places. (Autopens were used only in routine, repetitive matters.) Normally, however, the documents came in with files and summaries of the subject matter, so that the chiefs were not acting in the dark. Consequently, some would be returned for correction or improvement, and occasionally a letter would be changed and mailed by a chief on his own, with copies of the amended version inserted in the files and sent back to the drafter. The practice contributed to the chiefs' control over policy and external relations by limiting what could be done in their names, but it was also a source of intelligence for them as they reviewed the files and the correspondence placed before them. The process was largely automatic; the chiefs did not see many of the things they signed until the documents were before them, and the staffs quickly learned their chiefs' styles and attitudes so that little or nothing would have to be altered. Routine though the process was, however, it helped keep the chiefs apprised of developments in or affecting their bureaus.

Items were quite often sent for approval even when subordinates were authorized to sign them. This happened when the specialists who would sign as well as draft the documents were sufficiently concerned about the documents' sensitivity to seek advance authorization by the chiefs. Logically, one might expect anything important enough to justify clearance by a chief to be signed by a chief, and anything discretionary enough to be signed by a subordinate to be disposed of at a lower level, perhaps with information copies for the chief. But real life is seldom so symmetrical. Sometimes subordinates reckon that their chief's signature will carry more weight than their own in strategic places. They also vary in their willingness, or at least their eagerness, to exercise discretion. And anyway, signature rules do not always divide tasks perfectly. The chiefs therefore found themselves reviewing things that other people would sign as well as signing things that other people had written.

Documents sent by subordinates to prepare chiefs for decisions or public appearances added still more to their reading burden. If extensive oral briefings on particularly intractable problems or difficult choices were in store, the chiefs would be supplied with reports, analyses, and arguments on all sides; though compressed, these still aggregated to considerable length, and the chiefs ordinarily studied them carefully before assembling their advisers for discussion and decision. Similarly, before testimony, press conferences, interviews with journalists, and the like, their staffs would load them liberally with written homework (followed, if time permitted, by conferences and dry runs to perfect their mastery of the material). Even issues or

appearances of interest only to narrow audiences and decisions provoking little controversy engendered documentary briefings of the
chiefs.

Most of the reading matter of the chiefs was therefore provided by
their own bureaus. Even materials originating outside the bureaus
came to the chiefs through bureau channels. Each morning, for example, they received photocopies or digests of journal articles and of
newspaper items from around the country in which their agencies
were mentioned. Communications from other parts of the government and from nongovernmental sources were often summarized and
underlined by their staffs to shorten reading time. Printed government documents—the *Congressional Record,* committee reports, bills,
laws, GAO reports—were flagged, marked, and digested for the chiefs.
Internal channels thus were their main conduits for written intelligence from all sources.

In fact, it was through their aides and lieutenants that they learned
about many of the materials addressed to them directly. The incoming traffic was screened in mail rooms, in correspondence control
units, by administrative assistants, and by the chiefs' secretaries. Matters judged not to need their personal attention were diverted to the
agency specialists best equipped to respond to them so that the chiefs
were not overwhelmed by the influx. The people who made these
judgments quickly became sensitive to their chiefs' wishes. If somebody mistakenly diverted something a chief should have seen, it was
certain to be referred back to the chief by the recipient—immediately
in most cases, but for approval of a proposed response or for signature
in any event. At the very worst, the chief could count on getting an
information copy of any important actions or statements.

So the chiefs did not worry about not receiving or knowing about
things that should have come before them; they were far more likely
to get more than they needed or wanted, and some of the items in
their in-boxes were merely scanned quickly. In many cases, the chiefs
decided who should handle them, sometimes sending them off with
brief statements of what was to be done or said.

The volume of materials from outside the bureaus to which the
chiefs gave close attention was thus kept within manageable bounds.
These materials included all congressional mail of a nonroutine character, especially if it came from the chairmen or key members of
relevant committees. (All congressional mail was logged in and

flagged, however, so that it was answered promptly no matter to whom it went for response and no matter how routine the inquiry or request.) Included also were communications and information copies of actions, public statements, and testimony by departmental officials; correspondence from the Executive Office of the President; and communications from other government agencies, top state officials, and the leaders of organizations in the bureaus' respective constituencies. At least two of the chiefs made a point of periodically sampling mail from the general public for an independent reading of public sentiment and attitudes and an external perspective on themselves and their agencies.

They also scanned the daily press, trade journals, professional journals, and books when they could. Although their jobs consumed their days and evenings, their interests extended beyond their agencies, and they tried to satisfy their curiosity by ranging more widely. (However, they had to fit these independent excursions into their schedules as they could, and a far larger number of relevant items were likely to be called to their attention and summarized for them by their subordinates than they had time to discover independently.)

But all their written sources of intelligence, both hierarchical and independent, were less important in terms of the chiefs' time they consumed or the harvest of information they produced than conferences and conversations were. If you dropped in on a chief at random and found him reading, he would probably be going over something that came to him from inside his bureau rather than outside. The chances were much greater, though, that you would have found him deep in a discussion, not reading.

OBSERVING. No matter how much talking and reading they did, the chiefs also took pains to see for themselves at least a little of what went on in and around their agencies. Direct observation, it is true, was an incidental benefit of other activities described below—efforts to motivate their work forces or to conduct external relations. The chiefs almost never went out simply to gather or check intelligence unless something was flagrantly wrong; they usually took advantage of opportunities to pick up information in the course of their other duties—for instance, when visiting lower echelons of their headquarters or field stations of their bureaus, or attending professional or interest-group meetings. When they traveled for any purpose, even pleasure, they usually dropped in on one or more field installations.

Since I was not able to accompany them on such field trips, my impressions are based on discussions of them. From this hearsay evidence, it appears that the purpose of the observation was neither inspection nor investigation. The visits are best described as conducted tours, led by the senior officers in the organizational units visited. They were always arranged in advance, with a schedule of things and people to see, both inside and outside the bureaus, set by the tour leaders and the chiefs' staffs after general review and approval by the chiefs.

Inevitably, therefore, the intelligence they yielded was limited. Yet the chiefs valued these direct contacts for conveying a sense of the world beyond headquarters, a "feel" for the problems of the front-line employees, a taste of administrative reality. Administrators in Washington can grow isolated and lose touch with things outside the narrow compass of the capital. Direct observation, however circumscribed it may have been, reduced the chiefs' anxiety on this score and enabled them to visualize what some of their decisions and actions would mean in the field.

Intelligence-Gathering in Perspective

While the chiefs aggressively sought intelligence, they would have received a good bit had they never asked for any. It was thrust upon them.

Some of it came without planning or effort. It was simply "in the air." News travels fast in modern society. It moves especially fast in the Washington community. Officials as prominent as the chiefs of important government bureaus are inevitably athwart many lines of communication. Information comes to them from all directions.

Also, people trying to influence their decisions and actions put carefully selected data before them to shape their perceptions and evaluations. Briefs advocating specific positions and defending particular points of view are not dependable sources of information, but by comparing and contrasting them, decisionmakers can often piece together a good picture of a situation. Some intelligence thus falls, as it were, into their laps.

But no chief in this study depended on chance or volunteered intelligence. All of them requested information from their staffs and pursued it on their own. Their sensors were always out, always seeking, always pulling it in. Their own demands made receiving and reviewing intelligence the major activity.

Another contributing factor may have been an occasional desire to defer decisions under conditions of great tension and uncertainty. Taking a controversial matter under advisement, holding it off pending completion of further studies, sometimes allows tension to subside, tempers to cool, and differences to be reconciled, so that a situation in which no action seemed possible gradually becomes resolvable. Making a great show of receiving and reviewing intelligence is occasionally an oblique method of giving such processes a chance to take effect. Receiving and reviewing intelligence served so many ends—avoiding embarrassment, preparing for decision, appraising performance, as well as narrower tactical goals—that it became the primary activity of the chiefs I observed. Probably as much as 55 to 60 percent of their time went into it, and it is what they were most likely to be doing at any moment randomly chosen.

CONDUCTING EXTERNAL RELATIONS

Yet not a week—indeed, hardly a day—went by without some demand on them to represent their bureaus to the world outside.

The importance of external relations to the bureaus needs little explanation. The bureaus depend for their very survival, as well as for their programmatic success, on what other people do. They require the compliance of the public with the laws and regulations they administer. They must have legal authorizations and money from Congress and their administrative superiors to elicit compliance. They must be able to head off actions that would reduce their ability to elicit compliance. All these requirements oblige every bureau to deal extensively with its environment.

Why this responsibility fell so heavily on the bureau chiefs personally may not be so obvious. It would seem that they could have hired experts to perform much of this function for them. In fact, since they all had staffs for legislative liaison and public information, one might argue that the chiefs could have stayed free of this work altogether. By this reasoning, the elevation of external relations work to the status of one of their major functions seems something of a mystery.

But only because the reasoning is faulty. The chiefs of government bureaus become the personifications of their organizations, the symbolic embodiments of their agencies. They speak with an authority nobody else in their hierarchies can muster. Many people with power will not accept anybody else's word about their programs and organizations; some will not even listen to anyone else. By the same token, when a bureau wants an audience to listen to its message, the chief can almost invariably command greater attention. "Take me to your leader" (and its reverse, "Bring your leader to me") is not merely an amusing slogan; it is an expression of a deep-seated attitude toward hierarchical relations that apparently pervades society.

Consequently, the chiefs could not have escaped responsibility for external organizational relations even if they had wanted to. They did not want to, however. Their unique position protected them against circumvention by their subordinates and people outside the bureaus. They therefore would not have used their legislative-liaison and public-relations staffs as substitutes for themselves had that been possible. They depended on these staffs to monitor external relations, furnish advice, draft statements, maintain contacts, and explain policies to outsiders. But the chiefs themselves usually appeared as the official spokesmen for their organizations, a burden that often grew heavy yet was too useful to them to relinquish even if they could have.

Of course, the border areas between the bureaus and the environment did not involve the chiefs immediately and directly and took little of their time from day to day. These included such things as routine applications for established benefits and entitlements, policing clientele compliance with the law, service to clients, applications for employment in the agencies, appeals from the initial decisions of first-line employees, and the first stages of bureau consultation with the public about projected rules. The internal procedures of the agencies took care of most of these contacts with the environment.

The chiefs' role in external relations concentrated on those elements of the environment whose support, hostility, or neutrality could make the bureaus' operations easier or more difficult, more successful or less so. The traditional classification of these elements— the congressional set, the executive-branch set, clients and their organizations, hostile interests, professional groups, and the communications media—is particularly useful here.[13] From the perspective of the chiefs, these categories, though some of them overlapped, were the compass points on the map of the administrative, political, and social environment.

In general, relations between the chiefs and the constituent elements of each category consisted largely of efforts on each side to get the other side to do what it wanted. The external clusters constantly told the chiefs what the bureaus should do, and they employed every means from threats to cajolery to impress their respective preferences on the bureaus. The chiefs, in turn, strove to induce the outside elements to do what they wanted, which was to help the bureaus get on with their tasks as the chiefs saw those tasks. The relations were intricate, involving negotiations, exchanges of favors, accommodations, and endlessly shifting alliances and lines of conflict among the participants. The chiefs were almost always right in the middle of them.

The Congressional Set

At the center of the pattern of relationships for all the chiefs was Congress—its members, collectively and individually, its committees, its staffs, its evaluative arms (the General Accounting Office in particular). This set of congressional and congressionally related workers in the machinery of government seemed rarely to be out of the administrators' consciousness. The chiefs were constantly looking over their shoulders, as it were, at the elements of the legislative establishment relevant to their agencies—taking stock of moods and attitudes, estimating reactions to contemplated decisions and actions, trying to prevent misunderstandings and avoidable conflicts, and planning responses when storm warnings appeared on the horizon. Not that cues and signals from Capitol Hill had to be ferreted out; the denizens of the Hill were not shy about issuing suggestions, requests, demands, directives, and pronouncements. But even if they had been less assertive, they would have commanded the attention of the chiefs because of what Congress is empowered to do to and for the agencies.[14]

13. Walter G. Held, *Decisionmaking in the Federal Government: The Wallace S. Sayre Model* (Brookings Institution, 1979); and William W. Boyer, *Bureaucracy on Trial: Policy Making by Government Agencies* (Bobbs-Merrill, 1964).

14. See pp. 164–65, below.

For the chiefs, these powers, and the willingness of the congressional set to use them, led to what I thought was greater sensitivity to congressional influences than to any other category of factors outside the bureaus.

THE COMMITTEES. Since most of the work of Congress is done in committees and subcommittees, and the whole body usually defers to the judgments and recommendations of its subdivisions, the legislative relations of administrative agencies consist largely of contacts with the chairmen, members, and staffs of the committees and subcommittees that have jurisdiction over the administrators. This can be a demanding undertaking because jurisdictions overlap, and many agencies must answer to many committees for different aspects of their operations.

In the Ninety-fifth Congress, for example, FDA representatives appeared before a total of thirty-two congressional bodies—eleven Senate subcommittees (under seven committees), one Senate committee without subcommittees, seventeen House subcommittees (under eight committees), and three House committees without subcommittees. Moreover, they appeared before some of these groups a number of times—fifteen times in the case of one Senate subcommittee, fourteen in the case of one in the House—eighty-five times in all. The diversity and frequency of the FDA's appearances in that Congress were unusually great as a result of new administrative initiatives by the bureau and its new chief, legislative initiatives affecting the bureau's operations, and public and media interest in its programs. Ordinarily, the FDA would not face so many demands, and most agencies would encounter considerably fewer. Still, the demands are never negligible. The Forest Service was called before twenty-three committees or subcommittees, the IRS before twenty, Customs before seventeen, the SSA before sixteen, and even APHIS, the most specialized of all the bureaus in the sample, was summoned before seven.

Fortunately for the agencies, only two or three subcommittees were likely to probe especially persistently and deeply into their activities. Most of the time, therefore, the leaders of the six bureaus were concerned primarily with a limited number. The dominant subcommittees apparently changed from time to time as the membership of Congress, the assignments of its members, current events, and the interests of subcommittee chairmen shifted; while the period of observation in this study was too short to encompass pronounced changes of this kind, discussions with bureau staffs indicated that, over longer intervals, the intensity of a given group's attention to an agency varied greatly. One would grow interested when the interest of another flagged, however, so at no time was an agency likely to have fewer than two subcommittees closely examining at least some of its activities.

Appropriations subcommittees, particularly in the House, were among the most zealous superintendents of every bureau. Legislative subcommittees with jurisdiction over legislation in fields administered by the bureaus were as searching in their inquiries but not as unremitting.[15] (Not always, however. A former chief of the Social Security Administration declared that legislative hearings were by far the most important ones for him, and added that it was common for SSA chiefs to sit in on the deliberations of the legislative committees as legislation was drafted, acting as advisers to the committee and representatives of the administration. These sessions, he said, sometimes went on for months, day after day, and were more significant than formal hearings. Perhaps because things have changed— or just by chance during my period of observation—or because such close cooperation was not the general rule, I did not catch such sessions during my period of observation.) Subcommittees charged with generally overseeing the operations of particular bureaus—in some cases the subcommittees of the House Committee on Government Operations or the Senate Committee on Governmental Affairs, in

15. The general primacy of the appropriations committees in superintending the activities of the bureaus puzzled one reader, who expected them to be involved only at budget time. But their involvement at other times as well is not really surprising. Appropriations hearings, reports, and some appropriations legislation get into details of day-to-day administration, which generates negotiations over particulars in budget formulation, execution, and planning. Moreover, because appropriations automatically come up every year while legislative enactments of comparable sweep are not as frequent or regular, many of these understandings are routinely renewed and reexamined annually. Appropriations subcommittees are thus both more likely and in a better position to reward and punish agencies swiftly and with surgical precision than many legislative committees are. That is why the members and their staffs have such extensive contacts with the agencies under their jurisdiction, and why the agencies are especially aware of these bodies.

Things may change as a result of the recent intensification of congressional oversight generally, the spread of the legislative veto over agency regulations (should the practice survive court tests), and the increasing power of the budget committees in both houses. At the time of this study, however, the appropriations subcommittees still were, in most cases, more continually engaged in the lives of the six bureaus than other committees were.

others the oversight subcommittees of legislative committees or of the House Ways and Means (tax) Committee—also were occasionally prominent among the close observers. Others were sporadically involved, usually in connection with a specific piece of legislation and only for the period of consideration of that bill. Otherwise, the demands on the bureaus probably would have been overwhelming.

The chiefs represented their bureaus at committee and subcommittee hearings more often than any other members of their agencies did, but in no bureau did a chief handle all the appearances. During the term of the Ninety-fifth Congress, the administrator of APHIS came closer to that mark than any of the others, testifying personally at ten of twelve agency appearances. Next closest was the internal revenue commissioner, who testified at 60 percent of his agency's fifty-three appearances. None of the others exceeded 50 percent— eighteen out of thirty-six for the customs commissioner, thirty-seven out of eighty-five for the food and drug commissioner, twenty-five out of sixty-four for the chief of the Forest Service, and nine out of twenty-eight for the social security commissioner (when, it must be noted, the SSA was headed by an acting commissioner for a good part of the time). When matters of great technical complexity were scheduled for discussion by the legislative bodies and when hearings had to be set for times at which a chief could not attend, the agencies were represented by experts or by the chiefs' deputies. Almost invariably, however, the chiefs were present for the most sensitive, the broadest, and the most policy-oriented sessions.

When a chief appeared, he was usually accompanied by specialists who either furnished him with the information needed to answer committee inquiries or were permitted to answer directly. Often he was also accompanied by representatives of the department in which his bureau was located, presumably to answer questions beyond the scope of the bureau's responsibilities, including questions about the policies of the administration generally. Appropriate assistant secretaries were commonly the departmental spokesmen.

The testimony of the chiefs virtually always began with a prepared statement that was inserted in the printed record in its entirety but orally only summarized. The statements and summaries were drafted by members of their staffs who were especially well informed about the subjects to be discussed, reviewed by the bureau officers responsible for legislative liaison, and amended by the chiefs themselves. Preparing the introductory statement, however, was a lesser part of getting a chief ready for testimony than the briefings given him by his staff in anticipation of questions that might be put by members of the committees. Bureau experts in the matters under consideration assembled briefing books covering every topic that might arise at hearings; for appropriations hearings, which could range over the breadth of a bureau's programs, virtually every aspect of each agency's responsibilities was covered, and the books, with tabs to mark every subject, were often several inches thick. Just before the appearance, the functional specialists and the chief held briefing sessions, each specialist going over his part of the bureau's responsibilities. The chief followed along in the briefing book, asking questions to make sure he was in command of the subject. If mock sessions were staged, with members of the staff taking the questioners' roles, they were followed by critiques of the chief's responses and suggestions about how to improve them. Not all hearings required such intensive preparations; sometimes a chief would be called as a witness by a committee with whom his bureau ordinarily did little business or would be asked to discuss a narrow topic in which he was already well versed, in which case the briefings were much shorter and the briefing books much thinner. But at least twice each year, usually for appropriations and oversight committees, the briefings ran for hours, and the testimony was followed by debriefings with the staff to identify strengths and weaknesses in the chief's performance and in the materials compiled by the staff to assist him. On average, therefore, the time invested in getting chiefs ready for each hearing was substantial in all the bureaus.

To keep the briefing time within manageable limits, the chiefs and their staffs tried to find out what topics were likely to be of special interest to the committee members so that the witnesses could be particularly well prepared to deal with them. In large measure, they accomplished this informally through personal contacts with the members and their staffs, as described below. In part, however, committees seeking to get the fullest and most accurate testimony possible routinely put the bureaus on formal notice about the topics the hearings would address. Furthermore, when topics came up unexpectedly and the information requested was not at hand, standard congressional practice permitted witnesses to furnish detailed information for the record after the hearing. By these means, preparation time was kept within reasonable bounds.

The records produced by congressional hearings undoubtedly contained masses of information useful to the committees, to individual members of Congress, to people elsewhere in the government, and to interested people outside the government. How much the personal appearance of witnesses contributed to those records is another matter. Many of the most informative parts of the records consisted of written submissions not presented during the actual conduct of the hearings. Many of the questions to the witnesses were apparently drafted by staff workers or absent committee members and were routinely read by the members present. And many hearings were attended by only the chairman of the subcommittee and perhaps one or two other members for part of the testimony, so the replies were not heard by most of the members. Occasionally, to be sure, a witness's reply would lead to follow-up queries developing a point that might not otherwise have been unearthed or clarified, but conducting even these exchanges by correspondence was not unknown. The actual physical confrontation was therefore not essential to the building of a record.

Consequently I presume that other objectives must have inspired congressional insistence on personal appearances by bureau chiefs. One was probably the legislators' wish to see how the chiefs handled themselves in such situations; written responses, after all, could have been drafted by anyone, but observing the bureau leaders personally was a way of learning about their qualities at first hand. Another may have been to demonstrate the power of Congress to the chiefs, the chiefs' superiors, interest groups, and the chairmen's constituencies; the questioners on the dais grilling and occasionally lecturing the chiefs in the witness chair symbolized the authority of the legislative branch, and the deference of the chiefs emphasized the relationship.[16] A third probable reason was the attention thus drawn to the hearings, the chairmen, and the issues. The hearing process was more open and visible than exchanges of correspondence. Fourth, it was a long-established tradition. So the system has persisted even though

16. Jere Goyan, Donald Kennedy's successor at the FDA, testified before one committee only days after assuming his post informally and several weeks before he was formally sworn in; he had been summoned to Washington only a couple of months earlier. Inevitably, he had to admit that he did not know the answers to many of the questions put to him, and he was not in a strong position to rebut criticism of his agency by committee members. See *Infant Formula,* Hearings before the Subcommittee on Oversight and Investigations of the House Interstate and Foreign Commerce Committee, 96 Cong. 1 sess. (Government Printing Office, 1980), pp. 39–45. Providing the committee with information could not have been the main reason for his appearance so early in his administration.

the most common justification for the hearings, the record, is not self-evidently the strongest one.

Whatever the reasons, the chiefs took their appearances seriously and prepared diligently for every one. Preparation paid off; crisp, informed testimony apparently won respect and appreciation in Congress. The reputations of administrators seemed to rest to a considerable extent on their effectiveness at hearings. Such effectiveness was not enough to get the chiefs everything they wanted, nor could it overcome grave deficiencies in bureau performance if any existed. But it made their dealings with all groups, both in the government and in the nongovernmental sphere, easier and more efficacious, and it reinforced all their other administrative accomplishments.

It also worked to their advantage in two other ways. Impressive performances on the congressional witness stand gratified subordinates and roused their support for the chiefs. The members of their organizations, particularly in Washington, followed reports on their testimony and offered congratulations and expressed pride when their bosses made good showings. And getting ready to testify informed the chiefs about many practices and problems in their bureaus that they might not otherwise have bothered to investigate because other matters were more salient. A committee hearing was for them a little like an academic examination; the persons being examined presumably benefited more from what they learned while studying for the test than from the test itself. Thus even if the examiners learned little new about the subject and even if the procedure often looked like an exercise or a ritual rather than a search for information, it could still enrich the governmental process.

The chiefs' role in relations between the bureaus and Congress was not confined to testifying, however. They also went out to gather intelligence about the interests and concerns of members of Congress. At least once a year, they all visited the members of Congress in important positions on the committees with jurisdiction over their respective agencies; one, indeed, visited all the members of his principal House committee, which meant seeing more than four dozen representatives in that body alone, "to find out," he said, "what's bothering them." Another was described by members of his staff as "prowling the halls of Congress" from time to time to chat with legislators. A third had a warm friendship of long standing with a chairman. The six chiefs were not equally assiduous in cultivating such contacts, but none of them slighted the personal factor.

I never directly observed any contacts of this kind. From conversations with both sets of officials, I gather that meetings were useful for alerting agencies to what was likely to confront them in Congress and forewarning members of Congress about impending agency actions that might concern them. Whether the meetings were ever employed as well by chiefs to conspire with members of Congress against fiscal or policy or programmatic restraints and requirements imposed by the secretaries of the departments or by the White House, as some students of government have suggested,[17] I am in no position to say. There is no doubt, however, that the meetings helped clear up misunderstandings, avoid potential clashes, sharpen the focus of hearings, and provide opportunities to pay respects and get on a friendly footing. Without Byzantine conspiratorial intent, therefore, the chiefs had strong incentives to become personally involved in relations with Congress.

CONGRESSIONAL STAFFS. Members of Congress, both individually and in committees, rely heavily on their staffs to collect information, discern opportunities for legislative initiatives and investigations, and master technical details in many areas, as well as to handle the routine chores of serving constituents and running offices. For many years sophisticated officials in the executive branch have therefore made it a point to establish contacts with strategically situated staff people on Capitol Hill as well as with legislators. In recent years, rapid increases in the size of personal and committee staffs have made cultivation of such relationships even more urgent than in earlier generations, for hearings and questions and bills and investigations originate more than ever with the aides of the legislators whose names they bear.[18]

The six bureau chiefs in this study certainly knew the staff direc-

17. The classic statements of the divergence of interest between the president and his cabinet officers on the one hand and the alliances of bureaus, congressional committees, and interest groups on the other are Arthur A. Maass, *Muddy Waters: The Army Engineers and the Nation's Rivers* (Harvard University Press, 1951), chap. 3; and J. Leiper Freeman, *The Political Process: Executive Bureau–Legislative Committee Relations,* rev. ed. (Random House, 1965). See also David B. Truman, *The Governmental Process* (Knopf, 1951), pp. 410–15.

18. Michael J. Malbin, *Unelected Representatives: Congressional Staff and the Future of Representative Government* (Basic Books, 1979), chap. 10; and Harrison W. Fox, Jr., and Susan Webb Hammond, *Congressional Staffs: The Invisible Force in American Lawmaking* (Free Press, 1977), pp. 23–24, 88–89. See also David E. Price, *Who Makes the Laws? Creativity and Power in Senate Committees* (Schenkman, 1972), pp. 329–33; and Kenneth Kofmehl, *Professional Staffs of Congress,* 3d ed. (Purdue University Press, 1977), chaps. 8, 9.

tors of their major committees and were apprised of other staff assistants who concentrated on their agencies. (In one unusual instance, a senator's aide for a time spent the equivalent of several days a week at one of the bureaus to get information for a projected overhaul of the relevant legislation. The senator was not hostile to the agency or its program; relations were friendly, cooperative, and mutually beneficial. According to bureau personnel, the aide became quite expert in the bureau's responsibilities and operations. Though few congressional staffers were this deeply immersed in the agencies in this study, a good many of them were reportedly very knowledgeable about the bureaus within their purview.) But while the chiefs wanted to know about congressional staff, they did not invest much of their own time in relations with them; this task they left mostly to their headquarters staff. It was performed jointly by the bureaus' legislative liaison officers, substantive specialists, and assistants to the chiefs, who kept the chiefs informed about the interests and concerns of the congressional aides. Important as dealing with the legislative staffs was, the chiefs kept up with these relations indirectly rather than by personal participation.

CONGRESSIONAL ORGANS. Four staff agencies—the General Accounting Office, the Congressional Research Service, the Congressional Budget Office, and the Office of Technology Assessment—assist Congress by providing it with information.

The CRS also was in touch with bureaus from time to time—usually in connection with research it was doing to answer congressional inquiries and requests for data. (Its contacts with the Forest Service, however, have been especially frequent for several years, apparently because one of the committees with jurisdiction over the service has been particularly pleased with the work of the CRS and has therefore used it heavily.) The OTA likewise undertook studies that once in a while impinged on a bureau in this study, such as its report on the dangers of routine use of antibiotics in animal feed,[19] which touched the programs of both the FDA and APHIS. The CBO's occasional contacts with the bureaus were primarily to get data for economic and fiscal policy analyses, illustrated by its report on the effect of Forest Service timber sales on wood product prices.[20]

19. Office of Technology Assessment, *Drugs in Livestock Feed*, vol. 1: *Technical Report* (OTA, 1979).

20. Congressional Budget Office, *Forest Service Timber Sales: Their Effect on Wood Product Prices*, Background Paper (CBO, 1980).

It was the GAO, however, that was most important to the bureaus because of its special responsibility for assuring their compliance with appropriations laws and, as a result, for assessing agency performance. Among the four congressional staff organs, the GAO was the constraining force that most of the bureaus and most of the chiefs in this study felt most frequently. Acting in response to proposals by a committee or a member of Congress or on its own initiative, it often inquired into bureau policies, procedures, and organization and offered recommendations on how these might be improved. (And when it acted on its own, the head of the GAO division conducting the study reminded the secretaries of the departments, to whom the study reports were addressed, that they were obligated by statute to report from time to time on steps taken to comply with the recommendations.) There were even substantial GAO teams physically located on a full-time basis in the SSA and IRS buildings.

Contacts between the GAO study teams and the bureaus were mostly at levels below the chief officers of the agencies. But as a courtesy the consent and cooperation of the bureau chiefs were always solicited, and they were invariably given copies of the draft reports before the reports were cast in final form and submitted to Congress, to the secretary of the relevant department, and to the press. The chiefs were thus drawn into these relationships at the beginning and the end of a study. At the start, after discussions with their staffs, they and their top subordinates tried to define the scope of each inquiry. At the end, after review of the drafts with their staffs, they tried to eliminate findings and criticisms considered inaccurate or unfair, to soften the bluntest censure, and to increase the desirability and feasibility of the recommendations. Occasionally the inevitable differences of opinion would arouse tempers, and a chief might carry a protest to the comptroller general. Far more often, differences were sufficiently reconciled to result in bureau acceptance of GAO reports. And sometimes bureau leaders were delighted with reports that could be used to substantiate their petitions for more money, personnel, or authority.

The largest bureaus in the sample were the subjects of ten or more GAO reports during the period of observation. Others drew only one to three. Only APHIS had none.[21] Compared to relations with mem-

---

21. They covered a host of subjects—some broad, some narrow; some substantive, some procedural; some policy, some housekeeping. For example, in 1979, titles

bers of Congress, even the more frequent investigations claimed only a small proportion of the chiefs' time. But added to the other relations with Congress and its staffs, they reinforced an impression of almost continuous contact between the bureaus and the legislative branch.

The Executive Branch Set

The sensitivity of the bureau chiefs to congressional interests and concerns does not always sit well with people at the presidential and secretarial levels. The higher administrative levels no doubt understand why the bureaus must pay attention to the Congress and its affiliated units and personnel. But they tend to think of the bureaus as integral parts of the departments and the executive branch, and the responsiveness of these agencies to the legislative branch may therefore make them uneasy. Speaking of the executive levels above the bureaus as "external" to the bureaus, as I do here, doubtless violates their image of organic departmental unity. From the chiefs' point of view, however, although the higher levels have unique legal and moral claims on the bureaus, the bureaus are not mere appendages of their administrative superiors, but have a life of their own.[22]

From this perspective, the higher executive levels are essentially another cluster of groups intermittently making demands and telling the bureaus what they would like them to do.

---

of GAO reports on the agencies in this study included: "Social Security Should Improve Its Collection of Overpayments to SSI Recipients" (HRD-79-21, January 16, 1979); "Erroneous SSI Income Payments Result from Problems in Processing Changes in Recipients' Circumstances" (HRD-79-4, February 16, 1979); "Social Security Student Benefits for Postsecondary Students Should Be Discontinued" (HRD-79-108, August 30, 1979); "Taxpayer Waiting Time at IRS' Walk-In Service Offices" (GGD-79-53, April 10, 1979); "Who's Not Filing Income Tax Returns? IRS Needs Better Ways to Find Them and Collect Their Taxes" (GGD-79-69, July 11, 1979); "How Taxpayer Satisfaction with IRS' Handling of Problem Inquiries Could Be Increased" (GGD-79-74, September 18, 1979); "Food Salvage Industry Should Be Prevented from Selling Unfit and Misbranded Food to the Public" (HRD-79-32, February 14, 1979); "Does Nitrite Cause Cancer?" (HRD-80-46, January 31, 1980); "U.S. Customs Service Misclassifies Tobacco Imports" (GGD-80-19, November 6, 1979); and "Allegations Regarding Small Business Set-Aside Program for Federal Timber Sales" (CED-79-8, April 5, 1979). From year to year, of course, the number of reports on any given agency fluctuates, depending on what problems are brought to the attention of, or are discovered by, GAO personnel and on who demands investigations.

22. See the section called "The Differences They Made" in chapter 4, below.

THE PRESIDENTIAL CLUSTER. Take the president and the units in his executive office, the headquarters of the executive branch. Their direct claim on the time of the chiefs in the course of this study was slight. Of course, much of their influence was exerted through hierarchic channels—that is, through the offices of the secretaries and their staffs—so the impact of the presidential cluster on the bureaus was probably greater than the infrequency of direct relations might suggest. Still, they were relatively distant figures in the day-to-day life of the bureaus.

Most of the direct contact between the bureaus and the executive office was with the Office of Management and Budget. The OMB is responsible for, among other things, putting together the president's budget each year, overseeing agency compliance with appropriations laws, clearing agency policy positions in testimony and reports to Congress on pending legislation, and encouraging and assisting management and organizational improvements in the executive branch. So OMB officers work closely with the bureaus on budget formulation and execution, on review of presentations to Congress, and on structural and procedural matters, especially when large reorganizations are under consideration, as they were when this study was conducted.

The chiefs, however, were not deeply involved in budgetary details. Relations with OMB examiners were conducted mostly by their budget officers, who were guided by broad instructions from the chiefs and kept them generally informed. The chiefs took part in relations between the bureaus and the OMB mainly after the bureaus' budgets had been approved at the departmental level and the OMB had held its annual review of these figures. Then the chiefs themselves came to justify the requests at the OMB hearings. Budget examiners could be highly influential in these deliberations, producing decisions on minute details of bureau operations, to the irritation and dismay of bureau leaders. On a day-to-day basis, though, the chiefs usually left the specifics of dealing with OMB staffs to their budget offices.

Two of the chiefs were also engaged with the OMB on the reorganization side. Both Customs and the Forest Service were, in the period covered by this study, proposed for inclusion in major realignments of departments and agencies by reorganization teams. The chiefs as well as their staffs dealt more extensively with these OMB

groups than with all the others put together. As it happened, the
reorganization plans affecting them were dropped while I was observing the bureaus, and this area of contacts between the chiefs and
the executive office tailed off, too.

There were a few contacts between the chiefs and other units in
the executive office. The commissioner of customs, for example, was
part of a group consisting of White House staff and some line agencies that assembled periodically to discuss strategies for controlling
narcotics. The chief of the Forest Service heard from the Council on
Environmental Quality about his role in environmental management, from the Council of Economic Advisers about the effects of
timber prices and grazing fees on inflation, and from presidential
assistants about resource planning and about public lands in Alaska.
Occasional requests for information or opinions or material for presidential messages, or, more rarely, expressions of views, came in from
the White House staff (the second largest component of the Executive
Office of the President, after the OMB), the Domestic Policy Staff,
the Council on Wage and Price Stability, or the Office of Science and
Technology, and from time to time one of the chiefs would have a
meeting with those officials. These contacts could be delicate, for the
offices of the secretaries looked with distaste on direct, personal meetings between the departments' subordinates and the presidential
level. Furthermore, presidential aides were not always of one mind
on controversial issues, and bureau chiefs had to pick their way with
care in such cases. The initiatives in these relationships therefore
came from topside rather than from the bureaus; in fact, a bureau
initiative would have been considered unwise, if not improper. Consequently, the contacts were infrequent for any individual chief.

So the extent of direct relations between the bureau chiefs and the
cluster of presidential organizations, even for bureau chiefs who were
presidential appointees, was modest. This was not where their time
and energy went.

DEPARTMENTAL SUPERIORS. Much more of their time and energy
went into contacts with their departments. The chiefs saw a great
deal more of department officers than of the presidential group.

This is not to say that the chiefs personally conducted most of the
relations between the bureaus and the departments in which they
were lodged. On the contrary, their personal interactions were but
a small fraction of all the interactions between the two levels of

organization. Most bureau-department exchanges took place between bureau staff specialists (budget analysts, personnel administrators, public relations officers, property managers, and so on) and their departmental counterparts, or between bureau line officers and departmental legal officers, policy planners and evaluators, inspectors, auditors, legislative affairs officers, and public relations officers. The chiefs were informed only if the contacts were anything other than routine. Streams of communications moved in both directions without touching them at all.

Still, they were drawn into the center of these relationships, especially when the levels joined forces to advance legislation. They were the experts in their own jurisdictions on whom the secretaries called for information and advice. They were the sources of policy proposals and requests to the secretaries. They brought the secretaries warnings of hazards and embarrassments in their areas of responsibility. They were called to account when things went wrong. They were the ones summoned to receive orders, to brief the secretaries, to present budgets. They were the representatives of their bureaus who sought clearance from the secretaries before taking action. Reports to the secretaries on bureau operations went out over their names, and most written departmental directives were funneled through their offices. They were the spokesmen for their agencies when differences with other agencies obliged secretaries to resolve the arguments. On the average, therefore, each of the chiefs had four or five personal contacts with people at the departmental level each week, and about as many exchanges of correspondence.

One of the chiefs mentioned that when such contacts were made at his instance, which was not as often as initiatives came down from above, they sometimes required great sensitivity. The division of labor between a secretary and his main lieutenants—deputy secretary, under secretaries, assistant secretaries—blurs at the margins and varies. Approaching the wrong official might provoke rancor and charges of violating channels. As a preventive, the chief in question took pains to find out who was interested in what and to make sure that everybody was informed of every exchange. Over time, however, the risk of error diminished; it was not a significant source of anxiety anywhere during my study.

Most of the contacts and exchanges were not one-on-one encounters with the secretaries or even with the secretaries' deputies and assistants. Rather, most of them were conferences at which the chiefs appeared along with other high officers of the departments in much the same way as bureau officers participating in bureau conferences with the bureau chiefs, and a good many of the gatherings were recurrent. Four of the chiefs had more contact with the assistant secretaries assigned jurisdiction over their bureaus than they did with most other departmental officials. The IRS and the SSA were the exceptions, because no assistant secretaries stood between them and their respective secretaries. But even they dealt more extensively with top secretarial aides (the deputy secretary of the treasury and especially the assistant secretary for tax policy in the case of the IRS; the under secretary of HEW in the case of the SSA) than with the secretary. This is not to say that the bureau chiefs never saw the secretaries individually; of course they did. The commissioners of customs and social security, for instance, were close friends of their respective secretaries. But one-on-one meetings with the department heads were not the major consumers of the chiefs' time in their relations with the departments; group sessions and meetings with other departmental officers took much more time.

Both the group and the individual meetings at the departmental level were much like the meetings of the bureau chiefs with *their* lieutenants; that is, the meetings were given over largely to the exchange and review of information for essentially the same purposes and in much the same way as meetings inside the bureaus. At some, a chief would apprise superiors of projected actions by the bureau, both to get their approval and to prevent them from being taken by surprise. At others, a superior would expect progress reports on the implementation of past decisions or deliberations on pending ones approved or initiated at the higher level. Sometimes a meeting would focus on an impending announcement of a decision or brief the secretary or one of his deputies for a press conference or prepare them for testimony on Capitol Hill. Occasionally it would be the setting for reaching a decision. Often, however, as at the bureau level, a meeting would be taken up with exchanges of items about developments in both bureaus and departments, explanations of measures contemplated or taken, intelligence about relevant sentiments in Congress, the White House, and elsewhere, and similar bits of information that kept departmental and bureau leaders abreast of events and plans throughout the department and alerted them to larger trends not detectable from any single vantage point.

Correspondence from departments to bureaus was likewise primarily informational and addressed to groups of agencies rather than to individual agencies. I never saw any commands written in military fashion, with higher headquarters giving substantive marching orders to lower ones. Only in procedural and housekeeping matters was there anything akin to such direction, in the shape of department-wide regulations or of inserts for departmental administrative manuals (described in the next chapter). In matters of substance, which is to say the conduct of bureau programs, the intervention of the secretaries themselves was slight and of other departmental officials only a bit greater, and it generally took the form of negotiations over bureau actions rather than of formal departmental directives.

Nevertheless, the total volume of contacts and correspondence constantly reminded the chiefs that the departments were watching over them. One of the secretaries was especially active in his oversight and was always checking, prodding, inquiring, suggesting, and giving guidance. But in none of the departments were the chiefs free of constraint from the departmental level.

At the same time, the chiefs did not invest huge blocks of their time in relations with the departments, or even in preparation for them, except at budget time and when pressing for major new policy or legislative initiatives. The investments were noticeable, even irksome at times, and they were considered important. But they did not dominate the chiefs' schedules by any means.

OTHER FEDERAL AGENCIES. Possibly as much time was consumed by relations with other bureaus and other departments and agencies as by relations with superiors in the chiefs' own departments and the Executive Office of the President combined, though not with any single unit; each of the bureaus impinged on at least several other agencies. For this reason, the total time invested in lateral exchanges by the chiefs was, in most of the cases, of the same order as that invested in upward relations in the hierarchy. The number of points of tangency of each of the bureaus was striking. Customs, for instance, counted some forty sister agencies helped by customs officers to guard against illegal entry of forbidden and controlled substances and even against illegal immigration. Although many of these cooperative efforts had long since become routine, changing circumstances forced periodic readjustments of joint programs. Shortly before this study began, the commissioner of customs instituted regular, formal conferences with the chiefs of the Immigration and Naturalization Service and APHIS to discuss ways of stopping the entry of aliens without proper permits, of prohibited drugs and plants, and of animals and meat that might introduce disease into American herds, flocks, and pets.

Similarly, APHIS worked with the FDA on keeping carcinogens from entering the food chain through additives to animal feed; with the Environmental Protection Agency and the Fish and Wildlife Service to reduce the dangers of disease transmission from game to domestic animals; with the Forest Service to control, without fouling the environment, forest pests and diseases that might attack orchards and other sources of food; and with the State Department on fashioning agreements with foreign governments to prevent the importation of such pests and diseases from abroad and to permit the exportation of American foodstuffs.

The Forest Service, in turn, had to deal with other federal land management agencies, including the Soil Conservation Service, the Fish and Wildlife Service, the Bureau of Land Management, and the National Park Service. The Department of Energy, looking at biomass as a possible source of energy, sought out the Forest Service to find out about such resources in the national forests. Camps for training youth and young adults were operated in the national forests in cooperation with the Department of Labor.

The FDA and the Federal Trade Commission jointly sponsored a campaign to promote prescription of generic in place of brand-name drugs. In 1977 the commissioner of food and drugs signed a formal agreement with the Environmental Protection Agency, the Consumer Product Safety Commission, and the Occupational Safety and Health Administration for closer coordination of their activities; and he acted to implement a 1976 agreement with the National Cancer Institute to reduce excessive X-ray exposure in mammography facilities and persuaded the Departments of the Army, Navy, and Air Force, as well as the Indian Health Service and twenty-six states, to participate in the program. He also worked with the administrator of the Food Safety and Quality Service in the Department of Agriculture to coordinate their overlapping programs.

The IRS and the SSA impinged on fewer federal agencies than some of the other bureaus in this sample. But they touched each other at several points. Since the IRS collected social security taxes that furnished the basis for social security claims, the SSA depended on the IRS for these data and therefore had an interest in how many people were assigned to performing these services. Also, coverage under social security was defined in both the Internal Revenue Code and the Social Security Act; though the words were identical, the two agencies had to cooperate to standardize their interpretations of the provisions. They also had to work together to divide responsibilities for gathering information on pension systems under the Employee Retirement Income Security Act of 1974 and develop a Combined Annual Wage Reporting system that reduced the reporting burdens of employers. The SSA had joint programs with the Veterans Administration, the Railroad Retirement Board, and the Office of Personnel Management to avoid overpayments of benefits (and to arrange trust-fund interchanges with the Railroad Retirement Board); with the Department of Defense to take account of military pensions and military payments to social security retirement (all military employees being under social security); with the Department of Labor to coordinate black-lung payments to miners; and with the Department of Justice in cases of fraud and other violations. The IRS also had to deal with the Department of Justice—especially its Tax and Criminal Divisions—on litigation to enforce the Internal Revenue Code, and with the State Department about agreements on double taxation, services to taxpayers quartered abroad, and administration of tax laws applicable to both foreign and American companies and individuals in other countries. And the SSA worked through the State Department to administer its program for beneficiaries, both citizens and noncitizens, living abroad. So even the bureaus obliged to work with comparatively few other federal agencies were drawn into the web of interagency contacts.

The chiefs were not personally involved in all these contacts. Many of the contacts, after all, had been reduced to routines and were handled at lower levels. But the relationships generated meetings, telephone calls, and correspondence that now and then claimed the chiefs' attention. In a given week or even a given month, these claims might amount to little. The demands tended to be sporadic, however, and in the course of a year added up to something approaching the demands of hierarchical superiors on the chiefs' time.

The demands, incidentally, were not invariably congenial. I was present when an officer of a federal agency tried to get one of the chiefs in this study to rescue the caller from an embarrassing position in which his own agency's policies had placed him. Had the chief assented, his bureau would have been subject to intense pressure and a massive workload not strictly within its jurisdiction. He therefore declined. But he did not rest there. Anticipating that the caller would try to outflank him, he quickly made a number of calls to explain his position to various officials he was sure the caller would appeal to. Eventually, it was the other agency that changed course.

Similarly, I saw a delegation from an agency vehemently protest a procedural improvement suggested by one of my bureau chiefs that would have rendered obsolete a proposed practice the agency had been working publicly for many years to perfect, a mortification to which the protesters would not agree. Evidently, tension was not unusual in interagency negotiations. And the tenser they were, the more likely the chiefs were to be drawn into them.

Tense or amicable, though, relations with other agencies were sure to absorb a portion of the chiefs' time. While the chiefs met or talked or corresponded with their counterparts partly as a matter of courtesy, interagency contacts were also useful as a means of emphasizing their interest in a subject of mutual concern and of getting external intelligence at first hand. Anyway, the chiefs were usually the only officers of their bureaus in a position to make binding commitments. So dealing with sister agencies was not a trivial part of their duties or their schedules.

In the aggregate, then, taking stock of both lateral and hierarchical links, the chiefs probably spent as much time with elements of the executive branch as they did with components of the legislative branch. The time was divided into fragments of varying duration, from brief exchanges to hours of meetings, and many of these were spontaneous, triggered by unpredictable events that impelled them and their colleagues to get in touch. Over a year, these contacts added up to a substantial total because the parts of the executive branch are too interdependent for any of them to function in isolation.

Nongovernmental Sets

The chiefs probably averaged about as much time with a host of nongovernmental interests as with either branch of government. The majority of these relations were with organized groups, not individual persons or firms. Each bureau was surrounded by constellations of groups telling its leaders what they wanted it to do, criticizing its operations (or, more rarely, commending them), and seeking information about its actions and its plans for the future.

The effectiveness of the bureaus as organizations, and of the chiefs themselves, is perceived by students and practitioners of administration as depending in large measure on the attitude of the constellation associated with each agency. Unanimous denunciation, even for mutually contradictory reasons, is assumed to result in decreased support in Congress, reduced cooperation in the executive branch, and diminished compliance with bureau policies in the outside world. Unanimous approbation, on the other hand, is regarded as too much to expect in an arena of diverse, often clashing, interests. The best a chief can hope for, presumably, is backing from some quarters and neutrality from most so that he is not confronted by a solid phalanx of detractors. To this end, all the bureaus in this study had programs to explain their policies to the outside world, to discover the views and concerns of external groups and the media so that avoidable irritants and provocations contained in agency programs and proposals could be eliminated or softened, and to enlist the active support of favorably disposed interests when adversaries were on the attack.

Most of these duties were performed by special staff units at headquarters and, at least in the larger bureaus, in the field. Still, some of it fell to the chiefs. To show respect for, and deference to, interest groups in their constellations, they would accept invitations to appear at meetings and address the assembled members. As gestures of solidarity with their natural allies, they attended professional conventions and conferences. They lent their prestige to some of these proceedings merely by showing up, and they gained opportunities to cement ties with influential people in their fields. Of the full array of public relations activities conducted by the bureaus, the labors of the chiefs were only a part. Nevertheless, they were an important part, and usually a part that nobody else in the bureaus could perform as effectively.

THE UNORGANIZED CLIENTELE. The part of the bureaus' external relations programs that took less of the chiefs' time than any of the others was the dissemination of information on laws and regulations affecting much of the population—information on services offered, actions required or prohibited, ways to claim benefits or comply with legal provisions or improve one's personal or business condition. All the bureaus published booklets, pamphlets, and leaflets describing these opportunities and obligations in nontechnical language and distributed them widely. The field staffs of most of them gave talks to groups in their communities. The IRS, the SSA, and APHIS prepared spot announcements for television and radio stations. The SSA even furnished films and newspaper columns. The main purpose was to make sure that people knew their rights and responsibilities and to help them protect themselves against known hazards. These were efforts at education.

For the most part, they were performed by specialized staffs without much intervention by the chiefs, though new materials were customarily passed before the chiefs for their information and comment before release, and it was not unusual for a chief to express opinions that would influence a product or start work on a new one. One former social security commissioner reported that he considered these communications so important for the public's understanding of the programs administered by the agency and for the public image of the organization that he had on occasion devoted a whole morning to the drafting and format of a single publication to be printed in tens of thousands of copies. Mostly, however, these tasks were left to the professionals, and the chiefs' participation was not extensive. More of the chiefs' time was claimed by relations with their organized constituencies and the media.

THE ORGANIZED CONSTITUENCIES. Nearly every time a bureau did anything—especially when it changed anything—some people gained and others lost. (The "losses" were often deprivations of *expected* gains rather than reductions in existing benefits, but the reactions of the affected parties were much the same in either case.) Consequently, any action aroused opposition and generated support and approval at the same time.

While actions were under consideration in the bureau, the interests on both sides vigorously pressed their suits. After decisions were made, however, only the critics were likely to continue their campaign by bombarding the bureau, Congress, the president, other interests, and the media with their objections and denunciations. The beneficiaries were usually much less active and vocal. Perhaps deprivation is a more powerful stimulus than gratification. Perhaps the gainers did not want to draw attention to their benefits. Perhaps they took their good fortune for granted as their due. Or perhaps they saw it as the result of their strategic skill in influencing the bureau rather than as evidence of the bureau's largess. At any rate, once actions were taken, beneficiaries were less apt to applaud the bureaus voluntarily than losers were to attack them.

Under these conditions, opinion could seem unanimously hostile to a bureau even when there was widespread latent support for it. And apparently unanimous criticism could shake confidence and cause contractions in financing, authority, and compliance that generated still more complaints and alienation. In this fashion, the snowballing of half-true impressions could turn appearance into reality. Bureau chiefs' own public relations programs therefore aimed at maintaining balance by keeping known friends in line and encouraging their overt expressions and demonstrations of backing. They concentrated on working with consistent supporters.

The most consistent supporters of the bureaus were found among two clusters of outsiders: the professions strongly represented in the work force and the major associations of people and organizations (the "clienteles") served or regulated by the bureaus. The relationship between the bureaus and these clusters was a typical blend of love and hate. The outsiders were almost invariably angered by requests denied, proposals declined, constraints and inconveniences imposed. The bureaus were annoyed by the endless lists of demands and unsolicited advice presented to them. But the bureaus were also grateful for backing in times of need, and the backers had memories of benefits bestowed, protection against competition, special access to officials, and cooperation. Furthermore, no matter how irritating an existing agency was, its clientele and professional allies apparently felt more at home and secure with it than with what might have succeeded it if the bureau had been abolished and its functions transferred to other agencies. The unifying bonds were stronger than the sources of disaffection, and these groups furnished a core of support because their interests were so intricately intertwined with those of the bureaus.

Yet the bureaus never took the bonds for granted. They labored continuously to maintain and reinforce them. A defection of erstwhile friends was evidently more to be feared than the unremitting assaults of long-standing foes. Maintaining ties with natural backers had a high priority.

In particular, the chiefs took care to keep open their lines of communication with these groups. It was easy for spokesmen for groups associated with any bureau to get the chief's ear. Most of the outside speeches the chiefs made were at meetings of these professional or client associations (selected strategically from the abundance of invitations tendered). Correspondence from the associations was routed to the chiefs, and most of the replies went out over the chiefs' signatures. The chiefs conferred with such groups in a variety of settings ranging from formally constituted advisory committees to informal, ad hoc, open meetings, sometimes marked by candid, no-holds-barred exchanges of views. The groups did not invariably come away from these encounters with all they sought, nor did the chiefs. Still, even quarrels and freely expressed differences of opinion, like the strains inside a family, helped to enhance the solidarity of the parties involved.

But the bureaus' constituencies also included steadfastly hostile groups. For example, some people were so concerned about the harmful effects of certain food preservatives and artificial sweeteners and medicinal drugs and insecticides that they wanted them summarily and totally banned. When the agencies employing or regulating these substances declined to do so until they had assessed the benefits as well as the risks, they were accused of indifference to human life and welfare and, in the case of the FDA, of being more sensitive to the demands of the manufacturers than to the safety of the general public. Similarly, some organizations against almost all man-induced change in vast areas of the public domain were apt to fight every measure for development of the resources in those properties and to denounce any public official and agency not similarly inclined. Groups of this kind seldom had a kind word for the bureaus because the bureaus, trying to balance competing demands (such as criticism for being too slow to approve medicines, too cautious about the use of powerful insecticides against costly insect invasions, or too conservative about the use of resources on which many communities depended for their livelihood), could never do enough to satisfy the single-minded advocates. The bureaus therefore had little hope of changing their minds or winning their support.

The bureaus did not ignore them, however. In the first place, the arguments of the hostile groups often had merit, so the sensible course was to hear them out and to respond to their valid contentions as far as possible. Second, the consistently critical groups bombarded the bureaus' normal allies with their materials, so the bureaus were obliged to analyze and evaluate their arguments to make sure bureau supporters heard both sides of every issue. And third, refusal to yield an inch to these critics was seen as lending credibility to their charges that the agencies were bureaucratically rigid. So the bureaus not only heard them out, but tried to rebut their contentions and accommodate to them whenever possible. Unlike the relationships with natural allies, these relationships were thrust on the bureaus rather than eagerly seized or initiated and cultivated by them.

All of this meant that each of the chiefs dealt with a diverse set of interests. Associations and schools for accountants, lawyers, and other tax preparers figured especially prominently among organizations addressed by the internal revenue commissioner. The customs commissioner focused on customs brokers, importers, freight forwarders, freight and passenger carriers, and travel agents. Veterinarians, schools of veterinary medicine, beef and poultry and pork growers, animal and plant importers, dealers in pets and performing animals, and farm organizations generally occupied the administrator of APHIS. The commissioner of food and drugs dealt with the medical and nursing professions and their schools, hospitals, manufacturers and distributors of pharmaceuticals and medical devices and food additives, and processors and distributors of food for animals and humans. The Forest Service list encompassed associations of professional foresters, schools of forestry and environmental sciences, wood-producing and wood-using industries and workers in those industries, developers of mineral and gas and oil resources, grazing interests, wildlife biologists and enthusiasts (including hunters and fishermen), recreation consumers (associations of snow skiers, water skiers, campers, backpackers, snowmobilers, boaters, and motorcyclists), and recreation purveyors (such as the Recreational Vehicle Industry Association and the Campground Owners National Association). In the case of the social security commissioner, the constituency comprised the insurance industry, including underwriters and actuaries; labor unions; organizations of elderly, retired, disabled, and handicapped people; and associations of women, people on welfare, and ethnic minorities.

This inventory is by no means exhaustive; it merely suggests the character and variety of interests with which the chiefs strove—or were forced—to maintain relations.

THE COMMUNICATIONS MEDIA. The bureaus were also attentive to the media. The bureaus' public relations operations were not simply propaganda machines; their primary function was to provide information about agency actions and policies to anyone who inquired. Much of the time the inquirers were journalists gathering information for a story or a feature, but occasionally they were individuals trying to find their way to the proper channels for their own cases. Without the public relations offices, both sets of information seekers would have been left to their own devices, which would have cost them more time and money and would at the same time have imposed heavy burdens on the bureau work forces whom they called and visited blindly. Consequently, public relations staffs often served as research assistants to callers; staff members worked up the answers to their questions by consulting agency specialists and then passed the replies along to the inquirers. The procedures were economical for all parties to these transactions, especially since many callers asked the same questions and one search could do multiple duty.

Public relations offices were also control points for statements and articles originating with the bureaus. They made sure the substance of these pieces was cleared through all the proper units, that they were consistent with announced policy, and that they were properly and legally publicized. They also distributed the press releases.

And finally, they scanned publications for items about the bureaus and for news that might affect the bureaus' workloads in the future. The daily clippings supplied to the chiefs came through and from public relations people.

The activities of the public relations staffs made them excellent sources of intelligence for bureau leaders, according to a couple of chiefs. They said that public relations contacts with journalists, interest groups, and the general public made for reliable estimates of attitudes toward the agencies generally and toward specific contemplated measures. The staffs were also particularly helpful when, in response to prudence and law, an agency sought to induce the public to express itself about actions under consideration. Consequently, these chiefs turned to their public relations officers not only for the distribution of information, but also for the acquisition of information.

I was surprised to discover that trade and industrial publications, in whose areas of specialization each relevant bureau must have loomed large, were not prominent in either respect. Neither were the professional, scientific, and technical journals with specialties encompassing the bureaus' respective missions. For each of the bureaus, there were dozens of relevant publications of these sorts. Except for automatically receiving all announcements and releases, however, they did not figure conspicuously in the public relations activities of the bureaus. The general press, especially regional and local newspapers, was far more noticeable.

The routine flow of information in both directions between the bureaus and the media was thus almost entirely in the hands of the public relations offices. The chiefs were apprised of the public opinion trends and the media concerns revealed by these contacts. They were consulted on sensitive and troublesome items. For the most part, however, they were not involved in the day-to-day public relations work of their agencies.

All the same, they had significant responsibilities in this field because they were obliged by circumstances—even when, as was sometimes the case, they initiated the action—to perform certain public relations functions in person. As in their dealings with Congress, these were personal appearances that amounted to command performances; the hosts would not accept any substitutes. So the chiefs were called on (or arranged to be called on) to grant interviews and provide comments and appear on public affairs television programs and even to write articles. They joined the secretaries or assistant secretaries of their departments at press conferences for announcing important measures. They were consulted by their staffs and their superiors on the handling of public relations problems. These things did not take place every day, of course, or even every week. It is difficult to generalize about the frequency because there was so much variation between agencies, and even within agencies at different times; for example, new chiefs of big or controversial bureaus were the subjects of much press and television attention in their early days, but the excitement tapered off after a while. The chiefs were thus likely to have only a few media contacts a month. Consequently, even allowing for preparation time for some appearances, this was not one of their most demanding duties. They never took it lightly, but it was not a principal consumer of their time.

Officials of Other Governments

The bureaus were also linked with officials of state and local governments and foreign governments.

The points of tangency with the states and some of their subdivisions were numerous. The IRS, for example, had arrangements with many states for sharing certain data on tax payments and adjustments and refunds, and states had access to IRS magnetic tapes of selected data. In the Forest Service, a deputy chief was responsible for state and private forestry, which included cooperation with state forestry agencies to administer agreements on cooperative fire protection, forest management, and insect and disease control programs. The social security commissioner in 1979 established the position of associate commissioner for intergovernmental and community affairs to be "the agency's voice and listening post with state and local governments" in connection with grants to the states for assistance to the aged, blind, and disabled, and collection of social security premiums for covered state and local employees, among other things. An associate director of federal-state relations in the FDA was the channel for agency-state communications on such programs as mammographic quality assurance, exemption of state and local requirements from preemption by federal legislation in some matters, and advancing the use of generic drugs in place of brand-name products by appropriate state laws. APHIS depended heavily on the cooperation of state authorities with its field forces to control and eradicate plant pests and diseases and ailments of poultry and livestock, and its laboratories assisted state agencies in their campaigns against these afflictions. Customs agents worked with state and local law-enforcement officers in the struggle against narcotics and illegal immigration.

Once again, most of these relationships were routine and were conducted mainly by functional specialists, field personnel, and designated liaison officers. But the chiefs could not keep out of them entirely. For one thing, they had to sign or approve agreements and understandings between their bureaus and state and local officials, which meant they had a ceremonial as well as a substantive role. For

another, national associations of state and local officers performing
related functions (such as the National Association of State Social
Security Administrators, the National Council of State Public Welfare Administrators, the National Council of Local Public Welfare
Administrators, the National Association of Tax Administrators, the
National Association of State Departments of Agriculture, and the
National Association of State Foresters) wanted, like the nongovernmental groups, to see chiefs in person, and this demand furnished
opportunities for cementing alliances. So while the chiefs left the bulk
of these intergovernmental connections to their subordinates, they
did step into them from time to time. The involvement usually consisted of no more than an occasional speech to a national association,
prompt attention to communications from state counterparts, occasional visits with them in the course of field trips to their areas, and
granting them ready access to the chiefs when they came to Washington. The chief of the Forest Service even sat with the executive committee of the Association of State Foresters. These contacts did not
prevent storms once in a while, as when state officials rose up against
a move by the SSA to require monthly deposits of payments to the
old age, survivors, and disability trust fund on behalf of state and
local employees in the system instead of quarterly deposits so that the
trust fund instead of the state treasuries would earn the interest on
those moneys in those intervals. (The dispute was eventually settled
by a compromise.) On the whole, however, the contacts contributed
to smoother relations and stronger alliances. So the chiefs invested
willingly what little time was required.

Similarly, most of them invested modest amounts of their time in
relations with their counterparts in governments abroad. Most of the
bureaus were involved in one way or another with foreign officials in
the conduct of their programs, such as the cooperation of APHIS
with governments all over the world to prevent the introduction of
farm diseases and pests into this country and to assure other countries
that American products were similarly free of threats to their agriculture. American customs officers were stationed abroad and foreign
officers were stationed in the United States to facilitate the flow of
people and goods, and customs representatives were sent to other
countries to investigate allegations of dumping of foreign products in
the United States. The IRS provided taxpayers based overseas with
service, assisted foreign governments in developing and administer-

ing their own internal revenue systems, and administered the terms of international tax treaties. The FDA's responsibilities for regulating medicinal drugs, biological products and foods, medical devices, and similar items in foreign commerce led to interactions with regulators in other countries. The SSA, in collaboration with the State Department, negotiated treaties defining tax liabilities and benefit arrangements (called "totalization" agreements) applicable to American companies with operations in other countries, to their employees abroad, and to foreign counterparts in this country. Most of the bureaus also participated in international associations in their specialties and entertained visitors from counterpart agencies abroad. But these relations had long since been routinized, and the repetitive contacts were handled by specialized offices: both the IRS and Customs had international operations divisions, APHIS had an international programs liaison staff, the SSA had an office of international policy, and the FDA had an international affairs staff. And two of the departments had their own international units—under an assistant secretary for international affairs in the Treasury Department and an assistant secretary (under secretary since 1979) for international affairs and commodity programs in the Department of Agriculture. Consequently, the bureau chiefs ordinarily left these matters largely to others.

The administrator of APHIS, however, involved himself more than the others. The continuing struggle against diseases and pests that could travel overland from the country's southern neighbors kept him engaged in personally advising, assisting, consulting, and negotiating with his counterparts in this region, and he was also his department's principal resource for such negotiations in other parts of the world. He therefore spent a great deal of his time—probably 10 to 15 percent—in travel abroad and in receiving visitors from other nations. At the other end of the scale, the chief of the Forest Service had very limited demands for official international contacts. The other chiefs were somewhere between, closer to the low than to the high pole.

Thus, except for the APHIS administrator, the officials of other governments, both at home and in other countries, did not take up large amounts of the chiefs' schedules. Nonetheless, at irregular intervals they did require attention, and this was one more thing for the chiefs to deal with.

The General Public

Hovering in the background—nebulous, inarticulate, divided, and volatile—was the general public. The administrators heard from self-selected, interested parties, not from the general public, though all the special groups in the congressional, executive, nongovernmental, and other governmental sets of interests claimed at various times to speak for "it." And because "it" encompassed such diverse and mutually incompatible interests, nobody could reasonably argue that "it" wanted something, let alone what that something was. So the general public was an abstraction. Yet in some vague, indefinable sense, "it" was a factor in the behavior of the bureau chiefs.

They felt, I think, an obligation to balance the competing, narrow claims in a way that was reasonably fair rather than merely expedient; a duty to the long-range maintenance of the system rather than to actions that would relieve them of immediate pressure to the future detriment of the bureaus; a responsibility for the unorganized and the voiceless as well as for mobilized battalions of claimants. The IRS commissioner, for example, instituted a correspondence control system to expose and thereby to reduce delays in responding to inquiries because, as a citizen, he was indignant at the slowness of the procedure as well as because the delays adversely affected the bureau's reputation. Every chief had a personal interpretation of these moral injunctions and the appropriate steps to satisfy them. The chiefs' concern for these facets of their jobs, however, meant that the general public entered into their calculations and affected their attitudes in some fashion.

Practical considerations joined the moral imperatives that obliged the chiefs to take the general public into account. A good general reputation is a valuable asset in dealing with the environment. In the business world, goodwill is a salable commodity. In the government sphere, it is a political advantage. An agency in excellent repute is less vulnerable to the claims and charges of its adversaries and better able to resist demands it opposes than one without such an image. Administrators therefore prize esteem and they worry about it. For example, the social security commissioner publicly voiced his concern about a relatively small number of supplemental security income payments to ineligible aliens: "That's the kind of expenditure if there is only one case of it, much less several thousand, you really could not tolerate because it gives the general public the feeling that the system is being ripped off."[23] Similarly, the internal revenue commissioner testified that "the public's perception of the Internal Revenue Service as an efficient organization . . . is a crucial element in maintaining voluntary compliance."[24] The chiefs were ever mindful of the general public.

This does not mean that they devoted substantial amounts of their time to activities specifically aimed at the general public. The social security commissioner was unique in investing a good many hours in planning and participating in what were termed "outreach symposia"—a series of conferences with over a hundred "opinion leaders" at a time, held in Washington and the field—"with the aim of improving the public's understanding of social security."[25] Except for the occasional appearance on television or at a press conference at the side of departmental spokesmen, the others seldom worked personally on reaching a general audience. The public was a factor in their judgments rather than a consumer of their hours. The factor is difficult to trace or prove, but I am convinced that it did operate.

Time Taken by External Relations

Because the external elements with which the bureaus and their chiefs had to come to terms were so numerous and diverse, and because the chiefs' roles in the process can be understood only as part of a larger set of external relationships maintained by other members of their organizations, it has taken almost as much time and space to describe this activity of the chiefs as to describe the receipt and review of information. Their actual performance of this function absorbed much less time proportionately than it has taken me to tell of it. The balance would be different if information gathered for external-relations purposes were counted as external-relations time rather than as intelligence-collection time. In this section, however, I have been speaking only of their *conduct* of relations with outside groups

23. *Departments of Labor and Health, Education, and Welfare Appropriations for 1980,* Hearings before a subcommittee of the House Committee on Appropriations, 96 Cong. 1 sess. (GPO, 1979), pt. 6, p. 235.

24. *Treasury, Postal Service, and General Government Appropriations for Fiscal Year 1980,* Hearings before a subcommittee of the House Committee on Appropriations, 96 Cong. 1 sess. (GPO, 1979), pt. 1, p. 876.

25. Letter, Stanford G. Ross to participants of the National Symposium on Social Security, September 18, 1979.

and individuals rather than of their preparation for such conduct. On this basis, whereas the reception and review of intelligence occupied in the vicinity of 55 to 60 percent of the chiefs' working time, their direct participation in external relations amounted to no more than 25 to 30 percent. It was easier done than told.

MOTIVATING WORK FORCES

Describing the last of the major categories of chiefs' activities, the motivation of work forces, can be accomplished more easily because the chiefs put less of their time into this one than into the others— probably some 10 to 20 percent of their hours on the job. And the tasks were not as varied.

Once again, the figures are low because activities that contributed only incidentally to work force motivation, as practically all the chiefs' activities did, are not included here; they were counted in the categories already discussed. This section takes up solely those things the chiefs themselves did to whip up enthusiasm, build loyalty, raise morale, and generate pride throughout their bureaus. These formed the smallest class of the chiefs' functions, but a separate and distinct one.

Why Motivation Was Needed

Why they should have allocated a substantial proportion of their time to this function requires some explanation. After all, the employees of the bureaus were not forced to work there. Presumably, they joined in the first instance and stayed thereafter because their jobs in the bureaus were preferable to any alternative they could realistically hope for. That does not mean that they did not wish for something better; it means only that they were unlikely to get anything better. Whatever they felt about their pay levels, their salaries were enough to keep them in place. However dull and repetitive they found their jobs, they were not likely to find much better alternatives. No matter how much fun people made of bureaucrats, the significance of the bureaus' missions was attested by the continued financing of their operation by Congress. Why should the chiefs have felt any need to add to these basic motivations to contribute one's labor to the organization of one's choice?

The chiefs clearly believed that the levels of output, the quality of the product, and the rate of innovation would decline without special endeavors to sustain them. Most officers and employees, once they had attained career status, could do nearly as well materially without pushing themselves as they could by working at capacity. Maintaining their drive therefore required something more than the standard tangible incentives. The promise of material improvement and the threat of significant deprivation were not great enough by themselves to stoke the inner fires of the work forces.

Take salary, for example. Government compensation is not niggardly when retirement benefits are considered. Still, in the higher ranks, many career civil servants find themselves at pay ceilings where they earn no more than some of their subordinates and with years of continued constriction before them. (This is one reason the Civil Service Reform Act of 1978 promised higher salaries and bonuses for outstanding performance.) High rates of inflation for a long interval may have held down real wages and even reduced them in some cases. A bureau chief therefore could not rely on the pay structure to keep his work force at a high pitch of intensity.[26]

What is more, although more people are dismissed from the federal payrolls than prevailing myths indicate, the threat of removal for anyone who does merely adequate work is ordinarily small.[27] So fear of loss of livelihood is no greater an incentive than hope of substantial material advancement.

At the same time, the novelty of the job and the sense of achievement that people feel when they start in an agency diminish over the years for those who reach their respective career ceilings, as many do after a while in any large organization. The annual cycles repeat. Things change and then change back again. The old problems persist. The rhetoric stays the same. Few people can sustain much enthusiasm under these conditions.

And with it all comes the drumfire of criticism and complaint, denunciation and derision, aimed at civil servants. Elected officials find

26. Robert W. Hartman, "The Effects of Top Officials' Pay on Other Federal Employees," in Robert W. Hartman and Arnold R. Weber, eds., *The Rewards of Public Service: Compensating Top Federal Officials* (Brookings Institution, 1980), pp. 203–29.

27. In 1978, 19,200 were discharged, but this came to less than 1 percent of total federal civilian employment. U.S. Bureau of the Census, *Statistical Abstract of the United States: 1979*, 100th ed. (GPO, 1979), p. 275.

great sport in attacking them.[28] They are portrayed as stupid meddlers or clever villains. The work of their bureaus is characterized as not merely useless, but as downright harmful—and they are blamed for it even though they and their missions are decreed by law. If programs fail, rarely do the sponsors say the policies were ill conceived; instead, they say the bureaucrats sabotaged them. If government employees try to speed things by cutting corners, they are accused of arbitrary action; if they observe the letter of the law, they are charged with obstruction.[29] Seldom does anyone have a good word for them. No wonder some of them stop trying with all their might.

Despite the improbability of finding better jobs outside the government, however, many quit; the rate of resignations in the federal executive branch is high.[30] Among those who leave are able people

28. Members of Congress, doubtless reflecting what they hear from their constituents, are among the most vehement critics. For example, Representative Max Baucus of Montana, in the *Congressional Record* of September 21, 1976, p. 31637: "The major problems with most executive agencies and departments today is bureaucrats who have forgotten that they are servants of the people, and not our masters." Representative Elliot Levitas of Georgia, in ibid., p. 31634: "That is who is running the lives and businesses of the citizens of this country—unelected bureaucrats, not elected representatives. It is no wonder that our citizens have become cynical and angry and frustrated with their Government." Senator Jesse Helms of North Carolina, in the *Congressional Record* of July 19, 1976, p. 22589: "I do not need to remind my colleagues of the rising complaint of the citizenry over ever increasing harassment by Federal bureaucrats. This harassment often is coupled with an arrogant attitude on the part of many bureaucrats that we are doing this for your own good because we know what is right—we know what is better. But rather than wisdom from the bureaucracy, what we are seeing is a plethora of absurdities." Senator Paul J. Fannin of Arizona, in the *Congressional Record* of March 4, 1976, p. 5318: "The economy is being influenced . . . by the whims of a faceless army of unelected, unresponsive bureaucrats." See also the lampoon of civil servants by Representative Levitas in *Improving Congressional Oversight of Federal Regulatory Agencies,* Hearings before the Senate Committee on Government Operations, 94 Cong. 2 sess. (GPO, 1976), pp. 189–91.

29. For an interesting illustration of this dilemma of bureaucrats, see Allan N. Kornblum, *The Moral Hazards* (Lexington Books, 1976). When plainclothes policemen enforcing gambling laws were enjoined to display greater vigor by making more arrests, they arrested large numbers of petty members of illegal gambling operations for minor offenses. Since these did not reduce the operations significantly, the plainclothesmen were directed to get more of the higher-ups. But the higher-ups were adept at concealing their activities, so the enforcers employed improper methods of collecting evidence and even fabricated it. Consequently, many of the cases against the higher-ups did not stand up in court. The police were therefore instructed to adhere meticulously to proper procedures. The number of arrests then declined, whereupon the cycle began again.

30. In 1978, 223,200, or over 8 percent of all federal civilian employees, quit. Bureau of the Census, *Statistical Abstracts of the United States: 1979,* p. 275.

in demand elsewhere; among those who stay are a number who would depart if they could, but find no opportunity. The quality and morale of the work force may thus suffer a secular decline. Newcomers surrounded by dispirited colleagues grow dispirited themselves. Unless something is done, the culture of discouragement and cynicism takes hold. The organizations then tend to run down.

All six chiefs in this study therefore took pains to counter these tendencies. Besides the incidental motivations they provided when engaged in other activities, they reserved some of their time and energy specifically for stimulating and inspiriting the people who worked for them. Their labors in this regard took up an appreciable portion of their schedules.

Methods of Motivation

All the activities that counteracted the tendency toward lassitude strengthened organizational solidarity. That is, they intensified the employees' feelings of organic unity with their bureaus, deepened their sense of belonging. In the language of organization theorists, these measures increased member "identification" with the bureaus, meaning the members were more predisposed to act as though what was good for the bureaus was good for them personally.[31] The more complete the identification was, the greater the employee receptivity to organizational directives and the smaller the chance that personal advantage would be put ahead of organizational welfare. Under these conditions, members can presumably be roused to do better work and more work and to feel better about themselves and their occupations. The leaders of all organizations strive toward greater solidarity for this reason.

The institutional methods of building solidarity in the six bureaus were familiar.[32] They included training and indoctrination, filling high-level vacancies largely by promotion rather than by wholesale recruitment from the outside, publication of house organs that kept employees informed about each other and about their bureaus and were a channel for complaints to the top from all levels, formation

31. See Herbert A. Simon, *Administrative Behavior: A Study of Decision-Making Processes in Administrative Organization*, 3d ed. (Free Press, 1976), chaps. 10 and 15 and pp. xxxiv–xxxv.

32. Herbert Kaufman, *The Forest Ranger: A Study in Administrative Behavior* (Johns Hopkins Press, 1960), chap. 6.

of athletic teams, sponsoring of social functions, gatherings of the clan, and rotation of personnel through numbers of placements. Most of these were routine or performed by specialists, and the chiefs devoted little of their own time to them.

What the chiefs did do to strengthen solidarity was go forth to meet the troops by visiting various field stations at least several times a year and assembling top-ranking field officers in Washington at least twice a year. In the larger agencies, they also made the rounds of the central office. (In smaller agencies, the normal course of receiving and reviewing information sufficed to bring them into contact with much of their headquarters staffs.) Career chiefs who had come up through the ranks put less emphasis on such contacts than appointees brought in from the outside, probably because they already knew and were known to their co-workers. But all the chiefs put time of their own into this function.

If their meetings with groups of field officers in Washington are any guide, their field visits must have been mixtures of intelligence gathering, consensus building, and solidarity reinforcement. The techniques of strengthening solidarity—of cementing organizational bonds—were a combination of inspiration, exhortation, and consultation.

The chiefs delivered inspirational extemporaneous speeches in the fashion of football coaches firing up their teams between halves. They lauded the achievements, conceded the deficiencies, urged greater efforts, and indicated generally where improvements were needed and how they might be effected.

They exhorted subordinates to do what the chiefs wanted, enlisting their help and cooperation to improve output in particular programs in order to fend off critics among their clienteles and in Congress. In theory, they could simply have given orders, handed out rewards, and imposed penalties to compel the behavior they wanted. And often they did use these techniques. But they also demonstrated their conviction that command has its limits and that subordinates sometimes have to be won over to the position of their superiors.

They consulted with their subordinates, and bargained with them, about policy—not merely to tap their expert knowledge, but also to get them committed to top-level decisions. Giving people a role in shaping decisions secures their commitment in two ways. One is to produce decisions that meet many of their substantive objections. The other follows the principle that people are more likely to comply with a decision in which they have had a chance to participate than one imposed on them, even if some of their objections to a collectively adopted decision are overridden in the course of the deliberations.[33] Consequently, the chiefs sought the opinions and suggestions of officers and employees throughout their bureaus whenever issues of significance came to the point of decision, they adjusted their own proposals to the responses, and then they often systematically strove to "sell" the outcomes of the deliberations to those who would have to carry them out. They did not take obedience in every matter for granted; they worked hard to motivate their work forces to obey.

I heard one chief try to persuade some of his subordinates to be more vigorous in enforcing a law that an interest group complained was laxly administered, another appeal to regional officers to increase their activity in a certain program so as to reduce the discrepancy between performance and targets by the end of the fiscal year, and still another mobilize some of his regional representatives to counteract a possible rebellion by others against a draft directive on a problem of internal administration to which the chief thought all of them had agreed. The chief of one bureau, employing a form of "management by objectives," went so far as to negotiate written "contracts" with his immediate subordinates, spelling out (quantitatively, when possible) their priorities for the year ahead, detailing each of the intermediate steps to be completed on the way to those goals in the course of the year, and appraising their performance according to how close they came to hitting the targets—an example apparently followed later by other federal agencies. Also, the chiefs were occasionally visited by leaders of the associations and unions formed by their employees. They probably would have been obeyed in most of the individual matters had they been less conscientious about cultivating acquiescence. But it was not just getting their way on one or two issues that they wanted; they wanted to forge links of loyalty of a broader and more enduring kind. They put themselves out to attain this end.

From time to time, the chiefs appeared before groups of their em-

33. Much of the evidence comes from the work of Kurt Lewin and his followers; see, for example, Dorwin Cartwright and Alvin Zander, *Group Dynamics* (Row, Peterson, 1953), especially chaps. 19, 20, 21, 39, and 40. See also Victor H. Vroom, "Industrial Social Psychology," in Gardner Lindzey and Elliot Aronson, eds., *The Handbook of Social Psychology*, 2d ed. (Addison-Wesley, 1969), vol. 5, pp. 227–40.

ployees to answer questions. This practice had a triple benefit for the chiefs. It sharpened their responses to probing, informed interrogation. It gave many employees who would not otherwise see their leaders in the flesh a chance to experience the force of the leaders' personalities and fervor. It reassured people in lower echelons that the communiqués reaching them through long channels accurately reflected the wishes of the leaders. The result, presumably, was greater unity.

Other things the chiefs did for this purpose took less of their time. For example, they all conducted ceremonies presenting awards and prizes to their subordinates; the rites were usually brief, but the chiefs took part in them. All were careful to stand up for their bureaus and to see that some words of praise for their work forces were included in statements they delivered in person or sent out over their signatures. The commissioner of internal revenue, for example, applauded "the extraordinary efforts of many dedicated employees" in one annual report, and observed, "Administering our tax laws is an enormously complex task, one which is handled with a high degree of efficiency, sensitivity and integrity by the 85,000 career Civil Service employees of the Internal Revenue Service.[34] The commissioner of customs prefaced a report with the comment, "It is appropriate that the theme of this annual review centers on the people of the Customs Service. Our progress to date is due in large part to their dedication and enterprise."[35] The commissioner of food and drugs complimented the members of his agency for shielding the American people from grave dangers to the public health, and added, "News value being what it is, you have not gotten much credit. . . . And this is one of the reasons why you have such a large claim on my admiration. You and your fellow FDA employees do not work in the limelight of public acclaim. Indeed, you often operate in a discouraging atmosphere of public misunderstanding, regulated industry hostility, and under working conditions that seriously and unfairly burden attempts at maintaining excellence."[36] I am sure words of this kind were often inserted by the chiefs' speechwriters without any special

34. Commissioner of Internal Revenue, *1978 Annual Report*, p. 5.

35. *Customs U.S.A.*, a special edition of *Customs Today* on the activities of the U.S. Customs Service for fiscal year 1978, preface.

36. Donald Kennedy, remarks prepared for delivery at the dedication of the new FDA facility, New Orleans, Louisiana, November 29–30, 1978, p. 7.

instructions from the head men. Yet I also have the impression that the chiefs watched carefully to be sure they were not omitted, partly for no other reason than that they were true and partly because saying them publicly contributed to the morale and the solidarity of the bureaus.

Sometimes, to dramatize the bonds between them and their subordinates, they went to considerable lengths to get something their subordinates wanted. For example, high-level permanent officers of the IRS were upset by an attempt of an assistant secretary of the treasury for enforcement to exercise direct authority over revenue agents in connection with a campaign to detect violators of narcotics laws, fearing that such a precedent would gradually erode the agents' traditional revenue role. The commissioner took up their cause (and succeeded in persuading the assistant secretary to proceed through channels so that control of the agents would remain in the IRS). Similarly, personnel and other staff officers asked to be shielded from corresponding claims of direct authority by staffers under the assistant secretaries for administration. Seldom are such issues among a chief's own top priorities. But the chiefs would occasionally fight for them just the same, using up political capital with their superiors to gain things of secondary importance to themselves, to symbolize their unity with their subordinates and win employee confidence and cooperation.

Did these efforts really solidify the bureaus and motivate their work forces? Did they raise morale, raise the level of employee satisfaction, increase efficiency, improve the quantity and quality of output? Did they strengthen loyalty and intensify employee receptivity to direction by the leaders?

Or did these stimuli, like all others, lose their effectiveness because of repetition? Did employees regard them cynically? Were they seen as gestures and ceremonies with little substantive value?

I have no way of answering these questions from the research at hand, and I have no reason to think the chiefs themselves know the answers. But no chief would casually put the practices to the test by suspending them. For one thing, an experiment on which to base an evaluation would undoubtedly be uncertain in its own right. For another, the negative effects on the bureaus if the practices *are* essential would be too serious to risk for the sake of an experiment. Furthermore, even if the practices were never as effective as their advocates believed, dropping them when they are so well established might have adverse repercussions—suspension would probably be seen by employees accustomed to being "cultivated" as a deliberate message of criticism and dissatisfaction.

In the last analysis, I think the chiefs felt intuitively that they were doing something right and useful. At any rate, their willingness to go through certain of the rites made their personnel managers happy. The chores did not eat up vast amounts of time, and the effects might well have been highly beneficial. Continuing the traditional measures for motivating their work forces thus had more going for it than against it. So all six chiefs, in remarkably similar ways, engaged in this effort.

TWO "MISSING" FUNCTIONS?

Seemingly missing from this portrait of the chiefs at work are two functions traditionally associated with leadership: command and coordination.[37] Didn't the chiefs order subordinates to do things? Didn't they send letters as well as receive them? Didn't they correct imbalances in work flows and inconsistencies in actions taken at lower levels? Didn't they "take charge"?

Of course they did, but not in an obvious, authoritarian fashion. Ordinarily, for example, chiefs did not find it necessary to impose their will by fiat. Not that they were unable to do so; the moral and legal authority of their office was a powerful implement. But they seldom had to express it in the form of outright orders because in the formulation and announcement of decisions, the gathering of information, the conduct of public relations, and the inspiration of their work forces, they conveyed their wishes quite clearly. The exercise of command more commonly emerged through the performance of other functions than as a separate and distinct function in its own right.[38]

Similarly, coordination was not a separate activity, but a by-

37. These have been core elements in the definition of administration at least since the work of Henri Fayol in the early part of the twentieth century. See L. Urwick, "The Function of Administration," pp. 117–19; Henri Fayol, "The Administrative Theory of the State," pp. 102–03; and Luther Gulick, "Notes on the Theory of Administration," pp. 13, 33–41; all in Luther Gulick and L. Urwick, eds., *Papers on the Science of Administration* (New York: Institute of Public Administration, 1937).

38. Corson and Paul, *Men Near the Top*, pp. 48–49.

product of bringing people together, asking questions, distributing information, and setting signature rules. Occasionally a chief might act personally to break a bottleneck or knock heads together. Most of the time he would promote and facilitate coordination by the way he did his other tasks.

Consequently, command and coordination do not appear in this analysis of the chiefs' activities as functions in and of themselves. They simply could not be distinguished, even as roughly as the other activities, as claims on the chiefs' time and energy. Cracking the whip and personally regulating the flow of work were not ways in which the chiefs spent their working days.

SUMMING UP

Figure 1 is a schematic diagram of the allocation of the chiefs' time among the classes of activity described in this chapter.

FIGURE 1

Allocation of the Chiefs' Time to Activities

External relations[a] 25–30 percent	Motivating work forces[a] 10–20 percent
Receiving and reviewing information for all purposes, including preparations for decisionmaking, external relations, and motivating work forces; steps to avoid embarrassment; and efforts to appraise performance 55–60 percent	

a. Actual execution of function, in addition to time spent on receipt and review of information for this purpose.

Receiving and reviewing information was an activity common to all other activities and functions and served all purposes, including orientation, avoiding embarrassment, appraising performance, making decisions, conducting external relations, and motivating work forces. But it could not be apportioned among the other activities, functions, and purposes because most pieces of information received and reviewed by the chiefs served at least several ends simultaneously and often served all of them at once. This activity is therefore represented as an undifferentiated block of time. That block, however, was the foundation for practically everything the chiefs did.

Besides the time the chiefs put into getting information for external relations and motivation of work forces, they invested many hours in the actual *execution* of these functions. These activities were therefore separate and distinct and are represented in the figure by areas of their own.

The time allocations were not the same for all chiefs; the chart for each would be a little different. But while the percentages would vary slightly from case to case, the general pattern is roughly the same for all. The main outline therefore constitutes a reasonable fit.

Thus a visitor dropping in on one of the chiefs at random would probably have found him getting information or evaluating it, and more likely from members of his own bureau than from any other source. Chances are the visitor would have found him talking with someone, on the telephone if not in person, for a good part of the chiefs' reading was done at home at night. Finding out what was going on inside the bureaus and beyond its boundaries, and then figuring out what to do about the conditions thus apprehended, made up most of the job of the bureau executives.

If the chief was not in the act of receiving or reviewing intelligence at the moment, he would probably have been engaged in presenting the bureau's position on some matter to someone outside the bureau. Congress and its instruments, the departments, other components of the executive branch, nongovernmental groups, and the communications media turned to the chiefs for information about all sorts of issues connected with their areas of specialization and for defenses and justifications of bureau actions, policies, and proposals. The chiefs probably spent about half as much of their time (excluding preparations) actually responding to such demands and to cultivating relations with these external friends and foes as they spent getting and appraising and interpreting information. Nevertheless, the total was a substantial block of every working month.

The chance that the random visitor would have found a chief performing another of his characteristic activities—inspiriting his subordinates—was about half that of finding him engaged in external relations. Again, however, the fraction of his total schedule taken up by these duties was sizable.

The probability of the visitor discovering a chief in the act of making a decision, in the narrow sense of that term used in this study, would have been very small. This function, though one of the most important things the chiefs did, in itself consumed little of their time.

Yet if the visitor stayed with the chief for a full day, he would be almost certain to see examples of most of the categories of activity. The days of the chiefs were highly fragmented. Inside and outside the organizations, the things that called for their attention, or to which they made it clear they wished to have their attention called, went on simultaneously, not in neat, discrete, sequential packages. Consequently, the chiefs were constantly shifting from one subject to another. External relations with components of their respective constituencies would be interlarded with briefing sessions and brainstorming conferences with their subordinates and with motivational meetings. Sometimes they would initiate contacts to impel or extract things they wanted, and at the same time they were the targets of such strategies by people inside and outside the bureaus. If there were intervals when they had some time to themselves, they would attack the piles of diverse material in their in-boxes, and what they did not finish would go home with them to be worked on at night. In the course of a day, therefore, they would have dealt with scores of different subjects and perhaps a score of different individuals and groups. And no two days were exactly alike except that all were mosaics of bits and pieces; each of the mosaics was unique. If variety is the spice of life, the administrative life of the chiefs was certainly highly seasoned.

In sum, when you examine the contours of their activities and the character of their work, the chiefs seem to have been very much alike, differences in their personalities and organizations notwithstanding. They were not identical, but they were certainly variations on a single theme.

As I suggested at the beginning of this chapter, perhaps the reason for the similarities is that all the chiefs were picked because they occupied comparable organizational positions in the executive branch. But what is it about their organizational situations that produced so many common behavioral attributes even though they as individuals and their bureaus as organizations diverged in so many important respects? It is not self-evident that location in an administrative structure should have overridden tendencies toward differences in administrative behavior, nor is it obvious how this result came about. Yet it is not at all mysterious, as I explain in the next chapter.

CHAPTER THREE

The Confines of Leadership

EVERY one of the chiefs was hemmed in by a set of constraints limiting his capacity to make things happen in and to his bureau as he wanted them to happen. The constraints were not identical in every case, though some of them were common to all the agencies. But in each instance, the effect of the constraints was to leave open similar opportunities and to impose similar imperatives on the bureau leaders. That is why the administrative behavior of all the chiefs gravitated toward common patterns, with only variations on a common theme.

The constraints channeling the activities of a bureau chief taking over the leadership of an established operation are of two kinds. One is the prior programming of the behavior of the bureau's work force. The other is the imposition of agendas on bureau chiefs by events and conditions and people not under their control. An executive building an organization from scratch might well be free of many of these limitations and therefore exercise, or at least appear to exercise, more influence on the course of events within and affecting his organization than any of his successors would be able to exert. Even the youngest of the bureaus in this study, however, had a history with which the administrator had to come to terms. To put the situation another way, the slate not only was not clean; in all cases in my sample (as in most agencies throughout the federal government) it was already quite full when the chiefs came to office.

"PROGRAMMED" DECISIONS AND ACTIONS

The work of a bureau flows along because most of its members know what to do and how to do it. Their conduct, in a sense, is programmed—partly by formal written directives; even more by learn-ing processes that implant behavior patterns firmly in their nervous systems. All this a new chief finds when he takes over.

Written Directives

All of the actions and decisions of federal administrative agencies derive their authority from statutes. Many, though not all, of the limits on their authority are similarly imposed by statutes—some-times through express prohibitions, sometimes through detailed orders, but more often through grants of discretion that go only so far and no farther. Most such statutes are specific to the bureaus to which they apply, even though they are officially addressed to the secretaries heading the parent departments rather than to the bu-reaus directly; many, however, apply to all agencies in the whole executive branch.

They are supplemented by presidential orders, regulations issued by agencies having jurisdiction over processes throughout the govern-ment, regulations issued by departmental headquarters, and adminis-trative and judicial interpretations of the regulations and orders and of the statutes under which they were promulgated. All the foregoing are then digested and translated into operational instructions to bu-reau personnel in the form of bureau regulations, manuals, and orders. An incoming bureau chief is therefore confronted by an im-posing documentary edifice the first day he walks into his office. And each component of the edifice is itself a complex collection of provisions.

BUREAU-SPECIFIC STATUTES. Take, for instance, the legislation ad-ministered by the Internal Revenue Service at the time this study was conducted. It included everything in the Internal Revenue Code except the sections on alcohol, tobacco, and firearms, which were handled by a different bureau in the Treasury Department. It came to over 1,400 double-column pages of print, a remarkably detailed collection of specifications to guide and control administrative behavior.[1]

The tax rates, of course, were specified, but quite briefly. Establish-

1. Mainly 26 U.S.C., subtitles A–D, F, appendix. All references to the United States Code are to the 1976 edition unless otherwise noted. All references to the Code of Federal Regulations (C.F.R.) are to the 1977 or 1978 edition, parts of both being in effect when this section of this book was written.

ing the base to which the rates apply was what built up the length of the legislation. Thus for income tax purposes it took thirty-eight sections just to define gross income, sixty-three sections to spell out itemized deductions, and thirty for capital gains and losses. "Surviving spouse" and "head of household" each required a column of fine print. And besides these definitional specifications, Congress had also, by law, prohibited the IRS from issuing regulations on particular subjects, such as taxation of fringe benefits[2] and denial of tax exemptions to schools held to be engaged in racial discrimination.[3] These illustrations by no means exhaust the provisions governing income taxes, but they are enough to convey a sense of the legislation behind the forms we all fill out.

And income tax law was not the whole of the Internal Revenue Code under the jurisdiction of the IRS. Large portions were devoted to estate and gift taxes, employment taxes, and excise taxes. Another 400 sections—nearly 300 double-column pages—were allocated to procedure and administration, adding specifications on *how* things were to be done to the abundant provisions on *what* was to be done.

Such legislation, both substantive and procedural, extensive and detailed as it was, did not by itself determine all the decisions and actions of the members of the IRS; the network of explicit directives was much larger and more intensive than even those hundreds of pages of statutory language suggest. But the laws administered by the IRS went a long way toward shaping the behavior of the agency's officers and employees, and were among the most unyielding of the considerations that channeled the efforts of the commissioner's subordinates.

The Internal Revenue Code was an extreme case. None of the other agencies in the sample for this study was governed by nearly such a large body of statutory language. Next in length were the laws administered by the Customs Service, occupying less than half as much space—a little over 500 double-column pages of the United States Code—and half of those were tables listing the customs duties on thousands of items.[4] Even the social security laws,[5] despite their great complexity, took up about a sixth—something over 200 pages—

2. 92 Stat. 996 (1978), sec. 1. Extended by 93 Stat. 1275 (1979).
3. 93 Stat. 562 (1979), sec. 103.
4. Generally, see 19 U.S.C. chs. 1, 3, 4, 10, 11. See also 28 U.S.C. chs. 9, 11. Duties are listed in 19 U.S.C. 1202.
5. Mostly 42 U.S.C. ch. 7, subchs. II, IV, VII, XVI, and 30 U.S.C. ch. 22, subch. IV.

of the space required by internal revenue statutes. The Forest Service was responsible for slightly less than 200 pages,[6] and the laws administered by the Food and Drug Administration[7] and the Animal and Plant Health Inspection Service[8] came to fewer than 100 and 75, respectively.

Nevertheless, the chiefs of all these bureaus found themselves subject to a host of statutory directives resembling those encountered by the commissioner of internal revenue. For example, the Customs Service, in addition to collecting the duties set forth in the law,[9] had to ensure that the masters of arriving vessels complied with the specified requirements, prevent the importation of forbidden articles, and seize and arrest violators under certain conditions.[10] Furthermore, the law contained many procedural requirements, such as how to calculate the value of incoming items, how duty should be paid, how to protest the decisions of customs officers, and how to obtain review of such decisions.[11]

Similarly, the commissioner of social security was by no means freer than the commissioner of internal revenue, even though there was a substantial difference in the length of the statutes they administered. Consider old age, survivors, and disability insurance benefits, one of the sixteen subchapters (the longest single one) in the chapter of the United States Code on social security.[12] It took only a few pages to specify the amounts of the benefits and set up the trust funds that finance them; it took perhaps 160 pages to describe who was eligible for benefits, how much they were eligible for, and what they could do

6. Mostly in 16 U.S.C. chs. 2–4, 5c, 6, 23, 27, 28, 30, 36, 37. Other parts of the code impinging on the Forest Service are in 7 U.S.C. chs. 14, 17, 33, 55, 59, 61; 29 U.S.C. ch. 17; 43 U.S.C. chs. 23, 35.

7. Mostly in 21 U.S.C. chs. 1, 9.

8. Mostly in 7 U.S.C. chs. 7, 7A, 7B, 8, 11, 30, 37, 40, 48, 54, 61; 15 U.S.C. ch. 44; 21 U.S.C. chs. 4, 5.

9. Actually, the powers and duties are vested in the secretary of the treasury; Reorganization Plan 26 of 1950, secs. 1 and 2. They have been delegated to the commissioner by departmental order; Treasury Department Order 165, as revised by Treasury decision 53654 in 19 F.R. 7241, November 6, 1954. The bureau and its commissioner, however, were created by statute: 19 U.S.C. 2071. The collection responsibilities of customs officers are described generally in 19 U.S.C. 1500 and 1505.

10. For example, 19 U.S.C. 29, 482, 1433-35, 1437, 1581-84, 1648, and ch. 5. See also 18 U.S.C. ch. 27.

11. 19 U.S.C. 164-65, 197-99, 1514-16.

12. 42 U.S.C. ch. 7, subch. II.

if they believed they had not been given all they were entitled to. There were also numerous procedural specifications, such as explicit instructions on what to do about overpayments and underpayments of old age, survivors, and disability benefits, and how individuals and state governments objecting to initial decisions could appeal them.

Even the three bureaus that administered less than 10 percent as much legislation as the IRS were governed by an abundance of substantive and procedural commands. Some were broad and sweeping: "The Secretary of Agriculture shall make provisions for the protection against destruction by fire and depredations upon the public forests and national forests."[13] But many were quite specific: "The Secretary [of Health, Education, and Welfare] shall promulgate regulations exempting from any labeling requirement of this chapter . . . small open containers of fresh fruits and fresh vegetables";[14] "The Secretary of Agriculture is directed . . . to initiate a national hog cholera program in cooperation with the several States."[15] Separate procedures were prescribed for the Food and Drug Administration in dealing with violations and violators of the food, drugs, and cosmetics provisions,[16] in handling petitions for the introduction of food additives,[17] in processing applications for approval of new drugs for humans and for animals,[18] and in setting performance standards for medical devices.[19] The agency was even commanded explicitly (through the secretary of HEW) to find unsafe any animal drug or food color additive that induced cancer in man or animal,[20] but forbidden to promulgate regulations banning the use of saccharin despite its carcinogenic properties.[21]

Long or short, then, the statutes specific to each bureau contributed heavily to programming the behavior of administrative officers

13. 16 U.S.C. 551. The powers of the secretary have been delegated to the Forest Service by departmental order; 1 C.F.R. 2.60.

14. 21 U.S.C. 345. The function was delegated to the commissioner of food and drugs by departmental order; 21 C.F.R. 5.1.

15. 21 U.S.C. 114g. The secretary delegated these functions to the administrator of APHIS by departmental order; 7 C.F.R. 5.1.

16. 21 U.S.C. 334.

17. 21 U.S.C. 348.

18. 21 U.S.C. 355, 360b.

19. 21 U.S.C. 360d.

20. 21 U.S.C. 376(b)(5)(B). The function was delegated to the FDA by the secretary; see note 14, above.

21. 91 Stat. 1452 (1977).

from cabinet level down to the rank and file in the agencies. And that is only one of the forms of constraint the bureau chiefs in this study faced when they took office.

GOVERNMENTWIDE STATUTES. They were also caught about equally in a web of statutes applicable to all executive agencies of the federal government. Many of the most constrictive of these were in title 5 of the United States Code ("Government Organization and Employees"), which included the provisions on personnel administration and administrative procedure, among other things. But requirements of various kinds were scattered through other titles as well.

The administrative procedure sections of title 5 are good illustrations. They encompassed most of the basic provisions of the Administrative Procedure Act[22] as well as the Freedom of Information Act,[23] the Privacy Act of 1974,[24] and the Government in the Sunshine Act.[25] All of these provisions[26] profoundly affected the way the bureaus conducted their business. So did the twenty-five chapters in title 5 covering government employment. Here were found the creation of the competitive and other classes of service,[27] the mandatory examinations, the requirements for registers of eligible people, the extra points for those eligible with various kinds of preference,[28] the prescribed hours of work,[29] the principles governing career service,[30] the rights of employees against whom adverse actions have been taken by agencies,[31] the pay structure,[32] the ban on partisan political activity,[33] the retirement provisions,[34] the legislation on labor-management relations,[35] and most of the other practices and standards that give the federal civil service many of its familiar characteristics. There are probably few government executives who have not at one time or another raged at some of these provisions, which control so much

22. 60 Stat. 237 (1946); amended 1946, 1947, 1948, and 1966.
23. 80 Stat. 383 (1966); amended 1967, 1974, 1976, 1978.
24. 88 Stat. 1896 (1974); amended 1974, 1975.
25. 90 Stat. 1241 (1976).
26. They are codified in 5 U.S.C. ch. 5, subch. II. See also 5 U.S.C. 3105.
27. 5 U.S.C. ch. 51.
28. 5 U.S.C. pt. III, subpt. B.
29. Generally, 5 U.S.C. pt. III, subpt. E; sec. 6101 especially.
30. 5 U.S.C. ch. 23.
31. 5 U.S.C. chs. 72, 75, 77.
32. 5 U.S.C. pt. III, subpt. D.
33. 5 U.S.C. ch. 73, subch. III; see also ch. 15.
34. 5 U.S.C. ch. 83.
35. 5 U.S.C. ch. 71.

administration in their organizations. The provisions have survived hosts of such complaints.

The statutes on agency finances in title 31 ("Money and Finance") were not as detailed as those on personnel, but the requirements and prohibitions on all agencies were still plentiful. Agency leaders were commanded, for example, to "establish and maintain systems of accounting and internal control" for information, management, accountability, and budget preparation;[36] to arrange "proper administrative examination" of all accounts and to submit them to the General Accounting Office within specified periods;[37] to require "precise and analytical statements and receipts" for money expended by their disbursing officers.[38] And they were forbidden to send the Office of Management and Budget, the president, or Congress any requests for legislation that would authorize appropriations without the approval of their department head,[39] or to spend or obligate appropriated funds in excess of OMB apportionments.[40]

Similarly, under title 40 ("Public Buildings, Property, and Works"), authority to construct public buildings was vested exclusively in the administrator of the General Services Administration,[41] and even then, proposed projects above a minimum sum required the approval of the Public Works Committees of both the Senate and the House;[42] bureau chiefs could not just go out and build new quarters for their organizations no matter how dissatisfied they were with the quarters they had. Nor could even they buy new furniture at will,[43] acquire their own supplies and equipment, or store and maintain their supplies and equipment as they wished to.[44] And the law imposed on each agency the duty to "maintain adequate inventory controls and accountability systems for the property under its control,"[45] and to survey its property continually and report excess property promptly to the general services administrator.[46]

36. 31 U.S.C. 66a.
37. 31 U.S.C. 75, 78.
38. 31 U.S.C. 492-2.
39. 31 U.S.C. 581b.
40. 31 U.S.C. 665(c), (d), (h).
41. 40 U.S.C. 601.
42. 40 U.S.C. 606.
43. 40 U.S.C. 483b.
44. 40 U.S.C. 481(a).
45. 40 U.S.C. 483(b)(1).
46. 40 U.S.C. 483(b)(2).

And in cases when agencies *were* permitted to buy or contract for supplies or services, they were bound by the specifications in title 41 ("Public Contracts") prescribing advertising, sealed bids, minimum wages for contractors' employees, use of American materials, and the like.

In title 44 ("Public Printing and Documents"), additional responsibilities and restrictions were placed on the bureau chiefs. For instance, "the head of each Federal agency shall make and preserve records containing adequate and proper documentation of the organization, functions, policies, decisions, procedures, and essential transactions of the agency."[47] But to throw out records he no longer needed, he had to follow a careful process for their disposal, administered by the general services administrator.[48] Nor could he proceed on his own to collect information from the public; he had to seek the approval of the director of the Office of Management and Budget.[49]

The bureau chiefs in this sample could not even go to court on their own to enforce the laws they administered because, "Except as otherwise authorized by law, the conduct of litigation in which the United States, an agency, or officer thereof is a party, or is interested, and securing evidence therefor, is reserved to officers of the Department of Justice, under the direction of the Attorney General."[50]

These examples by no means exhaust the list of statutes governing all or most of the agencies of the government,[51] but they illustrate the ways in which such laws restrict administrators' freedom of action by obliging them and their agencies to do things they might otherwise not have done and by preventing them from doing things they otherwise would have. Some of these laws individually did not weigh as heavily on the bureaus as bureau-specific legislation did. But collectively they added a significant set of constraints to the system of statutory requirements and prohibitions.

GOVERNMENTWIDE REGULATIONS. Yet the governmentwide statutes were sketchy and permissive compared with the body of governmentwide regulations they generated. Virtually all such statutes permitted or required a staff agency of the federal government to issue rules and

47. 44 U.S.C. 3101.
48. 44 U.S.C. ch. 33.
49. 44 U.S.C. 3509.
50. 28 U.S.C. 516; see also 519.
51. See, for example, the provisions governing tort claims against the government; 28 U.S.C. 2672.

regulations amplifying the legislation under their jurisdiction—to set up appropriate procedures, to make general terms more specific, to anticipate or respond to situations in which the statutory language was ambiguous, to balance the need for diversity with the wish for standardization, to assure agency compliance with the general provisions of law, and to assist and guide government officers and employees in their efforts to do what the law commanded or prohibited. Many of the staff agencies therefore promulgated volumes of materials governing the behavior of organizations in the executive branch.

Take the issuances of the old Civil Service Commission and its successors, the Office of Personnel Management (OPM) and the Merit System Protection Board. They appeared in three forms: regulations, the Federal Personnel Manual, and qualification standards for individual positions and groups of positions. Together, they were an imposing set of mandates, backed by the power of the OPM to suspend or withdraw the personnel authority of any agency that failed to comply with them.[52]

The regulations alone occupied 583 pages in the Code of Federal Regulations (the codification of all agency regulations currently in force) and touched virtually every aspect of personnel management; they were grouped into ninety-eight parts, each dealing with a subject. The Federal Personnel Manual was a multivolume, loose-leaf collection of directives containing both the regulations (so that they were available to personnel officers in the agencies in readily accessible form) and amplifications of the regulations indicating how they were to be put into effect and specifying in even greater detail what they required. Qualification standards issued by the central personnel agency described the qualities and preparation required for individual positions or groups of positions. In these, the skills, knowledge, abilities, and potential of job candidates, and the experience, education, and other conditions of employment were set forth. Separate handbooks of qualification standards covered white-collar, blue-collar, and prevailing-wage positions; and there were handbooks on the standards for classifying positions for hundreds of jobs and job series. Thus virtually anything an administrator wanted to do in the field of personnel management was governed by one or more of these provisions, and the bulk of his agency's personnel procedures and

52. 5 C.F.R. 230.201, 230.202.

practices was more likely to reflect them than to realize his own wishes.

In like fashion, the General Services Administration promulgated nearly 900 pages of federal procurement regulations[53] and nearly 600 pages of federal property management regulations[54] in the Code of Federal Regulations. The regulations included the GSA's policies on contracting for goods and services;[55] on the management of public buildings[56] and the assignment of space to agencies;[57] the management of records;[58] control of travel on government business;[59] provision of telecommunications, transportation, and motor vehicles;[60] and the provision and management of automated data services and equipment.[61] They were supplemented and amplified by other documents of equally binding effect, such as the GSA's Federal Travel Regulations,[62] the Federal Standardization Handbook[63] (product specifications and standards), the *U.S. Government Correspondence Manual*,[64] and the Federal Information Processing Standards Publications[65] (FIPS PUBS) put out by the National Bureau of Standards of the Department of Commerce.

Internal operations of federal agencies—chiefly, but not exclusively, financial and accounting practices—were regulated by the General Accounting Office. For this purpose, it relied more heavily on its *Policy and Procedures Manual*[66] than on official regulations in the Code of Federal Regulations. The eight-volume manual was full of directives to the agencies—the principles, standards, and require-

53. 41 C.F.R. ch. 1.

54. 41 C.F.R. ch. 101.

55. 41 C.F.R. subpt. 1–1.3.

56. 41 C.F.R. pts. 101-17 to 101-20, inclusive.

57. *Internal Revenue Service's Taxpayer Assistance Programs, Monitoring of Commercial Tax Return Preparers and Tax Form Simplification Efforts,* Hearing before a subcommittee of the House Committee on Government Operations, 95 Cong. 2 sess. (Government Printing Office, 1978), p. 61.

58. 41 C.F.R. pt. 101-11.

59. 41 C.F.R. pts. 101-7, 101-41; see also 4 C.F.R. ch. I, subch. D.

60. 41 C.F.R. pt. 101-35 and pts. 101-38 to 101-40, inclusive.

61. 41 C.F.R. pt. 101-32.

62. See 41 C.F.R. 101-7.003.

63. 41 C.F.R. pt. 101-29.

64. General Services Administration, *U.S. Government Correspondence Manual* (GPO, 1977).

65. See 41 C.F.R. 101-32.1302.

66. U.S. General Accounting Office, *GAO Policy and Procedures Manual for Guidance of Federal Agencies* (GPO, 1957, and subsequent editions as revised periodically).

ments of accounting, for example; the fiscal procedures to be followed in handling appropriations, receipts, collections, obligations, and disbursements; the kinds of financial records to be kept; and the methods of auditing to be used by the agencies in their internal reviews as well as by the GAO itself in checking on the agencies. Budgeting processes, however, were governed primarily by circulars from the Office of Management and Budget. Traditionally, the major directive was the annual call for estimates,[67] which ordered agencies to submit requests for the funds they wanted to operate in the next fiscal year. (In the case of the executive departments, the call for estimates was sent to the department heads rather than to the constituent agencies of the departments, but enough copies were supplied by the OMB to permit the departments to pass them along, with whatever instructions they wished to add, to their subordinate organizations.) It was not simply a general statement. It could run to a hundred or more pages, specifying the kinds of data to be submitted, the format in which to organize them, and the kinds of information to be included in the narrative justifications that supported the numbers. The Carter administration also introduced zero-base budgeting, which required a different array of information in addition to the traditional budget.[68] And OMB circulars, bulletins, and letters to department heads also provided explicit instructions for particular items in agency budgets, for execution of budgetary provisions, and for apportionment of appropriated funds through the fiscal year.

This inventory of governmentwide directives and instructions encompasses the largest bodies of such issuances, but not all. Some were promulgated as Executive Orders of the President (which could be agency-specific as well as general) and could touch almost any aspect of federal administration. Others, such as the regulations of the Federal Labor Relations Authority, the regulations and notices of the Office of Federal Procurement Policy, and the OMB guidelines to agencies on how to comply with the provisions of the Privacy Act of 1974, emanated from staff agencies. Still others came from line agencies, such as the regulations of the Office of Federal Contract Compliance in the Department of Labor, the requirements for environmental impact statements issued by the Council on Environmental Quality, Department of Justice guidelines on what agencies

67. "Preparation and submission of budget estimates (Transmittal Memorandum No. 48)," OMB Circular A-11 (revised), May 25, 1978.
68. "Zero-Base Budgeting," OMB Circular A-115, May 5, 1978.

had to do to comply with the Freedom of Information Act and the Federal Tort Claims Act, and Equal Employment Opportunity Commission regulations prescribing agency programs and procedures to achieve equal opportunity in employment and personnel operations. The Treasury Department issued the *Treasury Fiscal Requirements Manual for the Guidance of Departments and Agencies,* which prescribed practices for payroll deductions, withholding, disbursing, handling and depositing public funds, reporting, certain aspects of accounting, and other fiscal matters. The list of constraints, controlling fundamental aspects of management, thus went even beyond the extensive set described here, presenting bureau chiefs (and other executives) with a series of faits accomplis when they assumed office.

INTERPRETATIONS. Despite the volume and specificity of the governmentwide regulations, areas of uncertainty and controversy remained, occasioned mostly by ambiguities of language and by unanticipated events. Consequently, there were constant requests for clarification. Some took the form of appeals from administrative decisions as individuals, organizations, or state and local governments disputed the construction placed on various provisions by administrative officers. Some were initiated by administrative officers seeking instruction before acting. Moreover, members of Congress did not hesitate to indicate how they construed legislation that was in the process of enactment or previously enacted.

As a result, the behavior of administrative agencies was governed by judicial opinions and judgments, decisions of the comptroller general and opinions of the attorney general, judgments of the Merit System Protection Board, the contents of congressional committee reports and comments in hearings, and even remarks made on the floor of Congress in the course of debates. While some of these interpretations carried less formal weight than others, prudence dictated to most administrative leaders that none of them be ignored.

Numbers of interpretations came from the Supreme Court. The IRS found itself obliged to do something to comply with a court decision that seemed to deny tax exemption to church-run schools if they violated equal educational opportunity laws and rulings.[69]

69. *Treasury, Postal Service, and General Government Appropriations for Fiscal Year 1980,* Hearings before a subcommittee of the House Committee on Appropriations, 96 Cong. 1 sess. (GPO, 1979), pt. 1, pp. 894–97. See also *Green v. Connally,* 330 F. Supp. 1150 (D.D.C. 1971).

Scarcely a year went by without some decisions on the meaning of the Internal Revenue Code—usually quite specific rulings, such as whether certain cash meal allowances were to be included in or excluded from gross income.[70] Other agencies did not come before the Supreme Court as frequently, but all of them were affected by its decisions—including those in the distant past—bearing on their substantive duties. And all the agencies were affected by Supreme Court decisions on administrative procedure ranging from the character of adequate public notice about pending actions to the scope of judicial review. Some actions were even upset for failure to observe procedures established and announced by agencies themselves![71]

Since many cases were not appealed to the Supreme Court, agencies were also influenced by decisions of lower courts. The main ones were the U.S. district courts and the circuit courts of appeals, but the court of claims, which handled a variety of claims against the government, was also an important factor. For the IRS, the tax court also had to be taken into account, and for the Customs Service, the customs court and the court of customs and patent appeals were the major judicial bodies.[72]

A large majority of the judicial interpretations of administrative powers and actions were engendered by clients' appeals from agency actions. On the other hand, in some administrative matters, interpretations by the comptroller general and the attorney general were elicited by *agency* requests that these officers construe the law in advance of agency action. The official rulings of these counselors became instructions for the agency leaders seeking advice and for their successors. They were usually quite explicit; for instance, opinions on powers to attach certain conditions to permits issued to private parties for road construction across national forestland,[73] on a conflict between a demand by a congressional committee for tax return information and the confidentiality provisions of the Internal Revenue Code,[74] on a petition from an organization seeking financial assistance to meet the expenses of participation in adjudicatory and

70. *Commissioner* v. *Kowalski,* 434 U.S. 77 (1977). See also *Central Public Service Co.* v. *United States,* 435 U.S. 21 (1978).

71. Kenneth Culp Davis, *Administrative Law Treatise,* 2d ed. (K. C. Davis Publishing Co., University of San Diego, 1979), sec. 7:21, p. 100.

72. 28 U.S.C. chs. 9, 11.

73. 42 Opinions of the Attorneys General 127 (1962).

74. 42 Opinions of the Attorneys General 485 (1974).

rule-making proceedings,[75] and on authority to modify the terms of a timber sale contract.[76]

Administrative tribunals also were a source of interpretations controlling agency behavior. For example, the Merit System Protection Board (which inherited the judicial function of the old Civil Service Commission) acted on employee appeals from the actions of their administrative superiors. Thousands of appeals were filed each year throughout the government, and though each one was an individual case, the holdings of the board usually applied not only to the units in which they originated, but to personnel practices in the whole federal administrative establishment. Also, the accumulating decisions of the Equal Employment Opportunity Commission on appeals by federal employees grew into another set of interpretations governing the practices of the bureaus.[77] So did the decisions of the Federal Labor Relations Authority on other aspects of federal employment.[78]

All the foregoing opinions and decisions rest partly on judgments about the intent of Congress in passing a law. Agency officers, however, were aware that statutory language and its official interpretations were not the only indications of congressional expectations. Congressional suggestions and recommendations appeared in all sorts of congressional documents,[79] injunctions that chiefs felt obliged to weigh even though they were not legally binding.

Appropriations hearings, for example, abounded with expressions of legislators' wishes. Here are the words of a member of the House Appropriations Committee addressing the administrator of APHIS on the agency's budget request:

If I did not know you so well . . . I would certainly feel that I was being assaulted personally by this budget in terms of the area of Virginia that I represent. . . . You zero the research budget for poultry disease research and control. This is going to impact on the poultry industry which is centered in the district I represent.

75. 56 Decisions of the Comptroller General 111 (1976).

76. 56 Decisions of the Comptroller General 459 (1977).

77. EEOC decisions of governmentwide effect (as opposed to decisions of application only to the individual or the agency involved) are issued as management directives sent to all departments and agencies. They currently appear in 29 C.F.R. ch. XIV.

78. See *Decisions and Interpretations of the Federal Labor Relations Authority* (formerly the Federal Labor Relations Council) (GPO, published intermittently).

79. See, for example, Michael W. Kirst, *Government Without Passing Laws* (University of North Carolina Press, 1969).

Furthermore, you delete the research funding for contagious equine metritis. As you know, the horse industry is also centered in my district. In addition to that, the only area which you call an outlying infestation of gypsy moth is in the part of Virginia that I represent.

Now, all those areas are zeroed. . . . I hope that you do understand the difficulties that are affecting Virginia and other Southern States as a consequence of some of the provisions in this austere budget.[80]

Or take a question from a member (William H. Natcher, soon to become chairman) of a House Appropriations subcommittee, put to the acting commissioner of social security: "Your . . . budget proposes to expand overtime man-years again by more than a thousand years. Why are you losing ground on overtime again?"[81]

The appropriations subcommittees regarded commitments made to them by bureau chiefs as serious contracts. The following exchange in 1979 between the then chief of the Forest Service (John R. McGuire) and the chairman of his House subcommittee (Sidney R. Yates) illustrates the point.

MR. YATES. We had the impression that the Forest Service was going to be governed by the R[esources] P[lanning] A[ct].

MR. MC GUIRE. The way I understood it there was a question as to whether the law required the Forest Service to reduce the backlog of reforestation to zero by the end of 1984.

MR. YATES. Wasn't that the understanding you had with this Committee?

MR. MC GUIRE: It was my understanding that this was the intent of this Committee, but it is not my understanding that a law requires that.

MR. YATES. . . . It has been the understanding with this Committee for many years now?

MR. MC GUIRE. For many years. That is right.

MR. YATES. Now, all of a sudden, is it a contention of the Forest Service that the passage of the law changed the Committee's understanding with the Forest Service?

MR. MC GUIRE. No, sir. I think I had the idea that some of the members of this Committee might have felt that there was a legal requirement in the law as well as the understanding. There is no question about the understanding with this Committee.[82]

---

80. *Agriculture, Rural Development and Related Agencies Appropriations for 1980,* Hearings before a subcommittee of the House Committee on Appropriations, 96 Cong. 1 sess. (GPO, 1979), pt. 6, p. 57.

81. *Departments of Labor and Health, Education, and Welfare Appropriations for 1979,* Hearings before a subcommittee of the House Committee on Appropriations, 95 Cong. 2 sess. (GPO, 1978), pt. 6, p. 462.

82. *Department of the Interior and Related Agencies Appropriations for 1980,* Hearings before a subcommittee of the House Committee on Appropriations, 96 Cong. 1 sess. (GPO, 1979), pt. 9, pp. 745–46.

Oversight hearings, like appropriations hearings, are filled with injunctions. For instance, in 1978, a member of the Senate Finance Committee's Subcommittee on Administration of the Internal Revenue Code warned the commissioner that the legislators expected him to consult with them before changing his agency's dealings with the public:

SENATOR HASKELL. I think change is desirable. My only comment, sir, is that when you make a change which affects the relationship of the IRS—or is perceived to affect the relationship of the IRS to the public, just as a suggestion, it might be helpful if you could on an informal basis, talk to members of the Senate Finance Committee and the Ways and Means Committee and perhaps some of these problems could be ironed out in advance. . . .

MR. KURTZ. I happily accept that advice.[83]

Similarly, a subcommittee of the House Committee on Government Operations examined IRS programs to give taxpayers information about the tax laws and to provide them with assistance in filling out returns. Two years earlier, the subcommittee had found the services seriously inadequate and asked the General Accounting Office to conduct a survey to assess them. The subcommittee chairman complimented the commissioner on the improvements made since the critique but left no doubt that he thought there was still a long way to go. "I can only suggest to you," he observed, "that you persevere in your requests for additional fundings from the Congress and the administration so that you can maintain a full forward movement in the quality of service to which the public is entitled."[84] The bureau's priorities were responsive to the record of the hearings; service to taxpayers was a major emphasis of the leadership.

Even committees not central to the life of an agency sometimes gave instructions to the agency in the course of hearings. The Senate Committee on Foreign Relations, for instance, in 1977 held hearings on tax treaties between the United States and three foreign countries having to do with the treatment by the IRS of taxes on oil company earnings in those countries. Senator Frank Church put the commissioner on notice: "What should not happen is a repeat of the 1956 tax ruling, where the National Security Council's desire to provide foreign aid to Saudi Arabia led to the creditability of these taxes

83. *Proposed Reorganization of 12 Smallest IRS Districts,* Hearing before the Subcommittee on Administration of the Internal Revenue Code of the Senate Committee on Finance, 95 Cong. 2 sess. (GPO, 1978), p. 28.

84. *Internal Revenue Service's Taxpayer Assistance Programs,* Hearing, p. 75.

[permission to subtract them from the amount of taxes due the United States], regardless of their technical merits, and without review by Congress."[85] Hearings were strewn with such admonitions and advice.

So were committee reports. Take the report of the Senate Committee on Appropriations for fiscal year 1977:

The Committee finds the 23.7 percent case error rate to be totally unacceptable. Although we are pleased that the Social Security Administration appears to be assigning top priority attention to improving administration of the Supplemental Security Income program, we direct the Social Security Administration to advise us immediately if at any time the agency goal of a 15 percent error rate by the end of fiscal year 1977 appears unattainable because of staffing or funding constraints or for any other reason.

The Committee will be continuing to oversee the Social Security Administration's implementation of the Supplemental Security Income program and directs the Social Security Administration to provide to this Committee periodic reports of the progress being made to improve administration and reduce the error rate.[86]

Similarly, in 1976 the House Committee on Government Operations issued a ninety-one-page report on its oversight investigation of the FDA. The document was loaded with criticisms of various aspects of FDA operations and policy at the time, and ended with a long list of specific recommendations, including a suggestion that the "FDA's illegal moratorium on enforcement of the new drug requirements of the law be terminated immediately."[87]

Still more indications of legislative intent appeared in the records of floor debates on bills under consideration in Congress. For instance, when a congressman asked, during the debate on the National Forest Management Act of 1976, for a definition of the term "silvicultural systems," he was told, among other things, that it was meant "to cover any variety of silvicultural practices, and specifically it could include, for example, clearcutting," a practice that a federal court held to be in conflict with an 1897 statute.[88] He was also ad-

85. *Tax Treaties with the United Kingdom, the Republic of Korea, and the Republic of the Philippines,* Hearings before the Senate Committee on Foreign Relations, 95 Cong. 1 sess. (GPO, 1977), p. 2.

86. *Departments of Labor and Health, Education, and Welfare and Related Agencies Appropriations Bill, 1977,* S. Rept. 94-997, 94 Cong. 2 sess. (GPO, 1976), p. 100.

87. *Use of Advisory Committees by the Food and Drug Administration,* H. Rept. 94-787, 94 Cong. 2 sess. (GPO, 1976), p. 12.

88. See note 99, below.

vised that "it means that before they [the Forest Service] can have a timber sale, they must have developed a plan that has met these criteria [set forth in the bill]. . . . There are no timber sales without an approved plan, and the approved plan must contain this criteria [*sic*]."[89] In the give-and-take on the floor, the authority and the obligations of the Forest Service were specified in great detail.

So a host of interpretations added another story to the edifice of constraints facing bureau chiefs. But the edifice is still not complete.

DEPARTMENTAL AND BUREAU ISSUANCES. Extensive though the statutes and governmentwide regulations and the interpretations of these provisions were, they did not make up the largest part of the programming of bureau behavior. The actions of the bureaus were also bound by yet another set of constraints—the issuances of departments and of the bureaus themselves. Together, these typically exceeded in length and specificity all of the preceding sets of documents combined.

For despite the length and specificity of those parent documents, they did not spell out what individuals had to do to comply with them. They did not identify the places to write or call for information or for forms, explain the meaning of puzzling terms, indicate where papers should be filed or what the agencies that received them were to do with them, or set forth the recourse for those who objected to agency actions. They did not provide bureau employees with forms to give the public, tell them what to do with the executed forms, describe the criteria of judgment when discretion was to be exercised, or specify how questions should be answered. They did not tell particular officers and employees what their powers and duties were. They provided a full and elaborate *framework* within which all the necessary arrangements were to be made. But until the details were decided and publicized, people in government and in private life simply could not know how to satisfy the requirements of law.

It fell to the departments and bureaus to fill in these details. They did so by means of published and internal statements that bound and instructed the public and their own work forces. In general, these were codified, indexed, and cross-referenced so that people could quickly find the parts that applied to their own situations. The statements often included the contents or summaries of the statutes they amplified, and they guided their readers to other documentary

89. *Congressional Record,* daily edition (September 15, 1976), p. H10142.

sources as well. Most people therefore seldom needed to go beyond the departmental and bureau materials to find out what was required of them and how to claim what they believed they were entitled to. The departments and the bureaus furnished most of what the public and the bureaus' employees needed to know.

These materials took three basic forms. One was published regulations that appeared formally in the *Federal Register* and were eventually codified into the Code of Federal Regulations in much the same fashion as the regulations of governmentwide effect. The second was manuals for the guidance of agency personnel. The third, produced almost exclusively at the bureau level, was information booklets in varying degrees of nontechnical language for the general public.

Departmental regulations and manuals tended to concentrate on administrative matters common to all bureaus in the departments. Bureau regulations were mostly substantive, that is, related to the distinctive purposes and activities of the bureaus; their manuals usually covered both substance and administration. The information booklets were exclusively substantive. The total output of each bureau included in this study exceeded the output of its parent department; the bureaus wrote most of the materials that governed the public.

Thus the sections of the Code of Federal Regulations dealing with departmental administration in Agriculture, HEW, and Treasury, amounting to approximately 400 pages for each of the first two and 200 for the third, covered employee conduct, delegations of authority, privacy and freedom of information with respect to records, tort claims, claims collection, hearing procedures, employees' inventions, and similar selected subjects. They applied generally to all components of the departments.

The manuals of each of the three departments were multivolume sets of detailed instructions on all aspects of administration. At the time this study began, Treasury was consolidating its standing orders, budget manual, personnel manual, and various bulletins and circulars into a master Directives Manual. Agriculture already had a single set of administrative issuances called Administrative Regulations (not to be confused with the published rules in the Code of Federal Regulations), eleven loose-leaf binders containing all the "administrative requirements and authorities of general applicability issued at the Departmental level." But it still had a separate personnel manual (consisting of the department's personnel management rules interfiled with the pages of the governmentwide Federal Personnel Manual), a number of finance manuals produced by its National Finance Center, and several data-processing manuals. HEW had a General Administration Manual and twenty-one staff manuals, the former including "all administrative policies, standards, procedures, and delegations of authority which are of general interest and applicability" to the whole department, the latter setting out administrative materials of narrower interest, such as correspondence and management of forms and printing. Staff specialists in the departments and bureaus looked to these for guidance in their areas of specialization.

The specifics affecting most of the contacts between the public and the agencies, however, were in the bureau documents. The published regulations of the IRS, as usual, dwarfed all the others; they occupied fourteen volumes—over 7,500 double-column pages—in the Code of Federal Regulations, encompassing and enlarging upon the bureau-specific language of the statutes. In addition, IRS officers and employees were instructed by the Internal Revenue Manual, a set of over seventy loose-leaf volumes; five volumes of orders of the chief counsel; and separate manuals on tax court proceedings, general litigation, and enforcement. These were the bibles of the IRS work force.

The FDA was the source of more than 2,800 pages in six volumes of the Code of Federal Regulations, most of them originating with its subdivisions. The regulations were enlarged on by more than a score of manuals, some administrative (the Administrative Guidelines Manual, the Regulatory Procedures Manual, and the Staff Manual Guides to Organization and Delegations), most technical (the Laboratory Operations Manual, the Pesticide Analytical Manual, and the Inspector Operations Manual). It was to these documents that the agency's personnel turned for descriptions of their duties, authority, and procedures.

The Social Security Administration, APHIS, and Customs each generated between 600 and 700 pages in the Code of Federal Regulations, and all three bureaus supplemented the regulations with extensive systems of internal issuances. Customs, at the time of this study, was in the process of instituting a master Customs Issuance System to replace the old Customs Manual, circular letters, handbooks, and other manuals. A multivolume Policies and Procedures Manual was to contain all the policies and operational instructions and guidelines in effect, with sections extracted and separately issued as handbooks for the convenience of specialists. The SSA employed an agencywide Administrative Directives System to transmit instructions on housekeeping matters, a Personnel Manual and Personnel Guides for directions on personnel management, and program manuals separately issued by the major operating components of the agency. (One estimate put the total pages in this collection at 100,000 —"enough loose-leaf folders to fill a cabinet 23 feet long and 12 feet high."[90]) APHIS had a Directives Issuance System for announcing agency policies and procedures, and two series of administrative and technical memorandums issued by its plant protection and quarantine and its veterinary services programs for their own staffs.

The Forest Service had the smallest volume of published regulations of all the agencies in the study—fewer than 140 pages. But the Forest Service Manual was a match for the internal issuances of any of the other bureaus. More than twenty volumes contained the statements of policy, procedure, technical methods, purpose, and sources of legal authority for everything the service did. These were supplemented by seventy-four handbooks containing step-by-step instructions for everything from preparing manuscripts and filing to smoke jumping and determining the causes of wildfires.

In all the bureaus, the regional offices and even the lesser field installations were authorized to supplement bureau issuances with issuances of their own adapted to their special circumstances. Neither in volume nor import, however, did the field issuances approach the products of the Washington offices. They constituted a small increment to the body of written directives confronting a bureau chief when he assumed his position.

Publications aimed at the public were of many kinds. Some merely described the agencies and their programs. Some explained how to comply with the law or apply for benefits or assert rights or report presumed violations of the law. Some told individuals what to do to help themselves. Even though they were primarily informational, however, they also served to program behavior—by creating expectations, plans, and practices on the part of bureau clients and contrac-

90. Thomas Hasler, "Words, Words, an Avalanche of Words," *Evening Sun* (Baltimore), March 10, 1978.

tors. An incoming bureau chief, if he wanted to alter anything, would have had to take these factors into account; they became another form of constraint.

LABOR CONTRACTS. So, too, did labor-management contracts between agencies on the one side and organizations of their employees on the other. At the start of this study, each of the six bureaus, under the provisions of presidential executive orders, had signed agreements with unions representing various of their employees. Things were in flux while the research went on; bargaining units were being consolidated, reducing the number of contracts to be negotiated, and title VII of the Civil Service Reform Act of 1978[91] put a statutory foundation under the whole process of labor-management relations in the federal government. Thus by 1980 the SSA was negotiating a master contract with a unit of the American Federation of Government Employees, the Customs Service had one with a unit of the National Treasury Employees Union, the IRS had a contract with its own unit of the same union covering most of its staff, and the Forest Service was working out a single contract to replace seventy separate agreements covering about half its employees. The FDA and APHIS, with more decentralized bargaining arrangements, had a variety of contracts with individual locals and specialized, unaffiliated groups.

In no case were all employees members of unions, even when a master contract covered all of them, and special local adjustments of general contract provisions were not unusual. While the specifics of each therefore varied, every one of the chiefs was confronted by labor-management understandings that were on the books when he took office. Many of these agreements, moreover, ran to over a hundred printed pages.

The documents, it is true, were of limited duration. Like all such agreements, they were in force for only a few years at most; then they came up for renegotiation. But they were not renegotiated from scratch. The concessions won by the unions in one period continued from then on, and the volume and specificity of substantive and procedural provisions accumulated, just like provisions of law. The completion of a contract's life did not free bureau leaders from past constraints; it meant only that they would have to bargain about additional ones. The terms were a constantly growing edifice in which many past union gains became permanent, irreversible features.

91. 92 Stat. 1191 (1978).

Many of the most important subjects covered by collective bargaining in the private sector, it is true, are set by law in the public sector. They are therefore decided in the legislative rather than the administrative arena. Consequently, if all labor contracts in the federal government were suddenly abolished, administrators would not experience a dramatic liberation from restraints or a great expansion of discretion; they would still be bound by a substantial body of law. All the same, the contracts between the bureaus and their employees added to the written controls by expanding on the law. Clauses in typical contracts covered union rights, management rights, employee rights, union stewards' use of official time and facilities, grievance procedures, arbitration, disciplinary actions, the withholding of dues, leave, overtime, training and career development, transfer and reassignment, and other matters of labor-management relations. These were all worked out within the framework set up by statutes and the regulations and precedents established by the Federal Labor Relations Authority (the federal government's counterpart of the National Labor Relations Board), but they amplified the official documents. Thus they elaborated the documentary requirements enveloping the chiefs and made the unions another factor to be taken into account in running the agencies.

THE BURDEN IS DIFFUSED. The total dimensions of the corpus of written directives—and this inventory, though it comprehends all the major elements of that aggregate of materials, probably does not include everything—were certainly staggering. Collectively, they are one reason for my contention that the bureau chiefs found much of the activity of their agencies programmed in advance (and for complaints from all quarters about red tape). But the inventory may exaggerate the oppressiveness of this burden. In the first place, the documents were highly repetitious because each level reproduced much of the language of the original materials on which its own issuances depended for legality. In part, this practice resulted from the caution of legal officers. If the language of higher authorities was reproduced, the risk of misinterpreting their wishes—and of being *accused* of misinterpreting their wishes—was diminished, the grounds for the lower levels' own administrative issuances were established, and the responsibility for annoying policies and courses of action was fixed on superior officers. And in part, the repetition was an effort to make things a little more convenient for agency employees and the public by locating everything they were likely to need in the documents of a single organization. For these reasons, the volume of paper was great, yet the oppressiveness of the documents was not quite proportional to the volume.

In the second place, nobody had to master the whole output. Most people, in government and out, came to know a great deal about what was relevant for them but were only generally aware of the rest of the mountain. They—and this includes bureau chiefs—therefore took a great deal on faith. The mountain of paper consequently did not overwhelm them.

In the third place, although I did not happen on specific inconsistencies and conflicts among the body of instructions to the bureaus, it seems likely that the directives to an agency, because they come from so many different sources at so many different times, did contain inconsistencies and conflicts. One would anticipate incongruities, for example, between the wishes of various political and administrative figures and the provisions of laws and regulations, between the provisions of different statutes and regulations, between the demands of divers congressional committees, or between legislators and executive superiors. In such cases, a chief might have been able to invoke the instructions justifying any course of action he preferred and thus to do what he wanted. Such opportunities did not occur every day (or I would have run across them), but to the extent that they did occur, they eased the strictures of the body of written directives at least a little.

So in their daily routines the chiefs did not feel constantly coerced or thwarted by the extensive written instructions that programmed so many of the actions of their organizations. Indeed, if they did not try to make sharp, swift, large changes in the behavior of their work forces, either substantive or procedural, they were hardly aware of the formal programming. But when they sought to introduce changes, they soon met it head on. The social security commissioner found himself unable to improve physical conditions in some of his local field offices that were depressing and, in his view, degrading to the clients of his bureau. The internal revenue commissioner could not expand or significantly alter the computer capacity on which the operation of his agency depended. The chief of the Forest Service was obliged to consult extensively with the public before recommending action on roadless areas in the national forest system. The customs commissioner discovered that it was not easy to prohibit extensive (but avoidable) accumulations of overtime by some of his inspectors that brought them higher salaries than top government officials. As techniques of chemical analysis improved, the commissioner of food and drugs found himself compelled by law to disapprove useful drugs and food additives containing minute traces of weak carcinogens though it was far from clear that the risks outweighed the benefits. The State Department directed the administrator of APHIS, for budgetary reasons, to vote at an international meeting against the creation of an international animal health center even though he strongly favored such a center. It was when chiefs wanted to modify things—policy, procedure, capital, or any other major feature of their agencies—that the constraints of programming became salient and inhibiting.

By the same token, changes forced on the agencies by directives sometimes made the chiefs aware of the constraints. One of them remarked, in terms strikingly reminiscent of the lamentations of businessmen, that complying with new commands often consumed bureau staff time and money, yet the costs were not recognized by those who imposed the new requirements nor were additional resources provided to meet the costs. Environmental impact statements, compliance with freedom of information requests, provisions for extensive public hearings, privacy laws and guidelines, demands for information not previously called for, and similar obligations placed on the bureaus multiplied their burdens without compensating allowances, forcing them to scrape and scramble to obey.

Thus it was under conditions of change—sought by the chiefs themselves or forced on them by others—that the chiefs were reminded of all the factors other than their own wishes determining what their agencies did. Prominent among these were the written programs setting the behavior of the organizations they headed.

Learned Behavior

Added to the explicit written directives governing the behavior of bureau personnel were the habits, routines, and practices that the members of the agencies brought with them when they started their jobs and that they acquired in the course of working. These were probably even more unyielding limitations on the ability of leaders to work their will on organizations than the written directives were because they were locked inside the nervous systems of individuals. I do not mean to suggest that all, or even most, of these patterns were immutable. But I do take it as axiomatic that they were generally harder to alter than written instructions and commands, difficult though changes of the latter kind sometimes turn out to be. Behavioral patterns are hard to change even when the organization itself, through its teaching and training efforts, has implanted them in its members. They therefore constituted another set of confines confronting every bureau chief.

LEARNING UNCONTROLLED BY MANAGEMENT. Most of the basic skills and information needed on most jobs in government and industry are acquired outside the employing organizations. Many of them are imparted in educational institutions, but the experience of living in a family, associating with a peer group, listening to radio and watching television, reading, going to the movies, attending church, watching and participating in sports and other forms of recreation, and all the other individual and social activities of which life is made up also equip us with knowledge that helps us survive in organizations. In these ways, we discover what other people expect of us and what we may expect of them. We develop our perceptions, understanding, attitudes, values. All of these come with us when we enter upon a job, and the executives in the organizations we join take them for granted as foundations on which to add the comparatively thin layers of special information and skill required to perform specific organizational functions.

Moreover, besides what people bring to their jobs and what organizations deliberately strive to instill in their employees, employees learn haphazardly from their fellows as they work.[92] By watching and talking with their co-workers, they find out what to do and how to do it. Chances are they become familiar only in general terms with

92. "Vocational education is based on the premise that one exogenously invests in skills and then brings these skills into the labor market to sell in much the same way that one would grow a bushel of wheat and then sell it. In fact, most skills in the United States are not acquired in formal education or training. Rather, they are acquired through on-the-job training from one worker to another." Lester C. Thurow, "Vocational Education as a Strategy for Eliminating Poverty," in Thomas J. Anton and others, *The Planning Papers for the Vocational Education Study: Vocational Education Study Publication No. 1* (National Institute of Education, 1979).

most of the formal directives with which they must comply; for the most part, they learn by doing. They also discover the shortcuts, the output standards, the informal social structures, and other realities of employee practice. The traditions, mores, and folkways of organizations are gradually absorbed by their members. The evidence of this socialization is abundant and has therefore been taken as a given in this study.

From the point of view of a bureau, all this unplanned learning is both advantageous and troublesome. It is advantageous in that it makes the most of what other institutions in society teach, lightening the burden of the bureau. But it is burdensome in that people's habits, attitudes, perceptions, values, beliefs, capabilities, and inhibitions are remarkably enduring once they are acquired or implanted, making most people rather resistant to change. Often they are resistant because they find they cannot change their ways of doing things even though they would like to be responsive to new circumstances. Sometimes they are unresponsive because they develop vested interests in established ways and ideas and persist in them even when it appears that they could change if they wanted to. In either case, established behavior patterns become obstacles to the exercise of influence on organizations by leaders in favor of change. Old practices continue, and the leaders can do little about them.

The more professional an area of expertise in an organization is, the more difficulty a leader is likely to have when he tries to move its practitioners. For one thing, a professional field is usually highly specialized and technical and takes a long time to master; consequently, its concepts and practices are particularly deeply ingrained and the sunk costs are particularly high. For another, to specialists, the head of their organization is a generalist, almost a layman when it comes to their expertise. They are bound not merely by the edicts of the organization, but by the canons of practice and ethics of their own disciplines as well. Organizations full of professionals and technicians tend for this reason to be exceptionally hard for a manager to manipulate.

Most bureaus of the federal government are full of professionals and technicians. The six in the sample for this study certainly were. The Forest Service had not only foresters, but also wildlife biologists, engineers of many descriptions, range conservationists, hydrologists, geologists, and soil scientists. The FDA had physicians, biochemists, food technologists, radiologists, toxicologists. The Animal and Plant Health Inspection Service had veterinarians, botanists, zoologists, entomologists, virologists, pathologists. In the Social Security Administration were social workers, actuaries, statisticians. Inspectors, appraisers, investigators, and narcotics experts abounded in the Customs Service. The IRS consisted heavily of lawyers, accountants, economists, investigative agents. In all the agencies there were management analysts, budget analysts, personnel administrators, data processors, information officers, and property managers. The list goes on and on. And every time a new chief took over any of the bureaus, he soon became aware, if he was not at the start, that the experts' knowledge, commitment, pride, and sensitivity meant that they could not be quickly turned around from what they were doing. Much of what they knew and did had not been learned under bureau auspices and therefore was not easily modified by bureau action.

MANAGED LEARNING. What is more, even the aspects of work force learning that are subject to some degree of agency control limit the ability of a new chief to modify the continuing activities in the agency. Each new leader after the first one enters an organization with a history of managed learning permeating its personnel. To be sure, the methods by which past learning was instilled in the work force may be used to introduce new patterns of behavior also. But it takes time and resources to effect such changes, to erase what has already been learned and substitute new patterns, and this task is particularly difficult if it must be accomplished while the work of the organization continues. A new chief is therefore likely to feel sharply constrained by what was deliberately infused into his work force by his organization before his accession to office.

Some of the methods by which organizations seek to provide themselves with appropriately disposed and skilled employees merely take advantage of the range of attitudes and prior preparation distributed in the society. Appointing officers, with the help of personnel specialists, try to induce properly qualified people to apply, then strive to select the most suitable candidates from among the applicants, and at least attempt to place the successful candidates in positions in which they can make their maximum contributions to the organizations. (All the bureaus in this study, for example, established demanding requirements for middle- and upper-level positions. Nobody went into those jobs without a great deal of preparation.) Managers try also to identify employees who display the attributes and values and capabilities that the managers prize, and to reward them and promote them. Not only are the hierarchical levels of each organization thus staffed with individuals who naturally fit the prevailing standards of the leaders, but all who wish to advance, seeing what is valued by the leadership, are motivated to mold themselves in the preferred pattern. Others do not get ahead and may either be weeded out or resign because the environment is not what they want. In this fashion, an atmosphere, a shared set of outlooks, and an established way of doing things are set up. They are reinforced in some organizations by rotating personnel through a variety of regions and divisions so that they pick up organizationwide norms rather than local customs. Even without formal programs of training and indoctrination, therefore, organizations manage to produce desired patterns of behavior among their members.

No matter how expert an organization may be in the techniques of selecting and nurturing personal qualifications developed elsewhere, it must still instruct personnel in its own unique features and procedures, in the specific requirements of the job each new or promoted or rotated employee will be expected to perform, and in new requirements engendered by changed conditions. Consequently, formal training and indoctrination sessions are conducted in every large organization, and they are vital to government agencies because employees must learn so many provisions of law as part of their work. A new chief therefore finds himself at the apex of a work force in whom norms and habits have been carefully infused by his agency in the past.[93]

For example, in one of the two largest bureaus in my sample, the IRS, there were over 78,000 employee enrollments in training courses and programs in fiscal year 1978, 99 percent of them within the agency, the balance outside. These constituted more than 2,200 staff-years of work time, devoted to 374 courses and programs—456 curriculum-weeks of offerings all together. "One copy of all printed IRS training materials," an IRS document proclaimed proudly, "takes 15 feet of bookcase shelves; and TV tape cassettes and film another 15 feet." Most of the training (63 percent, to be precise) was designed to ready recruits for their immediate duties, some jobs requiring as

93. See, for example, Herbert Kaufman, *The Forest Ranger: A Study in Administrative Behavior* (Johns Hopkins Press, 1960), chap. 6.

many as several months of classroom and on-the-job instruction. But another 17 percent was for advancement of personnel to more specialized and senior posts, 6 percent for supervisory and managerial training, 12 percent for updating and refresher work, and 2 percent for multifunctional and local tasks. This intensity of training, of course, was maintained year after year, mostly in the field, much of it at training centers in each of the seven regions. By the time a career employee reached a high-level position, he would almost certainly have been exposed to extensive formal preparation by the bureau.

Similarly, the smallest bureau in the sample, APHIS, had an elaborate training program, which was in the process of reconstruction during this study. The new plans called for a comprehensive orientation to the bureau as a whole, to be offered on both a group and an individual basis, and 120 hours of supervisory training offerings besides the 80 hours required by the Office of Personnel Management. The two major line components of the bureau—veterinary services, plant protection and quarantine—also offered a host of technical and professional courses. These included science and technology (pathology, virology, bacteriology, pesticide storage and disposal, entomology, biological control, and ecology), management and executive development, and specific job-related functions (such as detecting and blocking importation of prohibited animal products and identifying and quarantining plant-threatening organisms at ports of entry). Like the IRS, APHIS performed most of its training inside the bureau, but many of its employees also received instruction in the Department of Agriculture Graduate School, the Office of Personnel Management, and other "out-service" organizations.

The four bureaus between the largest and the smallest also conducted intensive training programs. In the Customs Service the technical preparation of patrol officers and special agents at the Federal Law Enforcement Center and of inspectors and import specialists at the Customs Academy was concentrated and comprehensive, and the regions, with the help of materials supplied by the Washington office, ran numerous courses for other employees. (The new commissioner and the new director of the personnel management division thought the quality of training for executives, however, sorely needed upgrading.) In the FDA technical training was conducted largely by the specialized constituent bodies within the agency and ranged all the way from basic instruction of new field investigators to continuing professional education for senior medical officers. There were also programs for clerical personnel, for supervisors, and for executives. The Forest Service employed courses and conferences at national, regional, forest, and district levels to develop technical and professional proficiency and managerial and executive competence. Technical skills were also honed at field encampments, and all supervisory officers were required to work up and carry out formal plans for on-the-job training. In the Social Security Administration, course offerings in the central office alone filled a booklet resembling a college catalog, and each of the regions provided a comparable range of training opportunities and requirements.[94]

Most of the officers and employees in the bureaus remained when new chiefs took over. A new chief was likely to bring new people into his immediate staff, reorganize and shuffle his staff about, and move some of his line officials in headquarters and the field until he got a structure and a group of aides and lieutenants he felt comfortable with. Still, the number who stayed on through changes in the leadership in a bureau outweighed by many times the number brought in by each newcomer.

The stability of the work force, especially in the upper echelons, is attributable only in part to formal civil service protection. Another factor is the knowledge and experience and connections developed by the work forces of the bureaus over the years; these are assets that a wise leader, especially a new one, does not lightly cast away. Besides, wholesale turnovers of personnel can disrupt operations and depress morale. So most people stay on because they are wanted as well as because they are protected in their jobs.

In four of the bureaus (APHIS, Customs, the FDA, and the Forest Service) the turnover for the agencies as a whole was very low— probably about 5 percent or less, including positions in the lower classifications, where the character of the work, the level of pay, and the career prospects were not overwhelmingly attractive and the number who could be expected to leave was comparatively high. In the two giant bureaus, the SSA and the IRS, the overall rates were somewhat higher—partly, I imagine, because massive operations entailed large numbers of dull, dead-end, repetitive jobs, and partly because, in the case of the IRS, the skills acquired in the agency were

94. I refer here mainly to work-related offerings. In some agencies, on-site college courses were also offered.

in strong demand for legal and accounting functions in the private sector. In any case, at the upper levels of all the bureaus, although each succession of chiefs brought some shifts and changes, many of the people from prior administrations turned up among the new leadership groups—not necessarily in the same positions, but still in major posts. The continuity was striking.

An incoming chief in any of these bureaus therefore encountered an entire hierarchy schooled and conditioned in the previously established policies and practices of the agency. That schooling and conditioning, preserved by the continuity of personnel, confronted him with yet another set of limits on the effect he could have, at least in the short run.

Benefits and Costs of Programmed Behavior

All the directives and the learned behavior that can frustrate a leader can give him aid and comfort, too. It must reassure him, after all, to know that the people in his organization have been told in detail how to keep the work moving, are trained to handle most of the problems they will face, and, because the programming is so deeply implanted, would do so for quite a while even if the chief failed to show up for days at a time. It must be comforting, if sobering, for him to realize that most employees are performing tasks that would bewilder and overwhelm him if he were suddenly thrust into their positions; their learning, both planned and unplanned, is an asset to him as a leader. It enables him to delegate authority to them with assurance. Certainly he has no choice but to depend on the people who work for him. If a chief were to try to handle personally all the demands for his attention and action or to supervise, review, and evaluate all the operations of his bureau, he would not have enough hours if he worked twenty-four hours a day seven days a week.

Nor can he anticipate decades in office to accomplish his ends. Between the end of World War II and the incumbencies of the subjects of this study, thirty-seven chiefs served in the six agencies in the sample. When APHIS, which at the time of this study had had only one chief since its creation in 1972, is excluded, twenty-six of the remaining thirty-six (over 72 percent) served six years or less, and only five (less than 14 percent) served over nine years; the longest term was twelve years.[95] Nine of the thirty-six (25 percent) served three years or less. Every new chief therefore had to choose carefully the things to which he would give his persistent and concentrated attention during his relatively brief period of hectic service, and had to rely on those around him to keep the rest of the organization's processes functioning properly.

The more ardently an executive aspires to seizing the initiative instead of merely reacting to what comes before him, the more selective he has to be about the use of his time; otherwise the routines will swamp him and hinder his efforts to find or open strategic opportunities and to devise measures to take advantage of them. Curiously, the boldest and most active leaders are frequently the ones whose subordinates have the broadest discretion and responsibility. At the same time, cautious, passive, or lazy ones who wish to avoid the cares and troubles of leadership are also likely to feel relieved that extensive, explicit programming controls the administrative behavior of their subordinates. The prior programming of work forces is therefore appreciated by both types of chief because it helps keep things from getting out of hand when the chiefs, for different reasons, are not engaged in policing all aspects of the system.

Moreover, programming gives active chiefs hope that traditional patterns of organizational behavior may eventually be changed. Since the patterns are products of identifiable, accumulated written directives and of habits and values formed at least in part by deliberate organizational training, they presumably can be altered by modifying the contents of the directives in force, the standards for recruiting, and the thrust of training. They do not seem to be utterly beyond managerial influence.

All the same, it would not be surprising if bureau chiefs were to express feelings of helplessness. In any large organization, so much momentum has built up and so many routines have already been formed that the prospects of having a profound effect in anything

95. These figures refer to years in the position of chief only. In the Forest Service all the chiefs were career officers with decades of employment in the agency before being appointed chief. The administrator of APHIS also had many years of prior service in the Department of Agriculture. And at least two earlier commissioners of social security—Arthur Altmeyer and Robert M. Ball—had had years of experience with social security before becoming commissioners. Such career service was not usual in the other cases.

short of a lifetime of concentrated effort must seem dim, especially in the early months. The programming of the members of the agency, whatever the benefits of this process, is sure to feel to the chiefs like a crushing burden of constraints much of the time.

But it is by no means the only such burden. Not only were the chiefs in this study constrained by factors governing the activities of their subordinates, but their own agendas were also shaped by forces beyond their control.

IMPOSED AGENDAS

Since public agencies are programmed to keep running without constant attention from their chiefs, one might infer that all the chiefs in this study would have had the luxury of allocating their time and selecting matters for deliberation according to their own preferences and perceptions of need. In fact, all sorts of tasks and problems were pressed on them by the organizational environment in which they found themselves.

Regular Cycles

THE BUDGETARY PROCESS. For example, the rhythm of the annual budget cycle pulsed through the administrative system of Washington with the regularity of heartbeats.[96] Unlike heartbeats, however, the budgetary rhythm was prominent in everybody's consciousness. Administrative activities kept in step with it, and schedules were built around it. Along with everyone else in the government, bureau chiefs marched to the rhythm of this governmental pulsation.

With a few exceptions (such as agencies with permanent appropriations, making money available for expenditure without annual action by Congress), most agencies would have little money for operations at the start of each fiscal year were appropriations laws not enacted by the first of October. Congress does not work on appropriations legislation for specific programs and agencies until it receives the president's budget request in January. The president's budget is assembled by a process of negotiation over departmental budget re-

96. David J. Ott and Attiat F. Ott, *Federal Budget Policy*, 3d ed. (Brookings Institution, 1977), chap. 3.

quests between the departments and the Office of Management and Budget, for the most part, in the late summer and fall. Departments put their budgets together in the late spring and summer by negotiating with the bureaus over the bureaus' budget estimates. Bureaus therefore have to present their cases to the departments, to the OMB, and to the relevant House and Senate Appropriations subcommittees on a generally predictable timetable. The bureaus in this study worked up their budgets in something between several weeks and several months in the late winter and early spring. Then the chiefs and their aides defended their estimates at each subsequent phase of the cycle, adjusting the figures as necessary to conform to departmental and presidential decisions. Consequently, even though the chiefs themselves were not deeply immersed in the details of the budgetary process, they still had to adapt to this timetable because so many of their top officers were engaged in it that it was difficult to get them to focus on anything else until the task was completed.

This scheduling pressure applied to the SSA despite the automatic transfer of social security taxes from the Treasury to the various social security trust funds under a permanent appropriations provision in the substantive law. For one thing, the SSA administered a number of programs, such as supplemental security income, aid to families with dependent children, and benefits for the victims of black lung disease, that were financed out of general revenues, and these depended on annual appropriations. And although the social security trust funds could be drawn upon for administrative expenses, Congress annually put a ceiling on the total amount that could be used for administration, and the agency had to propose and defend a ceiling each year. So the commissioner of social security, just like the chiefs of the other bureaus, followed the annual rhythms of the budget cycle.

CYCLES IN WORKLOAD. Some of the chiefs also were forced to adapt to waves of work that flooded their bureaus at fixed times each year. The IRS, for instance, as each calendar year drew to a close, had to arrange for printing and distributing tens of millions of tax forms and instructions for executing and filing them, and it had to be ready to receive and process them as they came pouring in during the three-and-a-half-month filing season. The SSA sent checks every month to 34 million beneficiaries of the programs in its charge. The Forest Service prepared for seasons of high fire danger, influxes of recreational visits during summer and hunting and fishing and foliage and winter sports periods, and for the running of livestock when the grazing lands were ready. At various times of the year the Customs Service was confronted by legions of foreign tourists and by American tourists returning from abroad. Although the workloads were handled mainly by subordinates, mostly in the field, and did not impinge directly on the chiefs unless problems arose, the chiefs felt their effects. During the extraordinarily busy intervals, staffs were so preoccupied with the tasks at hand that they were less responsive to unrelated demands and requests from any quarter, including the chiefs' offices, than they were at less stressful times. And questions and problems generated by the masses of work forced their way upward to the top levels. So the repetitive, predictable peaks and valleys of workloads helped determine the chief's own agendas.

Knowing what was coming and what had to be done to adjust eased the strain on the chiefs. They planned their own schedules to fit the circumstances, which made the conditions to which they adjusted seem less oppressive. But though they retained some opportunity to navigate, they were still prisoners of the river of events, obliged to accommodate to its twists and turns, to its rapids and shoals and backwaters.

Safe Channels through Minefields

Sometimes, to carry the metaphor one step further, the waters are mined. A host of understandings develop inside a bureau, and between a bureau and the people with whom it comes in contact, regarding the course the bureau will follow—the practices it will tolerate, the demands it will enforce, the services it will render—in doing its job. So long as everybody involved, including the chief, remains within the boundaries of these understandings, things tend to go on routinely and quietly. But let anyone step over the boundaries, and the reactions—of employees, other officials, politicians, interest groups, or the press—are likely to be explosive. The understandings thus mark a safe channel for a bureau and its chief, narrowing his options still further.

A particularly dramatic illustration of this constraint was provided by a bureau not in this sample. The director of the National Park Service was dismissed in April 1980 by the secretary of the interior because of morale and management problems in the agency and because of the director's poor health. According to informed sources, however, the removal was partly a response to political pressure, exerted through Congress, from concessionaires in the parks, whom he had been trying to "reform and restrain."[97] Yet just eight years earlier a director of the bureau had been removed "after conservationists charged that he was subjecting the parks to excessive development." Evidently there was a slim band between being too accommodating to concessionaires and not being accommodating enough. Chiefs who strayed from the safe channel in either direction found out about the consequences suddenly and swiftly.

The boundaries of such minefields are neither sharp nor fixed. The chiefs therefore were always taking soundings and probing the limits. All of them could be sure, from the experience of other chiefs if not from what they themselves experienced, that mines were out there, primed to go off if the helmsmen tried to depart from tested waters.

Erratic Agenda Items

The life of every chief was also affected by unpredictable events that thrust themselves onto their agendas. Unpredictable events were not unexpected; every chief knew that in the course of a year he would have to drop what he was doing and deal with problems he had not planned on. What he could not foresee was the specific content of those problems or when they would arise.

These items usually took one of four forms. The first, and probably the most common, consisted of unsolicited changes in the directives or interpretations of directives, including legislation, that governed a bureau. The second was sudden, undeclinable summonses to attend conferences, counsel superiors, testify before congressional committees, or the like. The third was natural emergencies within the jurisdiction of the bureau. The fourth was scandal. Any of these could compel a chief to make room for it in his schedule, usually reluctantly and unhappily.

UNSOLICITED CHANGES IN DIRECTIVES. During the period of observation, not one of the six agencies was free of change in its written

97. Philip Shabecoff, "Director Ousted over 'Problems' in Federal Parks," *New York Times*, April 25, 1980.

directives. Some of these changes, it is true, were introduced by the bureaus. But all the bureaus also received some instructions from Congress or its instruments, from their departments, from courts, and from all the other sources of such directives. The documentary under-pinning of administration was never totally at rest. If nothing else, appropriations were different from year to year.

The meaning and effect of written directives were also modified to some extent by instructions, expressions of preference, requests, demands, and inquiries presented informally, usually conversation-ally, to bureau leaders. They did not ordinarily become part of the permanent programming of behavior unless converted into official documentary form, and many of them were therefore of very short duration. But they meant that the wishes of strategically placed indi-viduals in the bureaus, elsewhere in the government, or even outside the government might for a time insert or remove, or advance or retard, an item on a chief's agenda.

In all likelihood, only a small percentage of the changes in direc-tives took up much of the chiefs' time. But that small percentage could push heavily time-consuming problems to their desks. When the issue of tax exemption for church-run schools alleged to have vio-lated equal educational opportunity decisions and legislation was raised by a court ruling, it involved the commissioner of internal revenue in many hours of deliberations, hearings, and testimony. The work of the commissioner of food and drugs was profoundly altered by the single statutory provision (the Delaney clause)[98] pro-hibiting the marketing of any food additive shown to cause cancer when fed to humans or animals. A court holding on timber sale prac-tices in the national forests[99] compelled the leadership of the Forest Service to devote much of its energy for a long time to getting appro-priate legislation allowing sales to be resumed. And the Forest and

98. 21 U.S.C. 376(b)(5)(B); see also 21 C.F.R. 5.1.

99. In two cases, *West Virginia Division of the Izaak Walton League of America* v. *Butz*, 522 F.2nd 945 (4th Cir. 1975) and *Zieske* v. *Butz*, 406 F. Supp. 258 (D. Alas. 1975), courts ruled that clear-cutting of timber, a silvicultural practice long used for some tree species, was forbidden by a provision of an 1897 law requiring that trees for cutting be individually marked (30 Stat. 35). Section 6(g)((3)(F) of the National Forest Management Act of 1976 (90 Stat. 2949, at 2952) specifically autho-rized clear-cutting in national forests under specified conditions, and sec. 13 (at p. 2958) repealed the old language. See Timothy Prior Mulhern, "The National Forest Management Act of 1976: A Critical Examination," *Boston College Envi-ronmental Law Review*, vol. 7, no. 1 (1978), p. 99.

Rangeland Renewable Resources Planning Act,[100] passed because Congress wanted an overall picture of the competing demands on forest and rangeland resources so that it could choose among them, imposed a burdensome (though not totally unwelcome) requirement of long-range, comprehensive planning on the Forest Service. Any strategically placed member of Congress, budget examiner, assistant secretary, White House aide, or spokesman for a lobby, among others, might, by voicing disapproval of a proposal or a request or by suggesting amendments or recommending additions, send a matter back to a bureau for further consideration and possible revision. In all these cases, only one part of the broad spectrum of agency activities was affected by the matters at issue. Nonetheless, they forced the chiefs to make room in their crowded schedules for things to which they would not of their own preference have addressed themselves at the time.

Ironically, unsolicited changes in directives could be brought about by the bureau's own initiatives. A proposed regulation, a recommendation for a modification of existing legislation, a novel ruling on a particular individual or firm, or any other attempt to depart from established practice could set in motion a process of struggle and negotiation whose outcome was uncertain and perhaps opposite to what the initiators intended. Awareness of this risk discouraged casualness in soliciting change. But most of the unsolicited changes were not of this character; they were imposed on the chiefs by the actions of others.

Whether some of the chiefs were subjected to more pressure of this kind than others I cannot say. It seems logical that the more extensive and specific the directives to which a bureau had to respond, the greater the frequency with which the directives were challenged and revised would be. The IRS, the SSA, and the FDA were, in fact, almost continuously grappling with their existing instructions (both on their own, to clarify or correct weaknesses or to change policy, and in response to other people's efforts to change them) and with propounded new ones. On the other hand, when I was watching the chiefs, all of the bureaus went through, or had recently gone through, modifications of their directives by one means or another. It was not possible to conduct detailed studies distinguishing the degrees to which the chiefs' agendas were taken up by imposed changes. What is

100. 88 Stat. 476 (1974).

clear, however, is that whether a chief was the head of a big bureau with volumes of directives or of a small one with a small body of controlling documents, his agenda was affected by this kind of reprogramming.

UNDECLINABLE SUMMONSES. All the chiefs were summoned from time to time by officials whose innovations carried the authority of command. When, for example, the secretary of a department wanted to consult or issue instructions personally, or an assistant secretary called a conference to get or give information, or a committee chairman decided to hold a hearing, or staffers in the Executive Office of the President known to enjoy a great deal of presidential confidence requested a chief's presence for a discussion of plans and actions (though this happened more rarely), or a prominent officer of an important interest group sought an audience, the chiefs usually complied even if it meant disruption of their own calendars. But even when they could not and had to negotiate the time and duration of such meetings, they had to accede to the summonses of these callers at some point, and their agendas were to that extent imposed on them by others.

It would be rash to generalize about differences among the chiefs in this respect because so many factors affected the frequency of such summonses. The style and interests of the relevant congressional committee chairmen and their staffs, of the secretaries and assistant secretaries, of the president and his aides, for instance, determined how often they called in various chiefs. The news value of the programs administered by a bureau, the degree of confidence in an agency and its leaders, the number of tangencies between the program of a given bureau and those of other government agencies, the number of complaints lodged against a bureau in a specific interval of time, the urgency of competing demands on the attention and the energies of potential intervenors, the support enjoyed by a bureau and its chief, and the state of relations with the bureau's constituency also determined the number of summonses each chief got. Consequently, there were marked differences in the frequency of undeclinable invitations to the chiefs in this study, and the incidence probably varied over time. Nevertheless, it may be said that demands of this kind generally had a significant, though not a paramount, effect on the agendas of all six administrators.

EMERGENCIES. Two of the chiefs, the commissioner of food and drugs and the administrator of APHIS, were also caught up in occasional emergencies that claimed priority over other items in their schedules. Whenever contaminated products were discovered in the food chain, the FDA removed them from the stream of commerce and destroyed them, alerted consumers who may already have acquired them, and sought to prevent recurrences. Such protection sometimes required action over large parts of the country and the destruction of millions of dollars worth of goods, not to mention its effect on the reputations of the firms responsible. Although the machinery to conduct such operations was ready to function without the personal intervention of the commissioner, such a problem would invariably move to the top of his list of priorities while it lasted; it kept him busy answering questions, making decisions, and policing progress.

The APHIS administrator became involved in much the same way when outbreaks of disease in animals or plants presented threats of potentially devastating epidemics. The response included quarantines of affected areas, and often the destruction of infected herds, and the identification and elimination of the source of the outbreak. If the spread and the threat were great enough, a campaign would be directed from what amounted to the bureau's war room. In such situations, nothing else was likely to get much attention from the chief.

The chief of the Forest Service, too, occasionally had similar experiences when catastrophic fires broke out in the national forests. But a fire had to be of monumental proportions before he would move in on his fire-control organization; even very large fires were left to it, and his own involvement was minimal.

Fortunately, such critical situations did not occur every day, though lesser ones, demanding much less time, were not unusual. That is why, for these chiefs, emergencies must be added to the list of erratic events that took their agendas out of their control.

SCANDAL. From time to time chiefs were also preoccupied with behavior in their agencies that offended propriety. Such failings commanded their attention for two reasons. If the offenses were not dealt with promptly and forcefully, employees might have interpreted the inaction as indifference or even tacit approval on the part of management. Furthermore, the reputation of the agencies and their leaders might have been badly tarnished, with harmful consequences for both. Such failings therefore got high priority when they surfaced.

Fiscal errors were one of the types of shortcoming that displaced other things on chiefs' desks. For example, revelations of overpayments of supplemental security income benefits by the SSA, and of payments to ineligible or fictitious claimants, provoked such storms of criticism and complaint that this problem became the bureau's first order of business.[101] Similarly, the discovery that income tax refunds had been paid on the basis of fraudulent returns elevated the problem to a high position on the list of priorities of the IRS.[102] These matters become high-priority items whether uncovered in routine checks within the bureaus, as was usually the case, or in external investigations by a department fiscal officer, the General Accounting Office, the staff of a congressional committee, a journalist, or other outside sources. There is little doubt, however, that the urgency of the response seemed a little greater when the irregularities were known in outside circles, pushing aside some of the other matters the chiefs had been working on.

The same is true of exposures, or even mere accusations, of misconduct by bureau personnel. Allegations that an inspector or auditor accepted money in return for unduly favorable judgments, that an official taking part in the deliberations leading to a decision had a conflict of interest in the case, or that workers falsely claimed and received overtime pay, all of which had occurred in recent years in one or another of the bureaus under study,[103] came quickly to the attention of the chiefs, who promptly leapfrogged them over other agenda items to assure themselves that action was taken promptly and fairly. Such abuses took center stage for the chiefs as soon as they were discovered, and they remained there intermittently until disposed of.

Allegations of impropriety brought *by* subordinates rather than *against* them also forced items onto the chiefs' agendas. In two of the

101. *Administrative Integrity of the Social Security Program,* Hearing before the Subcommittee on Social Security of the Senate Finance Committee, 96 Cong. 1 sess. (GPO, 1979), especially pp. 3, 11–12, 19–20, 24–31.

102. Disclosures of fraudulently obtained income tax refunds always make good newspaper copy; see *Multiple False Filings of Tax Returns for Refunds,* Hearings before a subcommittee of the House Committee on Government Operations, 96 Cong. 1 sess. (GPO, 1979), pp. 92–124. A special program to deal with the problem was started by the IRS in 1976–77; ibid., pp. 3, 28. Several cases came to light in March 1979, largely as a result of this program; ibid., pp. 116, 117, 119, 120. The hearings followed on the heels of these disclosures. Thus the problem was placed high on the commissioner's agenda and kept there.

103. Instances of bribery were reported in the IRS (*New York Times,* March 2, 1976; June 1, 1978) and the Customs Service (ibid., December 20, 1978). Conflicts of interest were reported in the FDA (ibid., January 20, 1976). Fraudulent claims of overtime were exposed in the Forest Service; see p. 29, above.

six agencies, the FDA and the IRS, under chiefs preceding those studied in this project, employees or former employees declared to congressional committees that their superiors had been delinquent in various ways.[104] The chiefs were thereupon obliged to devote substantial amounts of their personal time to investigations and defenses that they would unquestionably have spent in other ways had circumstances allowed.

Erratic agenda items by no means monopolized the chiefs' calendars; the chiefs were not constantly responding to summonses, emergencies, scandals, and unsolicited changes in directives. Yet hardly a week went by without one or another such occurrence imposing itself on the chiefs' agendas, disrupting other plans and forcing them to revise their schedules. Added to the inescapable regular cycles and the programming of subordinates, these compelling demands on them intensified the sense of constraint under which the chiefs labored.

AGAINST THE TIDE

If bureau chiefs commonly advanced to higher posts in the government or if they stayed for life in their bureau posts, as J. Edgar Hoover did in the FBI, the constraints might be less intimidating; then their power to reward and punish, however limited, would not decline and over time might be able to transcend such boundaries.[105] But in the six bureaus studied here, chiefs seldom remained in office for more than half a dozen years[106]—longer, it is true, than many

104. See pp. 140, 143, below.

105. Eugene Lewis, *Public Entrepreneurship: Toward a Theory of Bureaucratic Political Power: The Organizational Lives of Hyman Rickover, J. Edgar Hoover, and Robert Moses* (Indiana University Press, 1980).

106. Robert M. Ball of the Social Security Administration was a notable exception. He spent over thirty years in the agency, including more than a decade as virtual chief and twelve years as commissioner until removed by President Nixon in 1973. He would have to be classed with the charismatic leaders identified in the preceding footnote, both for his long tenure and his influence; see Martha Derthick, *Policymaking for Social Security* (Brookings Institution, 1979). Had this study been conducted when he was still in office, the findings would doubtless have been different. In the years between his departure and the completion of this study, however, the pattern changed. His deputy, Arthur E. Hess, was acting commissioner for eight months; James B. Cardwell then served from 1973 to 1977; Acting Commissioner Don I. Wortman followed until 1978; then came Commissioner Ross until the end of 1979. William J. Driver took over at the start of 1980; John A. Svahn replaced him in early 1981.

political appointees at the departmental level, but not as long as
some members of Congress, congressional staff, professional lobbyists,
and career civil servants remained in their jobs.[107] And none of them
moved to positions in or close to the cabinet or to elective office; they
went off to commercial or industrial firms, consulting, private professional practice, lobbying, international organizations, universities, or
public interest work. In these positions, some of them participated
actively in the policy areas in which their former bureaus functioned.
While they were the heads of their bureaus, however, they did not
enjoy the advantages conferred by expectations of long tenure and
higher office. This source of power was the exception rather than the
rule.

Assuming the leadership of an established bureau was thus in
many respects like first stepping into a large, fast-flowing river. The
leader had to contend with an array of forces not of his own making
that carried him and his organization along—sometimes at an unwanted rate and in an unwanted direction. None of the chiefs in this
study, not even the administrator of APHIS, had the luxury of taking
office with few such forces in effect.

The chiefs probably could have survived by simply drifting with
the current. That is, they could have restricted themselves to purely
ceremonial roles and inescapable obligations, such as command appearances and settlement of disputes their subordinates and aides
could not resolve. For the rest, since much of what went on in their
organizations took place without any action by them and since some

107. Hugh Heclo, in *A Government of Strangers: Executive Politics in Washington* (Brookings Institution, 1977), estimated the average term of office of an
assistant secretary at about two years, higher civil servants at seventeen to twenty-
five years, House committee chairmen at twenty-three years, and Senate chairmen
at twenty-one years (p. 118). Harrison W. Fox, Jr., and Susan Webb Hammond,
in *Congressional Staffs: The Invisible Force in American Lawmaking* (Free
Press, 1977), estimated the average period of employment of representatives'
administrative assistants at nine years, with ten to fourteen not unusual and
twenty years not unknown (p. 56); figures for the Senate were similar (p. 57);
and senior staff of committees rolled up long years of experience, though turnover in junior ranks was high (pp. 60–66). See also David T. Stanley, Dean E.
Mann, and Jameson W. Doig, *Men Who Govern: A Biographical Profile of Federal
Political Executives* (Brookings Institution, 1967), chap. 4; Dean E. Mann and
Jameson W. Doig, *The Assistant Secretaries: Problems and Processes of Appoint-
ment* (Brookings Institution, 1965), pp. 6–7, 277–31; and David T. Stanley, *The
Higher Civil Service: An Evaluation of Federal Personnel Practices* (Brookings
Institution, 1964), p. 27. Compare these figures with those on pp. 122–23, above.

of it was actually beyond their control, they could have watched without intervening. The organizations doubtless would have ground on in their accustomed ways, and the chiefs' lives would have been less trying.

But they did not elect to behave in this fashion. Instead, they hurled themselves into the fray they could have avoided, striving to influence the course of events despite the limitations under which they had to labor. Since the constraints were similar in outline despite their variations in detail, the chiefs' tactics and strategies were more or less forced into similar patterns as well. As they searched the boundaries for opportunities to impress themselves on their agencies and on the program in their charge, they found similar openings and chances for maneuver. Hence the similarities in their patterns of behavior.

Still, if the path of least resistance was to let their highly programmed and constrained organizations run themselves, why did none of the chiefs choose this path? Why did they all opt for the hard path instead of the easy one?

I cannot pretend to have any special insight into their reasoning or their feelings. But I did notice four properties of their environment that could account for much of this willingness to buck the odds and try to seize the initiative.

First, passive personalities do not readily make it to the top of federal bureaus. That is because they seldom come to the attention of appointing officers. By definition, wallflowers are not highly visible, and they are especially inconspicuous among the strong egos, unending turmoil, and interest in publicity characteristic of the Washington political stratum. Moreover, even if someone did call a high appointing officer's attention to a reserved, obscure individual, it is unlikely that such an appointment would commend itself to the political official. The reputations of the appointers as well as the appointees depend on the performance of the latter. Activists can be disasters if they seize on the wrong issues, but with any luck at all they can bring credit and favorable publicity to their superiors. Passive bureau chiefs, on the other hand, may also embarrass their superiors, but they are unlikely ever to add luster to the superiors' reputations. So even when new administrations in Washington embark on strenuous searches for fresh talent and competence, they usually end up picking men and women of force and vigor to head bureaus. Thus neither the career appointees in my sample (in the two Department of Agriculture bureaus) nor those who came from private life—two prominent and successful lawyers and a successful businessman so intrigued by the opportunities for public service that they accepted sharp income reductions when they entered the government, and an academic who had previously established an outstanding reputation in his scientific field and in the formation of governmental science policy—were disposed to let things happen; they were the kind who plunge eagerly into the struggle to take charge, no matter how high the obstacles to their leadership. Other types were not likely to survive the screening process.

Second, although the confines of leadership are indeed binding, they are not necessarily paralyzing. I shall have more to say on this point later. What is relevant here is that even leaders who recognize the limits on what they can accomplish during their terms of office are inclined, especially if they are the spirited, driving persons the system tends to select, to use all their powers for whatever effect they can have. After all, according to Darwinian theory, it is by increments so small as to be virtually imperceptible in any short period of time that evolution has produced the astonishingly diverse and beautiful edifice of life on this planet. To toil at making a small difference, then, is not inevitably an exercise in futility. Only irredeemable visionaries insist that the only worthwhile labors in the field of public policy are those with promise of quick, dramatic transformations. Pragmatists confronted by constraints do what they can within the constraints. And the bureau chiefs in this study were clearly pragmatic in this regard.

Third, bureau leaders quickly learn on the job, if they were not aware before taking over, that doing nothing does not mean that things will continue as they are. The formal constraints described in this chapter did not arise spontaneously; they were contrived by individuals and groups who wanted them for reasons of their own and had the political skill to get them adopted. Individuals and groups, pursuing their own interests, still do strive to impose their will on government agencies and their administrators. If administrative leaders are inactive, the opportunities to influence the course of events, circumscribed as these are, will fall to others. To be passive, then, is merely to make it easier for other people to have their way, to the extent that anyone can have his way. Thus even to preserve things as they are compels a chief to get aggressively involved. Withdrawal is not freer of consequences than engagement—and the consequences of disengagement are likely to be less to one's taste than those of engagement. So chiefs tend not to be passive.

Fourth, people constantly press them for decisions and actions. Two sets of factors turn the chiefs into lightning rods for the attentions of their subordinates, their superiors, other bureau chiefs, Congress, nongovernmental groups, and the media. One is their formal powers. The other is their symbolic position as the personification of their bureaus.

Their formal powers are rooted in the requirements that they sign all sorts of bureau documents to make the papers legally binding. If the chiefs do not sign them, many bureau actions will not stand up when challenged in the executive branch or in the courts. If the chiefs do sign, violators are subject to sanctions. Interests inside and outside the bureaus therefore converge on the chiefs, each maneuvering to influence the contents of the papers needing signature and to induce a chief to sign when a petitioner is satisfied with the contents or to dissuade him from signing if the contents are not to the petitioner's liking. From all directions, bureau chiefs are deluged with visits, telephone calls, and written communications from people seeking to influence their exercise of their formal powers. As the legal embodiment of their bureaus, they are sucked into the stream of activities whatever their personal predispositions might be.

Their symbolic personification of their bureaus also makes the chiefs targets for demands and pressures. People in government and out want to influence them not only because of what they are legally empowered to do but also because their positions lend them stature and legitimacy and visibility that magnify their authority and their publicity value. Their high offices make them a little larger than life, at least in certain circles. The result is constant effort from many quarters to get them to make personal appearances, public announcements, or official statements, to bless or to condemn or simply to inform. Though many of these duties could be handled as well or better by expert subordinates, the subordinates presumably would not carry the same weight with the intended audience. Furthermore, many legislators, department heads, and bureau chiefs try to avoid placing lower-ranking civil servants in the position of defending the policies of a particular administration. Chiefs are therefore obliged to testify personally before committees and subcommittees of Congress; to represent their bureaus in meetings in their departments and elsewhere in the executive branch assembled to inform superiors and colleagues, to plan strategies, or to arrive at policy decisions; to appear at press conferences for the announcement of important developments; to meet with the leaders of interest groups; to present awards for long service and notable accomplishments to bureau personnel; and in myriad other ways to incarnate the organizations for which they stand. They could not fade into the background even if they wanted the tranquillity of obscurity.

For all these reasons, the six chiefs became active participants in the lives of their bureaus. Only in theory could they have disengaged themselves and become detached and inert observers, even if they were so minded. But they were not so minded. The confines of their jobs notwithstanding, they threw themselves, and were drawn, into active, vigorous roles.

To what effect? Did they succeed in influencing the course of events? Did they make their weight felt? Or were their efforts scarcely more fruitful than passivity would have been?

CHAPTER FOUR

A Matter of Scale

IT SEEMS clear to me that the bureau chiefs in this study, for all the power and independence attributed to their office and for all their striving, could not make a big difference in what their organizations did during the period in which they served.

Admittedly, this statement is ambiguous. The chiefs do, of course, make some difference in the lives of their bureaus. In the absence of any commonly accepted measuring stick, how much difference would they have to make, and how quickly, before most observers would agree that the differences were substantial and important? An achievement that looks gigantic by one scale may look negligible by another. The concept is so elusive that talking sensibly about it is difficult.

Nevertheless, if you think of the chiefs' impact as a relationship between the continuities in the lives and situations of their organizations and the discontinuities that can be ascribed largely to their own efforts, the statement does begin to take on meaning. The continuities were far greater than the effects that could be convincingly linked to the chiefs, and factors beyond the chiefs' control evidently could or did produce results of larger magnitude. I contend that in this sense the chiefs were not as powerful or autonomous as they are sometimes alleged or inferred to be.

THE DIFFERENCES THEY MADE

The role of the chiefs was especially prominent in setting the tone and contributing to the image and prestige of their organizations and in the timing and sequence of certain organizational actions. The chiefs certainly do not single-handedly determine any of these attributes of their agencies; the characteristics are the results of many factors. But it is in these respects that the chiefs' activities seemed to produce their maximum effects.

Setting Organizational Tone

By organizational tone, I mean a combination of morale, crispness of task performance, and policy consensus. Morale is the level of unity, pride, confidence, dedication, enthusiasm, conscientiousness, and industry displayed by an organization's members. Crispness is a comprehensive term for the speed, accuracy, efficiency, and competence with which the members do their jobs. Policy consensus means the absence of sharp divisions among the members about the values emphasized in the organization's operations. For this study, I was in no position to develop or employ measurements of these attributes of the bureaus, so the evidence that a chief can influence them is circumstantial and fragmentary. But it points rather convincingly toward the conclusion that bureau chiefs do affect bureau tone.

As indicators, I sought clear changes in organizational tone, manifested unequivocally in the overt behavior and statements of bureau officers, employees, and other informed commentators. If conditions under a chief were far different from those under his predecessor or successor, the timing of such changes would be construed to mean that the leadership succession had something to do with them. If the changes took place when no change in leadership occurred, that would be interpreted as indicating that they were independent of the chiefs. If no oscillations of organizational tone occurred, no inferences could be drawn.

Pronounced changes in recent years had taken place in two of the bureaus in the sample. One was the Food and Drug Administration. Several years before the accession of Donald Kennedy, the commissioner at the time of this research, the agency's drug unit had been rent by internal conflict and division, assailed by both the industrial and the consumer wings of its clientele, afflicted with demoralization, and at war with the commissioner at the time. Some employees denounced it in congressional testimony, and the previous commissioner's own investigation of the charges only fueled the controversy instead of dampening it. An investigating panel appointed by the secretary of health, education, and welfare was at first divided on the merits of some of the allegations but, under a new chairman, eventually reached agreement and rendered its report in the same month that Commissioner Kennedy took office. The panel's final report was intended "to resolve long smoldering controversies, which have resulted in highly charged emotions on all sides."[1]

The depth of the rifts is suggested by the testimony of one of the major participants in these struggles some years earlier:

People—and I'm talking about division directors and their staffs, engaged in a kind of behavior that invited insubordination. There were people tittering in corners, throwing spitballs. I'm describing physicians. There were people who slouched down in a chair and did not respond to questions, moaned and groaned with sweeping gestures. A kind of behavior I have not seen in any other institution as a grown man.[2]

The discord is also indicated in the comment of one official to an investigative reporter from the *New York Times:* "The staff has been torn by dissension and strife, morale is bad, there's no direction, and stagnation has set in."[3] This view was corroborated by the official investigating panel's finding that "irregular procedures . . . kept FDA embroiled in a continuing controversy,"[4] and that

serious problems of managerial inefficiency exist at FDA, as reflected in the personnel actions described, in the frequent protracted delays in drug review, and in the agency's remarkable inability for six years to implement its decisions with respect to restrictive labelling for thyroid and digitalis.[5]

Small wonder that friends of Donald Kennedy, when informed that he had agreed to serve as commissioner of food and drugs, warned him that he had accepted "the captaincy of the Titanic."[6]

When he left office a little over two years later, things were entirely different. The evidences of internal warfare had evaporated; there were no signs of them in the attentive press or in congressional hearings, where they had originally surfaced, nor did I detect any in my

1. Review Panel on New Drug Regulation, *Investigation of Allegations Relating to the Bureau of Drugs, Food and Drug Administration* (Department of Health, Education, and Welfare, 1977), p. 10.

2. Rita Ricardo Campbell, *Drug Lag: Federal Government Decision Making* (Hoover Institution Press, 1976), p. 30.

3. Richard D. Lyons, "Demoralized F.D.A. Struggles to Cope," *New York Times,* March 14, 1977.

4. April 20, 1977, introductory letter to Joseph A. Califano from Norman Dorsen, chairman of the Review Panel on New Drug Regulation (reproduced in *Investigation of Allegations*), p. 4.

5. Review Panel on New Drug Regulation, *Investigation of Allegations,* p. 722.

6. *New York Times,* April 8, 1977.

narrow, but still revealing, observations and interviews. At meetings the atmosphere was businesslike, cordial, open, and relaxed, and at informal gatherings there was obvious cameraderie. For a time, at least, the ailing organization had been made whole again.[7]

Not all the credit can be given to Commissioner Kennedy. Some of his predecessors in the Nixon administration, according to the investigating panel, were philosophically at odds with certain of the drug regulatory policies of the FDA and transferred employees against their will and even punitively, in violation of civil service rules, to impose new policies on the organization. They then reportedly added insult to injury by lying about the reasons for the transfers.[8] Kennedy, however, was not separated by such a wide philosophical gulf from the agency work force, and he therefore had no incentive to employ such drastic and questionable methods. In any case, after the Watergate-connected exposés, administrators were inclined to avoid extreme personnel actions. One major source of unrest in his agency was thus excluded from the start.

Furthermore, the investigating panel laid out a course of action calculated to end the turmoil in the FDA, and its report was delivered two weeks after the new commissioner was installed. He did what anyone in his position might have done: he followed its recommendations, sending formal apologies to a dozen employees and consultants for what they had suffered earlier, issuing admonitions to several officers of the FDA for their parts in the affair, and putting the unhappy matter behind him.[9] This action must be regarded as institutional, not personal. Resisting the institutional thrust would have been a personal strategy; going along with a formula for relief devised by a prestigious body after two years of investigation was not.

According to an editorial in the *New York Times*, Kennedy car-

7. Within a year after Kennedy's departure, a new controversy erupted. An officer in the Bureau of Drugs was one of five employees temporarily detailed to other positions for possible violations of ethical conduct standards in the FDA. Two of his defenders (one a congressman) charged that he was being punished for his advocacy of generic drugs over brand-name products and not for any real offenses; Victor Cohn, *Washington Post*, March 29, 1980. After investigation, the five were admonished and restored to their original positions; FDA, "Talk Paper," T80-33 (June 13, 1980). But some of the old tension apparently had not been fully eased.

8. Review Panel on New Drug Regulation, *Investigation of Allegations*, pp. 569 ff.

9. Ibid., chap. 15; *New York Times*, October 27, 1977.

ried weight because he was a scientist rather than a physician. "His predecessors at the F.D.A., all physicians," wrote the editor, "were less comfortable with the controversies of scientific testing. When Mr. Kennedy said some animal study was solid, or shaky, his judgment carried authority."[10] It seems to me that not being a physician could just as well have been a liability as an asset, but if the editor's judgment is justified, then the advantage was a fortuitous result of status rather than a product of administrative skill and strategy.

So a good deal of the improvement in the FDA in 1977 and 1978 might have come about under a commissioner other than Kennedy. Still, he unquestionably exhibited great personal gifts that contributed to the improvement. He treated his colleagues with respect, was receptive to their ideas, encouraged inventiveness, and did his homework assiduously when they put proposals before him. He helped create a collegial environment, at least in headquarters. The rejuvenation of the agency might have happened without him, but it probably was speeded and intensified because of the way he conducted himself as commissioner. "He believed in himself and his agency," wrote one commentator, "and it caught on."[11]

In the Internal Revenue Service too, under a predecessor of Jerome Kurtz, the commissioner I observed, tension flared. In 1975 and 1976 relations between the commissioner at the time and some members of his senior staff became so hostile that a few of them resigned and, along with some of their former colleagues still in the agency, leveled serious accusations against him before a congressional committee. The allegations engendered investigations by the committee, the general counsel of the Treasury Department, and the Department of Justice, which impaneled grand juries to inquire into the possibility that criminal offenses had been committed. The commissioner contended that he was the victim of efforts to discredit him, and he was supported by the secretary of the treasury, who denounced vilification of the commissioner by a "mindless, invisible bureaucracy." Other officials of the Ford administration grew concerned about the diversion of IRS leadership energies from improving and simplifying the tax collection system. The conflict was front-page news.

10. *New York Times,* July 2, 1979.
11. Linda E. Demkovich, "A Tough Act to Follow," *National Journal,* May 5, 1979, p. 745.

Eventually every investigation cleared the commissioner of the charges against him and the battle subsided.[12] Under Commissioner Kurtz no signs of antagonism appeared; there were no media reports or rumors of strife or discontent in the agency, no disclosures or complaints at congressional hearings, no signs or intimations of clashes or dissatisfaction that I could detect in the course of my observations. I am not in a position to say more than that Kurtz administered the bureau in a way that did not stir up antagonism; it might well have died down under any new chief. But there can be no question that the prior history of the IRS, like that of the FDA, indicates that the tone of a bureau can be negatively affected by a chief's actions. And the two records at least suggest that a chief's actions can play a large part in making things better.

No comparable changes of tone in the other four bureaus in the sample turned up in congressional hearings, the press, studies, direct observation, or any other source I used. Maybe such changes did occur and escaped notice for some reason. But changes of the magnitude described above virtually force themselves on the attention of a researcher in a study of this kind. I am therefore disposed to assume that, while there may have been some variations in tone in the other four agencies, they were much less pronounced. Things seem to have remained on an even keel through changes of leadership.

What these facts seem to imply is that organizational tone in the majority of bureaus is comparatively steady most of the time but that occasionally it may vary greatly, and when it does, whether upward or downward, the way a chief conducts his office is likely to be a major factor in the variation. This is one of the areas in which chiefs, despite the constraints on their influence, can apparently make a difference in their agencies.

Contributions to Agency Prestige

There are also grounds for believing that the chiefs' behavior makes a difference in the reputations of their agencies, at least in the Washington community, and maybe more broadly if their standing in Washington is reported throughout the country. The apparent linkage between the image of a bureau and the performance of its

12. Jim Drinkhall, "CIA Helped Quash Major, Star-Studded Tax Evasion Case," *Washington Post*, April 24, 1980.

chief in public was mentioned earlier, in the discussion of external relations. Firmer evidence comes from the recent history of one of the six agencies in this sample—the FDA once again. As with organizational tone, the evidence consists of a sharp change in reputation associated in time with a change of chiefs. Such a swing of prestige following the installation of Commissioner Kennedy was dramatic in its swiftness and extent.

When he took over, the FDA's standing with Congress, the press, and its clientele was dismal. According to one reporter:

In 1976, in the waning days of the Ford Administration, the FDA was under heavy attack by congressional and consumer critics. . . . Talk of reorganization—transferring its functions to other departments—was in the wind.[13]

In 1977, just before Kennedy assumed office, another reporter observed:

Its bureaucratic problems have been so vexing that in just the last three years the agency has been the target of more than 100 Congressional investigations, 50 highly critical reports by the General Accounting Office and a series of internal inquiries despairing of ever setting the place right.[14]

A third commentator summed up its standing by describing the FDA as "a long despised bureaucracy in good odor with almost no one."[15]

Yet in just a little over two years, the new commissioner turned things around. Senator Gaylord Nelson credited him with raising "both the status of and morale within the beleaguered FDA."[16] One reporter declared that he "is getting the credit for silencing the critics and giving the FDA a fresh start."[17] And a writer for *Science*, the magazine of the American Association for the Advancement of Science, remarked:

The Food and Drug Administration . . . has recently undergone a most surprising transformation, and the reason seems to lie in the brief but enlivening reign of its now departing commissioner, Donald Kennedy. . . . Somehow or other, Kennedy managed to gain the respect of all the FDA's constituencies, a group whose members do not invariably see eye to eye with each other. . . . Kennedy also enjoyed an unusually cordial relationship with Congress, a body accustomed to batting the FDA commissioner about like a

13. Demkovich, "A Tough Act to Follow," p. 745.

14. *New York Times,* March 14, 1977.

15. Nicholas Wade, "Kennedy Leaves as FDA Commissioner: Stanford Biologist Brought New Approach to Agency," *Science,* July 13, 1979, p. 173.

16. *Congressional Record,* daily edition (July 12, 1979), p. S9246.

17. Demkovich, "A Tough Act to Follow," p. 745.

shuttlecock. . . . He managed to make allies, even friends, out of natural critics of the FDA's regulatory politics, such as the congressmen who represent agricultural interests.[18]

The consensus among informed commentators on the FDA seems to be that he accomplished this remarkable feat by the sheer force of his intellect, personality, and style. Even his adversaries came to admire him. He "turned a phrase as well as anyone I ever heard in my life," said an official of one interest group, and he displayed "fantastic ease at communicating with quite different audiences," one of his colleagues told a journalist.[19] Moreover,

the fact that Kennedy was not intimidated by the committee process, that he would answer his most vocal and hostile critics with an easy charm and tact, won the agency a renewed measure of respect on Capitol Hill, congressional aides say.[20]

Having seen him at congressional committee hearings, press conferences, personal interviews, appearances before interest groups, and a variety of meetings, I fully concur in these judgments. His performance glittered.

He also brought pending matters to a head and stood behind his decisions on them. As a representative of the drug industry put it:

He eliminated the fog and equivocation that existed at the top, and although many of his decisions were unfavorable from the industry's standpoint, it's a lot easier to deal with an SOB who's consistent than with one who's not.[21]

In this way, he "changed the FDA's image . . . to an agency that acted, and then stood behind its action."[22]

That the personal ability and demeanor of a chief could have achieved so much in just the twenty-six months or so that Kennedy was in office is astonishing, and perhaps students in the future will identify other factors as important as his own dynamism and talents. At this time, however, with the evidence at hand and in view of the conclusions of other observers, one would be hard put to deny his extraordinary role. A chief apparently can almost single-handedly shape the image of the bureau he heads.

He could not make his bureau seem like a model of efficiency and effectiveness if it were obviously failing; chiefs cannot work miracles.

18. Wade, "Kennedy Leaves as FDA Commissioner," p. 173.
19. Ibid.
20. Demkovich, "A Tough Act to Follow," p. 745.
21. Ibid.
22. Ibid.

But it certainly seems that he can restore the damaged name of a competent organization by ending the conditions that brought opprobrium on it and demonstrating through his own conduct that high standards prevail. By raising the tone of the FDA, Kennedy improved its public image. By reestablishing its good name, he helped raise its tone. Indeed, the two elements are so closely related that they may be two sides of the same coin. Presumably, they can spiral downward as well as upward. In the FDA they rose, thanks in large measure to the administrative behavior of the chief.

The other cases in the sample are not as graphic; the reputation and tone of the other agencies did not fluctuate so markedly. The Forest Service, for example, had enjoyed long-standing acclaim as a "center of excellence" before John R. McGuire, the chief during most of this study, took the helm. Doubtless he added to its luster by his personal performance, for he won the President's Award for Distinguished Public Service shortly before he retired. And he certainly handled deftly a flurry of attacks on the service by interest groups concerned with only one or two of the multiple uses that it tried to keep in balance; the early and mid-seventies were a period of controversy, change, and unrest, and he served under three presidents and three secretaries of agriculture. Some of the critics were factions of a conservation movement that previously had often supported the Forest Service with near unanimity. Despite these travails, the treatment of the agency in the general press and in the government remained largely favorable. Perhaps McGuire's adroit leadership fended off what could have been a decline of confidence in it of the same proportions as that suffered by the FDA. Given the long record of public and media approbation of the Forest Service, however, its continued high repute at the end of his term of office can hardly be credited mostly to his personal efforts.

Similarly, the reputation of the Animal and Plant Health Inspection Service seemed to be very high, and the conduct and ability of the only administrator it had had since it was established, Francis J. Mulhern, must surely have counted heavily in establishing this standing. But the consistency of its good reputation, the short history of the agency, and the absence of prior administrators to compare with Dr. Mulhern make it hard to demonstrate what seems so obvious intuitively.

The IRS and the Customs Service likewise experienced no wild swings of reputation, so the special contributions of their respective commissioners to the standing of their agencies cannot be isolated. Commissioners Jerome Kurtz and Robert E. Chasen, respectively, managed to avoid difficulties and to preserve confidence in their agencies despite budgetary strictures that cramped them, which required no small skill in agencies with such sensitive and politically delicate responsibilities. Critics might complain about particular decisions, but they did not question the integrity or administrative competence of the two organizations.

Only in the recent history of the Social Security Administration has there been a period that might be construed as confirming the FDA experience. In 1974 the supplemental security income program, a form of welfare assistance for people with low incomes, was set up and assigned to the SSA. It soon ran into trouble:

Errors in determination of eligibility or in payments occurred in about a fourth of the cases; overpayments approached a billion dollars a year; applicants waited hours for service at area offices and then were served by employees who were poorly informed of the rules and hampered by computer breakdowns. Newspapers carried exposés and congressional committees rushed to investigate.[23]

Yet even the agency's critics did not assail the agency for administrative incompetence. Instead, they ascribed its difficulties to the complexities of the new program. One could interpret this gentle response as indicating that the reputation of the chief and his colleagues was good enough to buffer the SSA against even so strong a shock. But other interpretations are also possible, especially since the agency survived for a year and a half with an acting commissioner before Stanford G. Ross, the commissioner during this study, took over; something besides the chief's personal standing, some institutional factor, was probably at work. So my evidence that chiefs can contribute significantly to the reputations of their agencies still comes mainly from the FDA experience. But that case is certainly striking.

Not even the FDA experience suggests that an agency's image is completely in the hands of its chief, however; a chief surely cannot make or break an agency all by himself. Yet after all the reservations are taken into account, the record of Commissioner Kennedy cannot

23. Martha Derthick, *Policymaking for Social Security* (Brookings Institution, 1979), p. 32.

be dismissed. Though far from conclusive, it indicates that a boss can affect the esteem in which his bureau is held in the capital.

Nudging Agendas, Priorities, and Decisions

Chiefs may also be able to affect the order, timing, and substance of work in their bureaus despite the constraints to which the organizations are subject. They do not—they cannot—control everything that goes on in the bureaus, of course. But their wishes result in emphases and sequences and decisions that would probably not be the same under someone else's leadership. This may be what they and other commentators refer to when they speak of the power of bureau chiefs. It is also, I suspect, the area of influence generally considered most important.

For example, under the administrators of the social security system from its inception until 1973, the emphasis was on increasing the number of people covered by social security, expanding the scope of protection (for instance, disability insurance and medicare), raising benefits, and taking pains to see that everyone eligible exercised his or her right to benefits. The focus of administrators after that shifted from growth to sustaining the system.

There are doubtless many reasons for this shift, but two factors clearly played a major part. Falling birth rates resulted in revised forecasts of the future age composition of the population and of trends in the ratios of workers to beneficiaries, which affected the assessment of the long-run financial future of social security. At the same time, short-run problems were created by rises in the price level greater than rises in the wage level, which meant that indexed benefits went up faster than the returns from social security taxes. These developments indicated outflows so much greater than income that social security tax increases planned for both the near and distant future would not have been enough to meet the demands on the system. Raising payroll taxes sufficiently to restore balance would have required increases so large as to rouse unprecedented opposition. In addition, in inflationary times, the new taxes would have led to higher prices, automatically generating higher benefits because of indexing and thus intensifying the drain on the system. The old strategies would no longer do, and anyone who became commissioner would have been compelled to adopt a new approach.[24] The system was in jeopardy.

Early warnings came from James B. Cardwell, President Nixon's social security commissioner, who took office in 1973. But it was Commissioner Ross who made limits on benefits the dominant theme of his term of office, contending that the solvency of the system depended on such restraint. Convinced that a new era for social security had arrived and that a new philosophy and a new set of policies had to be adopted, he set himself the task of selling them to political leaders, the staff of the SSA, and the general public. His aggressive campaign did not ignore revenues, which were recognized as inadequate despite a 1977 law pushing up payroll taxes. Moreover, like many of his predecessors, he called upon Congress to provide more funds to improve the quality and appearance of local social security offices, many of which were in such a sorry state that he considered them a disgrace and depressing for clients and employees alike. But his campaign was aimed in particular at what he publicly called inequities and irrationalities in the whole income security system, and it was designed to hold down the rate of growth of outlays. In this respect he departed sharply from the attitudes and practices of previous commissioners.

He relied heavily on public statements. Almost immediately after assuming office, he made a number of speeches stressing the need to head in new directions, and he wrote or stimulated reports pointing out the urgent necessity for reforms. He did not pretend he had any blueprint for such reforms; rather, his purpose was to "encourage public debate of the critical issues involved."[25] His encouragement was persistent and vigorous.

But making public statements was not all he did. He supported legislation imposing a lower ceiling on disability benefits than was

24. Ibid., pp. 381–84.

25. Stanford G. Ross, *New Directions in Social Security: Considerations for the 1980's*, U.S. Department of Health, Education, and Welfare, Social Security Administration, Office of Policy, SSA Publication 13-11950 (December 1979); the quotation is from p. 62. See also the same author's "Social Security: A Worldwide Issue," in Social Security Administration, *Social Security in a Changing World*, HEW Publication (SSA)79-11948 (September 1979), pp. 1–20; "Income Security: A Framework for Reform," paper prepared for the National Journal Conference on Retirement Income, November 17, 1980; and "Income Security Programs: Past, Present and Future," working paper for the President's Commission on Pension Policy, October 1980.

then in effect.[26] He reinstituted and reinvigorated checks on claims by students and disabled people and widows to ensure that their eligibility for benefits had not lapsed. He launched yet another study of means to curb fake social security cards and set in motion a new plan for collecting overpayments to beneficiaries in any category.[27] He embarked on a reorganization of the SSA's top echelons and brought in a number of new people to help him implement his philosophy in the agency. He lashed out at what he called the "superselling of Social Security" over the years by the "Wilbur Cohens and Bob Balls,"[28] arguing that the public would have had a better understanding of the "limitations of Social Security" had the people been given "a more balanced picture" of the system.[29]

Cohen and Ball vigorously denied the implication that they had ever misrepresented the costs or the fiscal state of the system, claiming that they had been accurate and truthful under the conditions and estimates within which they worked. But there is no doubt that they subscribed to a different set of priorities than Ross did,[30] and they fought tooth and nail against the benefit reductions he championed when these were under consideration in Congress.[31] Not that they denied the existence of a problem; instead, Ball wrote, "There were completely different ways of handling this situation that I believe would have been successful."[32] Unquestionably the public posture of the commissioner had changed dramatically.

It would be rash, however, to assume that the course of events changed equally extensively as a result. Ball and Cohen out of office still commanded attention and respect in the relevant committees of Congress, and Ross's policy recommendations were not promptly translated into a host of new legislative enactments. Moreover, economic, demographic, and political developments undoubtedly would

26. Signed into law on June 9, 1980 (P.L. 96-265).

27. Jane Bryant Quinn, *Washington Post*, May 28, 1979.

28. Wilbur J. Cohen is a former secretary of HEW and was one of the early program executives of the social security program. Ball was a long-time leader of the agency; see chapter 3, note 106. Both were prime movers in the development of social security.

29. Edward Cowan, *New York Times*, July 17, 1979.

30. Robert M. Ball, "Managing the Social Security Program" (prepared for internal SSA distribution), January 29, 1973.

31. Spencer Rich, *Washington Post*, June 6, 1979; Edward Cowan, *New York Times*, July 17, 1979.

32. Letter to Bruce K. MacLaury, December 15, 1980.

have forced any chief, whatever his or her philosophy, to seek adjustments in the system; Ball maintains that he did not hold that benefit rights could never be changed, but only that the changes should not be made if they were likely to undermine confidence in the system.[33] So factors other than the philosophy of the incumbent chief probably had a more important effect on the agenda and priorities of the agency than the chief's personal views did.[34]

Still, I cannot resist the conclusion that things would have been different in some respects in and for the SSA had Ball been commissioner instead of Ross at the time of this study. Possibly not as different as the philosophies of the two men would lead one to anticipate, but different nonetheless.

The SSA was the only one of the six agencies in which such a pronounced change in basic philosophy occurred. In the others, the indicators of the chiefs' influence were not as sharply etched. But they did appear. In the IRS, for example, the commissioner's interpretations of tax law shaped the tax rulings issued by the agency. They were judgments on whether particular transactions, operations, or institutions were taxable, and thus gave specific meaning to the general language and ambiguous provisions of the statutes. For thousands of taxpayers, they were important decisions—not only because they determined the tax liability of the taxpayers, but also because they affected business and personal decisions about investment and expenditure. About ten or so were published each week, and all of them came across the commissioner's desk. When he announced a decision, his judgment became the official position of the agency. Since most of his decisions either were not challenged or were not overturned upon challenge, they put his distinctive mark on the course of the IRS.

This is not to say that he could rewrite the tax code if he chose to. The framework of written law did not allow him that much discretion, nor would the courts or Congress. Moreover, he tended to accept the opinions of his staff in 85 to 90 percent of the cases. But when he differed with them, he did not hesitate to return their recommenda-

33. Ibid. Ross, of course, contended that his proposals would increase confidence in the system, not reduce it. The two men differed more on means than ends.

34. As though to illustrate the point, Commissioner William J. Driver and his three immediate predecessors—James B. Cardwell, Ross, and Ball—appeared together before a congressional committee to support a measure to finance medicare out of income taxes and thus free more payroll tax revenues for the endangered retirement fund. *New York Times*, February 19, 1981.

tions for redrafting or further research. Occasionally the staff would insist that law and precedent allowed no choice, but they had to convince him, and sometimes the arguments were strenuous—and unavailing. Often, however, they would agree that an issue could be settled either way, in which case his preference prevailed. Through the hundreds of decisions on which he signed off, he could thus edge tax administration toward what he regarded as the intended, fair, and technically proper practice. Rule-making and adjudication were areas in which different commissioners might produce different results.[35]

But they were not the only such areas. For example, under Commissioner Kurtz, the office of ombudsman was created at a senior executive level in the Washington headquarters and filled by a veteran official in January 1980:

By establishing the ombudsman position, the I.R.S. has placed high priority on resolving taxpayer problems and has decided to put someone with clout in charge of the task. For the first time, there will be someone in the I.R.S.'s national office who has sole responsibility for serving as a taxpayer advocate.[36]

The idea did not spring full-blown from the mind of the commissioner. The ombudsman as an institution, after all, is an adaptation of a Swedish office and has been much discussed in public administration for many years.[37] Furthermore, even within the IRS, experiments with complaint-handling offices had been going on since 1976, and units were set up in all the district offices around the country during 1978 and 1979. So the establishment of the Washington position and the appointment of an incumbent were the culmination of a process and might have transpired regardless of who was chief in this period. But from the very start of his term of office, Kurtz had demonstrated a special interest in improving service to taxpayers and devoted much of his time to exploring avenues to that end. His concern, his receptivity to fresh approaches, and his attention to this

35. The influence of a given commissioner, however, may be attenuated by inconsistencies in the application of rulings to specific cases by field officers. Kenneth Culp Davis, *Administrative Law of the Seventies* (Lawyers Cooperative Publishing Co., 1976), sec. 17.07-1.

36. Deborah Rankin, "Taxes: An Ombudsman for the I.R.S.," *New York Times*, January 15, 1980.

37. Herbert Kaufman, *Red Tape: Its Origins, Uses, and Abuses* (Brookings Institution, 1977), p. 95.

aspect of the IRS program, it seems to me, nourished the ombudsman innovation, among other ideas, and helped bring it to full flower earlier than might have been the case had he not been there to push and assist and encourage it.

In both Customs and APHIS, Commissioner Chasen and Administrator Mulhern, respectively, injected into the leadership levels of their agencies a heavy emphasis on management consciousness and techniques. Both were of the opinion that technical expertise in the specialized tasks of the bureaus did not equip people for the kinds of difficulties that would confront them, and the decisions they would have to make, as executives. At the same time, both chiefs valued the knowledge that the experts brought with them to leadership posts. And they liked the incentives to the work force provided by promotion of experienced personnel to managerial positions. So they decided to instill in their current and future executives, most of whom were specialists, a sensitivity to management and an ability to deal with managerial problems for which their specialized experience had not readied them. They allocated big blocks of their own time to this undertaking.

Commissioner Chasen introduced management by objectives as he had practiced it in business before coming to the government. This consisted of negotiating written contracts between the commissioner and his immediate aides and subordinates defining the main objectives of each individual for the coming year, the "milestones" to be reached on the way to each objective, and the dates for each step and for attainment of each goal. These were discussed in open sessions so that all top officers could learn what their colleagues were up to, objectives could be adjusted to one another, the chief could influence the activities of his work force, and all the objectives and milestones could be collectively evaluated. The top officers, in turn, were to employ the same techniques with their lieutenants, and the method was in this fashion to spread all through middle management. Executive development was one of its goals. But it was more than that: it was a means of trying to direct the activities of the organization. Chasen's approach to management by objectives certainly permeated top management in Customs, and there is no reason to think things would have been done this way had someone else become commissioner.

Administrator Mulhern personally organized and took part in

seminars with his top staff at which managerial problems and materials were analyzed. He also delivered formal lectures (which were taped and made available to other parts of the organization) on his vision of making APHIS a "model agency" in federal administration. And he exhorted ranking officers to be more aware of the managerial dimensions of their jobs and to treat them as no less urgent than the technical tasks under their jurisdiction. As in Customs, this approach was uniquely his, and while any other person serving as administrator might have found it necessary to do something of a comparable sort, the special emphasis on management and the personal energy he poured into it put his distinctive stamp on headquarters.

During Commissioner Kennedy's administration, the FDA took new steps to promote the use of generic prescription drugs in place of more expensive brand-name products.[38] He certainly did not invent the idea; it had been urged by consumer groups and by some members of the agency for a long time, and some action had been taken in years past. But movement had been limited, in part because of strong opposition from the manufacturers of brand-name drugs. Kennedy pushed generic identification ahead.

One could argue that pressure for such a move had been building up for years and would have come to a head anyway. But it is hard to believe that the pressure would have been fruitful after so many years of hesitation had not a skillful, informed, dedicated, energetic individual applied himself to the task without stint.

By the same token, his participation doubtless sped completion of a proposal for the reform of the laws on the regulation of medicinal drugs. He shepherded it along, winning agreement to the proposal at higher levels in the executive branch and persuading the White House to have it introduced in Congress. Maybe this, too, would have happened in any event. Without the personal qualities that he brought to bear on behalf of this policy, however, the forces that had blocked it before would probably have done so again.[39]

In the Forest Service under Chief McGuire, plans for the future of roadless areas in the national forests—determining which should be included in the wilderness system and closed to all development and

38. Department of Health, Education, and Welfare, "Statement by Joseph A. Califano, Jr., Secretary of Health, Education, and Welfare," *HEW News*, January 9, 1979.

39. See note 7, above.

which should be kept partly or wholly outside the system and opened to limited or full development—were completed, accepted by the secretary of agriculture, and forwarded to Congress by the president for required legislative action. To assure maximum public participation in the formulation of the plans, which had the close attention of both commercial and environmental interests, the service set up special procedures to invite, facilitate, and process comments by everybody concerned. More than a third of a million were received and taken into account in the formulation of the Forest Service recommendations. In the climate of the times, the procedures may have been virtually compulsory rather than the elective decision of the chief in office at the time. Yet there can be little doubt that McGuire, by lending his support to them, broadened the scope of public participation and its weight in the final recommendations.

Chiefs also influenced the rate of advance toward equal employment opportunity in their agencies. Commissioner Chasen placed heavy emphasis on progress in this area by the Customs Service, and he appointed the first black regional commissioner in the history of the bureau. In the Forest Service, where progress in the past had not been notable, Chief McGuire built up the equal opportunity staff, and his successor, Max Peterson, dramatized his commitment to improving the record when, at a meeting of top officers of the headquarters and field organizations, he warned one of them who seemed to be resisting that either the officer would do better or his successor would. One could argue plausibly that no chiefs in the social environment of the day could have ignored prevailing trends and pressures. And there is no denying that things change slowly in the bureaus despite such efforts by the chiefs. But determined statements and actions by the top officials at least moved the program from a back burner to a front one. After years of inaction and indifference, that must be reckoned no small accomplishment.

This list of indications that the chiefs did exert influence on the course and character of their organizations despite the currents that swept them along is illustrative, not exhaustive. Another observer might come up with a different inventory. It might be longer or shorter. But there would certainly be some kind of list. There is no denying that the chiefs had some influence on organizational tone and prestige and on agendas and decisions.

CONTINUITIES

Yet their influence should not be overestimated. As I have noted repeatedly, there is no way of demonstrating conclusively that achievements completed during the tenure of a given chief would not have been completed regardless of who assumed the leadership. The decisions and actions of organizations are end products of long processes, not discrete and instantaneous events.

When a long process initiated by a predecessor comes to a head, the chief in office is seldom inclined to scrap the whole operation. A large investment of time and money cannot be lightly sent down the drain. Also, rejection of the painstaking work of the permanent work force would be an expression of no confidence in them, if not of outright contempt. Furthermore, working out an alternative might take as long as it did to formulate the original, and the alternative might not be different after all the interests involved in the planning were accommodated. Rejecting the result of such a process entails high costs. It is not done casually.

Consequently, developments during a chief's term should not be construed as necessarily having originated with that chief. Each chief is the beneficiary (or sometimes the victim) of processes begun by his predecessor, and each chief starts processes that bear fruit in the administrations of his successors. These continuities must be borne in mind in evaluating the effects of a given incumbent on his organization.

Even in the FDA under Commissioner Kennedy, these carry-overs could be seen. Although the bill reforming drug regulation fashioned under his leadership certainly bore his imprint, it was not an isolated product. A long history of legislative ferment preceded it. The 1906 law had been enacted after a quarter century of debate in which more than a hundred pieces of proposed legislation were considered. The stream of bills and the debate continued afterward, too, resulting in significant amendments from time to time. In the 1970s the introduction of bills affecting the FDA accelerated, increasing not only in absolute terms, but as a proportion of all bills introduced in Congress on all subjects.[40] Pressure for change was obviously building. It did

40. *FDA Annual Report, Fiscal Year 1978,* preprint copy, pp. 2, 4–5, 15.

not originate with Kennedy, and the substance of the legislative proposals drafted under him was not forged entirely in his two years of service. By the same token, if they are ever enacted, his successors will benefit from his efforts.

The same is true of administrative initiatives of the FDA in this period. In its annual report for 1978, for instance, listed among the agency's accomplishments for the year were new regulations on labeling fats and oils and diet foods; an initial decision by an administrative law judge on cyclamates; a tentative order on protein diet products; a final rule on classification of medical devices; and the approval of a new preservative extending the shelf life of human blood for transfusion. These actions, however, were for the most part not the results of work done exclusively during Kennedy's term of office; the inquiries leading up to them began earlier. He helped move them along to realization, but they were already in the pipeline.

The same observation applies to the IRS. Creation of the office of ombudsman was the outcome of a process begun in previous administrations, brought to completion by Commissioner Kurtz but not initiated by him. And some of the studies under way in his term (but not for the most part started by him) on the improvement and simplification of tax forms and instructions to taxpayers, measurement of compliance with tax laws, exploration of new technologies (such as new ways to use computers and optical scanners), and revision of organization and procedures will undoubtedly continue to result in decisions and actions although he has left office.

In short, evidence ostensibly demonstrating the influence of bureau chiefs is often more ambiguous than it seems at first glance. The continuing functions of their organizations shape much of what the organizations do even when it looks as though the officials are prime causal agents.

And discontinuities, too, are often due to other causes. The very missions of the bureaus, for example, fluctuate according to the dictates of Congress, the president, and the department heads. Thus major programs once in the SSA—unemployment insurance and medicare—were removed from it; others—supplemental security income and aid to the victims of black lung disease—were added to its responsibilities; and still others—certain social services—were assigned to it, taken away, and then returned. The FDA, in one seven-year interval, had two functions transferred away—household product safety and pesticides surveillance—and five assigned to it—radiological health, biologics, toxicological research, medical devices and diagnostic products, and monitoring of bioresearch (premarket testing of regulated products of biological origin) in nonclinical laboratories. Alcohol, tobacco, and firearms taxation and regulation were removed from the IRS. At one time APHIS was temporarily in charge of meat and poultry inspection for the purpose of consumer protection. The Forest Service has a hand in a number of human resource programs in addition to its programs in natural resource management. As these words were written, administration of the statutory bans on the dumping of foreign products in this country was shifted from the Customs Service to the U.S. trade representative.[41] Every bureau has thus been subjected to sudden expansions and contractions of its duties by legislative, presidential, and secretarial actions in which the chiefs were merely one among many factors. At the same time, each of the bureaus was in charge of a distinctive core program defining its identity and character, and this it never lost.[42] Its other programs, even if they were large, were still subsidiary. The core program was the hallmark, the sine qua non. And it was not significantly manipulatable by the chiefs.

In the SSA it was old age, survivors, and disability insurance. In the IRS it was administration of the income tax. In the FDA it was protection against impure and unsafe foods, drugs, and cosmetics. In APHIS it was protection of plant and animal production from diseases and pests. In the Forest Service it was forest protection, management, and research. In Customs it was the collection of duties on imported products. Other activities might come and go, but not these. These *were* the bureaus.

The core programs were highly stable. Nothing is utterly immutable; they varied a little from year to year, usually expanding with economic growth, population increase, inflation, and technological developments. But wide swings were unusual. The programs went on steadily for the most part, changing gradually.

Compared to these massive continuities, the changes wrought by the chiefs I observed were diminutive. Consider the activities de-

41. "International Trade Functions," Executive Order of the President no. 12188, January 2, 1980.
42. Morton H. Halperin calls this the "organizational essence"; *Bureaucratic Politics and Foreign Policy* (Brookings Institution, 1974), p. 28.

scribed in appendix B. At this stage of the SSA's development, for example, the number of social-insurance beneficiaries served, the amounts of money disbursed to them by the agency, the flow of claims, appeals from decisions, and requests for information and aid, the opening of new accounts for people entering the labor force, and the number (113 million) of previously established accounts are unlikely to be much changed by what a particular commissioner does during his term of office. Even reduced error rates and tighter procedures in welfare programs administered by the SSA, on which Commissioner Ross and his recent predecessors concentrated their attention under congressional prodding, are not likely to change expenditures by more than a fraction of a percent.

Similarly, the tax collections by the IRS, the number of returns received, the audits and inspections, the investigations, and the appeals and protests by taxpayers, as well as all the other work of the service, would be roughly the same under any commissioner of internal revenue, the effect of whose personal wishes on these totals is barely discernible.

And the FDA's inspections, examinations, and chemical analyses are not substantially increased or decreased by the food and drug commissioner's actions. Even the disposition of applications for permission to market substances under FDA controls, a comparatively small number of items, will be changed only slightly by different commissioners.

So, too, with Customs policing and collections; Forest Service timber sales, grazing permits, recreational visits, and other services and sources of revenue, not to mention its research programs; and APHIS surveys, inspections, spraying, licensing, and research. The scale of these operations is not fixed by the bureau chiefs, and the decisions and actions of the chiefs usually do not visibly impinge on it during the chiefs' periods of service. Other factors, mostly beyond the influence of the chiefs, have greater effects.

The chiefs thus work at the margins of their agencies' operations. The gross organizational effort of each bureau, by which I mean all the activities of its members and all the materials and services produced by their endeavors, maintain the same broad contours through changes in leadership. If the broad contours change, the chiefs' labors are apt to have played a smaller part than other causes in bringing the change about. But the core programs are usually not very malleable, even under greater pressure.

The continuities in the lives of the bureaus, then, far outweigh the changes traceable to the chiefs while they are in office. The carry-over from one leader to another is sizable because the changes that do occur are the outcome of lengthy processes. The changes are like dents in a mountain. The mountain endures despite them.

Perhaps things would be different in new agencies embarking on new programs or in an agency whose chief serves for decades as its leader. On the basis of my observations, however, and under the conditions I found, I am forced to conclude that the continuities over-shadow what the chiefs can accomplish.

THE QUESTION OF AUTONOMY

If you think of autonomy as the ability to do whatever you want regardless of what other people want, the chiefs in this study obviously did not attain it. Their personal wishes—even their deeply held convictions about the public good—too often had to give way to factors they could not control, including the demands of other people inside and outside their organizations, and the changes they could accomplish were too circumscribed, to warrant calling them autonomous.[43]

Even if you define autonomy more narrowly as the ability of chiefs and bureaus to bargain as equals with all those trying to tell them what to do, they were not autonomous. Congress clearly had the upper hand in dealing with them, and many other constraints on them sprang from that relationship.

Nor were they autonomous in the sense that James Q. Wilson uses the term—"An agency is autonomous to the degree it can act independently of some or all of the groups that have the authority to constrain it"[44]—because at one time or another, and to one extent or another, they bowed to virtually all the groups with authority over them; the web of constraints was extremely confining.

43. But the reader should be aware that at least one expert on the Forest Service, Glen O. Robinson, would disagree vehemently with this judgment. In *The Forest Service: A Study in Public Land Management* (Johns Hopkins University Press, 1975), he asserted that, even in a system where all large bureaus are quite autonomous, "the Forest Service does seem to enjoy an autonomy unique in the federal bureaucracy" (p. 22). For the reasons presented in this section, I find the allegation of autonomy and uniqueness too strongly put.

44. *The Investigators: Managing FBI and Narcotics Agents* (Basic Books, 1978), p. 165.

Maybe the chiefs *wanted* autonomy. Maybe, as Wilson contends, they would have preferred, if forced to make such choices, autonomy to more money, more power, more personnel for their bureaus. Such choices rarely had to be made. And in the only instances I came across, the choices were not unequivocal. Both involved the IRS. In one case[45] the commissioner acceded to requests by his enforcement officers that they not be placed under the direct command of officials of Treasury and other departments in a campaign against narcotics smuggling and dealing; the issue, however, was more important to the subordinates than to the chief, who functioned as their representative rather than as champion of bureau autonomy. The other case was the commissioner's indifference, if not opposition, to a bill twice introduced to remove the IRS from the Department of the Treasury and make it separate and independent.[46] Theoretically, one might have thought a bureau chief who prized bureau autonomy above all else would have been pleased by the measure, even an instigator of it. In practice, however, more independence might have meant less autonomy; the sponsor of the bill complained explicitly that Treasury hampered the committee's access to, and presumably influence over, the decisionmaking processes of the IRS, and the purpose of "liberating" the bureau was to make it more responsive to the committee. The commissioner's attitude was governed in part by the permissiveness of Treasury as contrasted with what could be expected of the committee.[47] So Wilson's assessment of chiefs' values does get some support from the evidence here, even though the courses of action to which the values led were not always what one would infer.[48]

45. See p. 85, above.

46. *Foreign Tax Credits Claimed by U.S. Petroleum Companies*, Hearings before a subcommittee of the House Committee on Government Operations, 95 Cong. 1 sess. (GPO, 1977), p. 394; and *Foreign Tax Credits Claimed by U.S. Petroleum Companies*, H. Rept. 95-1240, 95 Cong. 2 sess. (GPO, 1978), recommendation 1(d), p. 4.

47. See p. 187, below. In any event, the bill stood no chance of enactment; it was mostly a means of serving notice on the IRS that the committee was displeased with Treasury. Under the circumstances, had the commissioner backed it, he would have incurred the wrath of the department and the administration to no purpose.

48. Wilson's contention gets still more support in Eugene Lewis, *Public Entrepreneurship: Toward a Theory of Bureaucratic Political Power: The Organizational Lives of Hyman Rickover, J. Edgar Hoover, and Robert Moses* (Indiana University Press, 1980).

On the other hand, there was one case in which a bureau chief opposed discretion others were trying to thrust upon him and his agency. The majority of the members of a panel of the National Academy of Sciences, responding to a congressional request for advice on what to do about carcinogenic food additives, proposed that the FDA be permitted to calculate the costs and benefits, in both health and economic terms, of each additive and to devise an appropriate strategy, ranging from total bans through restrictions on sales and requirement of warning labels to no controls at all, adapted to each case. Commissioner Kennedy demurred. Congress, he insisted, should balance the competing values, decide among health risks, and set weights for economic factors and such philosophical considerations as the worth of a human life. Then it should promulgate its decisions in specific, binding, legislative guidelines for the FDA. Otherwise, he reasoned, the FDA commissioner would become the main target of political pressure from interests favoring and opposing each additive. While he might be able to play them off against each other, effect his own bargains, and often impose his own will, thereby achieving a substantial measure of autonomy, the personal and political costs of such a role impressed him as excessive and distracting. He therefore wanted conflicts of this magnitude to be resolved in the legislative arena, where both the constitutional responsibility and the appropriate mechanisms for resolution were lodged, not in an administrative body. Visible discretion was the last thing he sought; he preferred to be told explicitly what to do.[49]

In short, the chiefs were not confronted by hosts of occasions on which the autonomy of their agencies was clearly at stake, and they did not opt for greater autonomy on every such occasion. Furthermore, autonomy for them seemed to mean securing a place for their bureaus under less exacting taskmasters, not the attainment of freedom to do all they wished. Loosening bonds, however, is not precisely what most of us mean by achieving autonomy.

The power of Congress was the predominant factor in their situation; the influence of other groups on the administrators derived from the central position of Congress in the system. That makes the

49. Elizabeth Wehr, "Saccharin Debate Heats Up as Congress' Delay on Ban Nears Expiration," *Congressional Quarterly* (March 10, 1979), p. 415; and Richard D. Lyons, "Scientists Seek Added Efficiency to End Confusion in Food Laws," *New York Times*, March 3, 1979.

administrators' reputation for independence all the more puzzling, especially since members of Congress themselves appear to believe in it. The puzzle cries out for explanation.

Congress's Preeminence[50]

The instruments with which Congress can punish—or, for that matter, reward—the behavior of bureau chiefs are familiar to all students of government and need not be rehearsed here. Legislation, appropriations, investigations, hearings connected with these functions or with the search for information, and vetoes of the administrative regulations of some agencies make up an awesome arsenal. They can be used with the discrimination of a stiletto or the explosive power of a bomb, and this flexibility rescues the legislature from the immobilism of too small a weapon to be a credible threat and too devastating a weapon to employ for any but the most drastic confrontations.

Congress can theoretically repeal the enabling legislation giving an agency life and authority, transfer all its powers to a different agency, or reduce its appropriations to zero, but the consequences of such extremism for the many innocent people who have come to depend on the agency are too painful to contemplate. Few chiefs are motivated by the fear that their bureaus will be abolished overnight.

However, Congress can write a specific mandate or prohibition or authorization into a law, or reduce the funds available for a particular program or part of a program, or inquire into an individual action. Such things happen all the time, as in the congressional denial to the IRS of authority to lift the tax exemption of private schools deemed to have racially segregated student bodies, the "Delaney amendment" banning the use of any substance in food if it were found to cause cancer in animals, and the grant of permission

50. Arthur A. Maass, in *Muddy Waters: The Army Engineers and the Nation's Rivers* (Harvard University Press, 1951), and J. Leiper Freeman, in *The Political Process: Executive Bureau–Legislative Committee Relations*, rev. ed. (Random House, 1965), also commented on the preeminence of Congress through its subdivisions. David B. Truman spoke of "formal, 'vertical' responsibility to the president and actual, 'horizontal' control by elements in the Congress"; *The Governmental Process* (Knopf, 1951), p. 410. This study confirms the impressions of all of them and indicates that (as Truman declared, p. 415) the phenomenon is not confined to the bureaus they examined. (It does not follow, however, that they would necessarily agree with my discussion of bureau autonomy in all respects.)

to the Forest Service to continue clear-cutting in the national forests according to congressionally specified guidelines. A body that can be so selective in the application of its great power cannot be ignored or flouted. All of the chiefs I watched were alert to the moods of Congress, sensitive to the attitudes of their committees, and careful not to give offense even when demands could not be fully met. So were the chiefs' staffs. No other external group or institution enjoyed quite so commanding a position as Congress.

Nongovernmental pressure groups, spokesmen for state and local governments, the media, and even the general public can influence bureaus and bureau chiefs mostly because they carry weight in Congress and Congress has such power over the agencies. These interests can do little to or for the agencies directly. But they can help them or hurt them in Congress, and the well-being of the agencies rests mostly with Congress. Thence come the incentives for the administrators to serve, listen to, court, and conciliate outside interests, and to plead or bargain with them to lobby and testify when necessary. Otherwise, the administrators might be disposed to heed them only as a matter of courtesy, and experience indicates that this is a slender reed for petitioners to depend on.

Members of Congress are motivated to heed interest groups by their constitutional and moral obligations to act as representatives and by their dependence on contributions of money, time, energy, and ultimately votes to electoral campaigns. The president is, too, but his constituency is so vast and diverse that he can attend to only a few claims, which often means those made by organizations with large memberships and large resources. Senators and representatives, with their smaller, more homogeneous constituencies, are accessible to lesser claimants as well, and the short terms of the representatives compel them especially to keep their political fences at home in good repair as well as to hear lobbyists in Washington. What they learn from listening to all these sources forms their attitudes toward administrative agencies, among other things. That is why bureau leaders devote themselves so assiduously to cultivating external support, reducing external opposition and criticism, and establishing as favorable a public image as they can manage; they want Congress to hear good reports about them. Were there no elected Congress, their behavior would surely be very different. "Autonomous" is therefore hardly the way to characterize them.

Since Congress is a microcosm of the nation, one might reason that being beholden to Congress is tantamount to having a free hand because the elements within the legislature can be played off against one another. The committee system militates against this strategy. Congress as a whole usually defers to the interests and expertise of its committees as a way of dividing labor, accommodating the special concerns of its members, and preventing every issue from having to be thrashed out on the floors of the two chambers. Ordinarily the members of one committee do not challenge the actions of another committee lest that set off a chain reaction of challenges. Consequently, Congress is, for a bureau chief, the committees with jurisdiction over his agency. The chance to play interests off against one another, while not entirely lacking in this more circumscribed arena, is severely restricted. Thus inside the legislative branch, as in the governmental system generally, the discretion of the chiefs is contained. None of the six in this study, at any rate, no matter how clever in strategy, could go his own way autonomously.

That does not mean the relationships between the chiefs and Congress were one-way streets. Members of Congress and their staffs have been known to defer to the judgment of the leaders of the agencies, accepting their reports and recommendations despite competing pressures from other quarters; influence ran in both directions. But the relationships were not symmetrical. Congress could rarely be led by the chiefs if it was strongly unwilling; the reverse was not equally true. Congress's displeasure therefore was not risked often or casually by the chiefs, and its favor and respect were diligently nurtured.[51]

The Hierarchical Ideal

Curiously, the responsiveness of the chiefs and their staffs to Congress, which diminishes their autonomy, is the very quality that creates the impression in some quarters of high autonomy. The explanation is simple: the lateral relationships with the legislative branch do not conform to the pattern of authority relationships pre-

51. So carefully were relations with Congress tended, said one of the chiefs, that he "could pick up the phone and find out more in ten minutes about what was going on on the Hill than the current White House staff could in a week."

scribed by the hierarchical ideal. The ideal hierarchy is a schematic diagram of what some people think the authority structure of an organization should be. It calls for all authority to flow from a chief executive to his immediate subordinates, who are few in number and controlled by their single superior. Each of them, in turn, is supposed to control a limited number of subordinates, and so on down to the level below which there are no subordinates—the familiar pyramid of authority with the chief executive at the apex, exerting his will throughout the organization.

No organization fits this scheme.[52] Everybody knows it is a vision, a mental construct, not a description of reality. Yet the idea is so firmly implanted in our culture that people give it lip service despite its conflict with the facts of organizational life. As a result, all sorts of arguments have been advanced to reconcile the ideal and reality. They are sometimes intricate.[53]

Nevertheless, some people apparently would like to shape the executive branch of the federal government, at least the regular executive departments, into the traditional pyramid with the president at the apex and with hierarchical directives unequivocally outweighing all other influences on everybody in it. They seek in a sense to restrict the flow of authority to vertical channels and reduce or eliminate the lateral contacts that induce officials in the system to respond to other instructions, demands, and requests. (In this spirit, one recent cabinet officer prohibited "meetings, calls or staff contacts" on a number of subjects between her subordinates and members of Congress, congressional staff, White House staff, and the Office of Management and Budget, unless approved by her or her assistant secretary for legislation,[54] and another secretary forbade informal

52. Herbert Kaufman and David Seidman, "The Morphology of Organizations," *Administrative Science Quarterly*, vol. 15 (December 1970), pp. 439–51.

53. For example, see Herbert A. Simon, Donald W. Smithburg, and Victor A. Thompson, *Public Administration* (Knopf, 1950), pp. 283–91.

54. Howie Kurtz, *Washington Star*, September 1, 1979. Admittedly, this example may have been a special case because the cabinet officer in question, Patricia Harris, had just taken over as secretary of health, education, and welfare from Joseph A. Califano, Jr., whose resignation the president had sought, and most of the top departmental officers and aides were not of her choosing. On the other hand, she justified the action by asserting that it was a way of ensuring that only authorized representatives of the department would present its views, which suggested something more than an ephemeral concern.

visits to the Hill by bureau personnel.) Deviations from hierarchy are regarded as undesirable, if not improper; hierarchy, in this view, must prevail.

In the American system of government, it obviously cannot. The preeminence of Congress, the diffusion of power in Congress, and the influence these conditions confer on groups outside the federal government thrust too hard in the other direction. At the same time, the presidential establishment and department heads and their staffs are preoccupied with matters other than the work of individual bureaus under them, for reasons discussed in the next chapter. The bureaus are thus not targets of a steady stream of directives, guidelines, and oversight from those above them in the administrative structure.[55] If they seem more receptive to other sources of influence, part of the explanation is that the other sources are in close, almost continuous contact—making demands, offering advice, and monitoring the responses. And with the power of Congress behind them, they cannot be ignored.

What is more, the interests of the secretaries of the departments do not always coincide with the interests of the president. The secretaries therefore do not always behave like extensions of the president's will. They may sometimes be more closely identified, in fact, with some of the bureaus under them than with their own superior, let alone with his staff aides. So the chain of command coming down from the chief executive to the bureau chiefs is not necessarily straight and clear; the bureau chiefs' administrative superiors are not a monolithic group.[56]

If hierarchy is your ideal, these violations of its precepts may seem intolerable. All those officials running around reaching accommodations with all those people not in the administrative pyramid are seen as out of control, autonomous, anarchic. Never mind that they are forced by their circumstances to do things they would not freely choose to do if they really had their own way. Never mind that some

55. This finding coincides with the observation by Francis E. Rourke that "inattention on the part of other actors or participants in policy-making" was a source of bureau discretion; *Bureaucracy, Politics, and Public Policy*, 2d ed. (Little, Brown, 1976), pp. 182–83. See also pp. 184–90, below.

56. The differences within the group are as evident to those who stress the "natural" alliances among its members as to those who emphasize the "natural" enmities. See Harold Seidman, *Politics, Position, and Power: The Dynamics of Federal Organization*, 3d ed. (Oxford University Press, 1980), pp. 84–87.

of their own cherished initiatives are blocked. Never mind that they often feel trapped by the overriding need to avoid disruptions of their agencies' routines at almost any cost. They do not behave in accord with the principles of idealized hierarchy. To some commentators, that means autonomy. But only to those who cleave to this single, narrow criterion.

Et Tu, Congress?

How does it happen, then, that members of Congress are among the most vehement complainers about the autonomy of the bureaus? You would not expect *them* to measure bureaucratic compliance by hierarchical standards. Only if bureaus were to disregard Congress and respond solely to *administrative* superiors would you expect Congress to denounce their autonomy. Why they should do so when the bureaus are so sensitive to congressional wishes is puzzling.

Answering this question takes me beyond my data into the realm of conjecture, for Congress was not the main subject of my research. All I can offer is hypotheses. But the congressional criticism is so contrary to expectation that it should not be left unexamined even if the explanations are conjectural.

Many conjectures suggest themselves.

1. When individual members of Congress denounce the autonomy of bureaus, they often seem to have in mind bureaus under the jurisdiction of committees other than their own. They are apt to be protective of "their" bureaus, even urging them to seek more money and personnel than were allowed them in the budget and previous appropriations. For example, the chairman of a subcommittee of the House Committee on Appropriations, reviewing the budget request of the Customs Service, declared:

> I am not in disagreement with you in wanting all prudence and efficiency and tightening up of the lines we can possibly justify. Our subcommittee's thrust has been in that direction at all times. But we also should not get carried away with budgeting to the point where we become penny-wise and pound-foolish and you are one of the major revenue raising agencies of our government.
>
> At a time when we are running an enormous deficit, common sense would tell you we need to be collecting every legitimate dollar we possibly can and not weakening our ability to do so. . . .
>
> Sometimes, after all of these years, I am getting the feeling there is some-

body in the Office of Management and Budget that is carrying on an endless vendetta against the U.S. Customs Service. We have tried and tried and tried to equip you with the tools we thought you needed, only to find somebody that we can't face, we never get to eyeball these geniuses that decide you don't know what you were talking about. . . .

This is efficiency? I just want you to understand that I am not appointed to defend Customs, but I think in the national interest we have to be concerned about whether you are going to be able to do this job.[57]

Similarly, a producer-oriented legislator is apt to consider a vigorous environmental- or consumer-protection agency as a wild-running burden on business that Congress never meant to impose, but the agency may simply be complying with the wishes of its own committees. By the same token, a legislator for whom the environment or consumer protection are paramount values will regard as rebellious an agency responsive to committees that give greater weight to production. Within any committee, a member holding minority views may be irritated by an agency's receptivity to the policies of the majority.

"Autonomous" therefore does not mean "independent" in this context; it means under the control of someone other than the accuser. That is a far cry from being a free agent.

The more responsive a bureau and its chief are to the wishes of a committee, and the better their reputations, the more ardent the committee's defense of the bureau against attacks will be. Such defensiveness is sometimes construed as the agency's adroitness in manipulating the committee. There may well be such cases. But the congressional partner in these alliances is likely to be the stronger one. If a committee rises to the defense of the agency, it is probably because the agency, by its performance and its docility, has found its way into the good graces of the committee and not because the committee is a tool of the administrators.

Agencies could probably achieve a high degree of independence if they could shop around and place themselves under the jurisdiction of a committee they liked. The jurisdiction of committees, however, is not decided by agencies. It is set by congressional politics. When committees and agencies display a community of interest and

57. *Treasury, Postal Service, and General Government Appropriations for Fiscal Year 1980*, Hearings before a subcommittee of the House Committee on Appropriations, 96 Cong. 1 sess. (GPO, 1979), pt. 1, pp. 204–05. See other examples on pp. 104–05 and 106, above.

philosophy, therefore, the agency probably defers to the committee more often than the committee bows to the agency. They doubtless learn from each other, but they are not equal partners.

The frustration of members of Congress when they cannot make particular agencies do particular things at particular times is genuine and deep, and it is easy to empathize with their anger. But when they describe the behavior of the agencies as uncontrolled, self-directing, and autonomous, their rhetoric must usually be construed as hyperbole provoked by their ire, or perhaps even as efforts to intimidate the agencies into complying with congressional demands of all kinds.

2. Legislation sometimes has consequences unanticipated and unwanted by its sponsors. Unintended authorizations and prohibitions slip into its provisions. People find loopholes. Provisions turn out to be ambiguous—sometimes by accident, sometimes by legislative design.[58] Administration proves to cost more than Congress is willing to appropriate. The projected effects are miscalculated.

For legislators to concede openly that they themselves may be the cause of these problems is not unheard of. But it is not common, either. People usually have a blind spot for the defects in their brainchildren. Consequently, when things go wrong with a program, it is natural for its sponsors to conclude that the administrators are at fault, that they are ruining the program by excessive or insufficient zeal, by extreme literalness or failure to adhere to the letter of the law, by laxness in enforcement or unreasonable severity. The administrators undoubtedly are at fault some of the time, in all these ways, but they are also convenient and plausible scapegoats on whom to put the blame for deficiencies that the authors of legislation would like to evade responsibility for.

3. What legislators request of an administrative official is usually special consideration for a constituent or an interest. The administrator, citing the legal, political, and practical constraints on him and his agency, often protests that he cannot satisfy such requests. Many legislators are disposed to perceive a refusal on these grounds as arrogant disregard of the representative body. They tend to assume that the criteria for administrative decisions are not as precise as the

58. See p. 163, above. When Congress is pressed to do something about a problem that it does not know how to solve or that is amenable only to politically controversial solutions, it may demand administrative action without giving clear guidelines—and reserve the right to criticize whatever action is taken by the agency.

administrators say they are in such cases—or that they have been more flexibly administered in practice than the administrators pretend when they do not want to be cooperative. A conscientious administrative officer may provoke an attack on his alleged autonomy by holding doggedly to legislatively prescribed, publicly announced standards, and the attack will be all the more vehement if the record shows that he ever departed from them to do someone a personal or political favor.

4. A legislator who is ideologically opposed to big government in general, or even to a particular governmental activity, may find it politically risky to condemn the substance of individual programs. The beneficiaries are sure to resent such criticism, especially if the criticism casts doubt on the propriety of the benefits. Condemning the way a strongly supported program is *administered,* on the other hand, tarnishes the program without incurring equal political risks; even beneficiaries will have had some unhappy bureaucratic experiences, and nobody outside an agency is against shrinking the work force without reducing the output. So some congressional pronouncements about unresponsive, irresponsible, autonomous administrators are probably oblique assaults on what they do rather than on how they do it. (In such cases, the better they do it, the more bitter the assaults.)

5. People do not write their senators and representatives to compliment agencies; they usually write to complain. The members of Congress know this, of course, and probably make due allowance for the inherent bias in their mail. They are also aware that many of the complaints stem not from poor or improper administration, but from impeccable execution of the law as Congress decreed. Still, they would be more than human if the constant bombardment with negative communications did not influence their perceptions and opinions, obscuring the pains administrators take to accommodate the legislative branch.

Administrative agencies are by no means always and everywhere innocent of the charges against them. The object of this argument is not to exonerate them; it is to explain how it happens that members of Congress are among those who lament the unresponsiveness of bureaus when Congress is the most prominent and powerful of all the influences on them. Legislators do indeed have incentives to join this chorus despite the deference of the administrators to the legislative body and its subdivisions and organs.

PERSPECTIVES

If you seek swift gratification of all your aspirations for your organization, you clearly will be well advised not to become the chief of one of the bureaus in this study, despite all the alleged power and autonomy the job is said to confer on the incumbent. If you dream of imposing your will on a broad area of public policy, shaping it to your wishes, this is not the position for you. If you need assurance that your labors will work enduring changes on policy or administrative behavior, you would do well to look elsewhere.

For, in the short run, the only perceptible changes are likely to be small compared to the continuities, your contribution to them will be so mingled with the contributions of others that you will have trouble identifying it and reconciling yourself to the final product, and you will never be sure that what you have worked on will last beyond your tenure.

The rewards of being chief of an established bureau thus are not staggering. But the job does have its satisfactions. In the first place, improving the morale and reputation of an organization makes life pleasanter for its members. As long as the improvement lasts, even if it is only for the duration of the chief's tenure, an executive can take pride in the achievement.

Second, improvements in service can ease the burdens on clients and reduce their aggravation and frustration. Rectifying an injustice to a single person, taking one step toward more equitable administration, or preventing one unnecessary hardship can be most satisfying for anyone who prizes the individual as much as the collectivity.

Third, lending support to policies one favors and arguing against those one opposes may not carry the day but may influence others, who influence still others, and thereby play an indistinguishable yet helpful part in producing an outcome more to one's liking than might otherwise have been the case. Because of their position, bureau chiefs are apt to have larger and more frequent opportunities of this kind than they would have had as private citizens.

Fourth, in large operations, small effects often aggregate into large ones. For example:

A 0.5 percent error in a checking account with a $100 balance translates into 0.50 cents [sic]. That is hardly an amount any of us would agonize over in an attempt to correct. Yet that same error rate applied to the $100 billion RSDI [retirement (old age), survivors, and disability insurance] program leaves us with an unacceptable $500 million.[59]

Fifth, actions hardly noticeable when they are taken may be the start of significant developments in the long run. They may launch—or stop—a process whose end no one can foresee. A modest move may later be regarded as the planting of an important seed or as the suppression of a mischievous tendency before it could gain a footing.

In short, being a chief is gratifying only for those who derive pleasure from accomplishments on a small scale and from the chance that some of these small accomplishments may lead to larger benefits in the future. The chiefs are like the rest of us. They live in faith and hope about the effect of their endeavors, not in certainty, their prominent positions and official authority notwithstanding. They certainly do calculate and negotiate to accomplish all they can. But they make their marks in inches, not miles, and only as others allow.

Although it is risky to extrapolate findings from a small, selected group of executives, I have no reason to assume that the modest incremental accomplishments characteristic of bureau chiefs set them apart from other executives. On the contrary, there are indications that even their administrative superiors experience similar limitations,[60] and some commentators have argued that the president himself, in domestic affairs, is frustratingly constrained.[61] The bureau chiefs in this study may, at least to the extent that their achievements are ordinarily on a small scale, be more or less typical of public officials in the federal system, perhaps of public officials everywhere, and perhaps even of all executives. One should not assume they are a unique breed.

If the chiefs in this study are not a unique set of federal executives, their administrative situation and behavior invite a fresh look at some of the tenets of public administration and at some of the practices and policies that proceed from these premises.

59. *Administrative Integrity of the Social Security Program*, Hearing before the Subcommittee on Social Security of the Senate Committee on Finance, 96 Cong. 1 sess. (GPO, 1979), p. 27.

60. Hugh Heclo, *A Government of Strangers: Executive Politics in Washington* (Brookings Institution, 1977).

61. Thomas E. Cronin, *The State of the Presidency*, 2d ed. (Little, Brown, 1980), pp. 150–53, 332–40.

CHAPTER FIVE

Inferences and Speculations

DRAWING inferences from the kinds of facts collected here is an uncertain art. Different people looking at these data may well find different lessons in them, even if they agree about the validity of the data. Some of their inferences might therefore contradict others, and what one analyst might consider a major implication could strike another as trivial. The further one moves from the observations, the greater the uncertainties. So I approach the search for implications warily.

That does not mean, however, that the data contain no larger indications at all. On the contrary, if my impressions are accurate, three sets of lessons are strongly suggested here: one about qualities to look for or develop in chiefs, one about organizing the federal administrative establishment, and one about administrative theory generally.

IMPLICATIONS FOR THE PERSONAL QUALITIES OF CHIEFS

If you distinguish the personal qualities you think you would *like* a bureau chief (or other public servant) to have from those you think he *needs* on the job, you would probably come up with two very different lists. The first would sound like a description of an ideal Boy Scout.[1] The other would sound like Machiavelli's prince.

1. David T. Stanley, "The Quality of Senior Management in Governments in the United States," Working Paper for the National Academy of Public Administration (Washington, D.C.: NAPA, 1979), pp. 6–8; and John J. Corson and R. Shale Paul, *Men Near the Top* (Johns Hopkins Press, 1966), pp. 43–60.

For people want their public officials to be intelligent, informed, industrious, honest, considerate, articulate, helpful, and public-spirited, and to possess all the other virtues of a wise, decent, hard-working, and creative human being. But people *suspect* that they need to be ruthless, aggressive, zealous, a little shady, cunning, cal-culating, and tough—exemplars of the practice of Byzantine politics —if they are to conduct their programs and administer their agencies (not to mention advance their careers) effectively.

Most would probably applaud a blend of these traits. Gentleness and forcefulness. Idealism and pragmatism. Softness and hardness. I think people would say they want a little of each—now more of one, perhaps, now more of the other, but enough of a balance in the individual leader to give him the advantages of each as required— and to permit each tendency to check the other and thus save him from extremism of either kind. Too much of either can render him ineffective.

A nebulous ideal, however, is neither a useful criterion for select-ing executives nor a helpful guide to understanding their work. Indeed, I believe one learns more from four specific attributes that seldom make the lists. Ability to switch from one topic to another quickly and easily, patience, self-restraint, and skill at interrogation, to judge from the experience of the chiefs in this study, are especially and almost continuously valuable to bureau executives. This fact alone indicates a great deal about what the chiefs' job is like.

A Juggler's Disposition

Some people do not function well when they have to shift their minds back and forth among different, widely disparate matters in rapid-fire order. They are at their best if they can stay with a single, coherent set of tasks until they complete it and then move to another. For them, dealing with things in sequence is the optimal pattern.

There are some, on the other hand, for whom dealing with many things simultaneously is more congenial. They find it stimulating and exciting to keep many balls in the air at once. Doing one thing at a time bores them.

The job of the bureau chief imposes a simultaneous rather than a sequential mode of life on the incumbents. Things come at them all at once, not in single file. Their days are splintered. They may go from an issue of national policy to the problem of a single employee, from an intense struggle over substance to a light-hearted ceremony, from giving testimony at a legislative hearing to receiving a presentation by an interest group or staff. The most constant characteristics of their work are its diversity, fragmentation, and velocity.

Nobody of a sequential disposition would be happy as a bureau chief. Most such persons would probably be overwhelmed by the work. Some would become bottlenecks throttling the flow; others would become ciphers isolated from the flow. The organizations would continue to function, but in the narrow areas in which the chiefs have an effect—organizational tone, prestige, and the order and timing of certain decisions and actions—the consequences would be detrimental rather than constructive or even neutral.

For appointing officers weighing the qualifications of candidates for the position of chief, for potential appointees assessing their own qualifications, and for programs intended to prepare people for such offices, tolerance for taking on a variety of chores simultaneously should therefore be a prime consideration. It certainly belongs on any list of executive qualities, for it is likely to prove more useful than either the Boy Scout or the Machiavellian roster.

Patience

The same is true of ordinary patience. Management doctrine stresses the desirability and techniques of control and change. After all, people turn to instruction in management to learn how to make things happen, so it has been contrived to answer their need. The qualities of a leader are therefore described in terms of action, aggressiveness, dynamism. Less is made of the patience that a government leader needs in abundance if he is not to be devastated by frustration.

The frustration stems not only from the limits on what a chief can accomplish, but from a number of other things as well. His time is not his own, and while he can bargain a little over the precise timing of meetings and hearings requested by his superiors or Congress or even by his staff, his schedule is shaped in large part by their demands and needs, and by the demands of outside groups as well. These can be exasperating when they interfere with other things he would rather concentrate on, particularly if the requirements are repetitive and ritualistic, but prudence and strategy dictate that he suppress his irritation and try to accommodate the claimants with good humor.

Furthermore, every chief is aware that events over which he has no control may overturn measures that he has slowly and painfully advanced, or wipe out gains won at great cost. A swing in the birth or death rate, for instance, or in the business cycle, an advance in chemistry or medicine or communications or transportation or computer capabilities, the appearance of a new virus, or a shift in public opinion or attitudes or fashions or in the political fortunes and prospects of various individuals and factions in public life, will impinge on one or several of the bureaus in this study more heavily than any factor a chief can manipulate. All his labors are, in a sense, as a leaf in the wind. People must all adjust to the impact of independent variables in their lives; public officials are not alone in this. But their high positions can create exaggerated expectations. It takes special patience to stick to your last when you know that what is possible is so much less than people anticipate and so far short of what you know is needed.

It also takes special patience to show deference to people with power who do not inspire admiration or, occasionally, even respect. Sometimes people with such power badger the chiefs simply to demonstrate who has the upper hand. Sometimes they demand special privileges that are costly, inequitable, or of questionable propriety. Sometimes they are so uninformed about the programs over which they have power that they must be given special courses to educate them in the basics. They turn up in almost all parts of the political system—the executive branch, the legislative branch, the communications media, the interest groups, and even the judicial branch in its activist manifestations.

To be sure, all of us encounter such people in our personal lives. We do not tell most of them off because the personal costs of giving vent to our resentment would be so high. The chiefs in this study, however, had alternative career opportunities—often more remunerative and of equal status. For them to put up amiably with arrogance, affronts, ignorance, and stupidity on behalf of their organizations took extraordinary equanimity. Anybody lacking the patience for such behavior would be wise to avoid a position of agency leadership in government.

Self-Control

These positions call for still another form of tolerance—the capacity to resist the impulse to meddle with things that are going reasonably well. As every physician knows, trying to make things better can make things worse,[2] and even when things *are* improved by executive intervention, the *net* improvement may be small when costs are put into the equations. An executive who responds enthusiastically to the apparent injunctions of management doctrines, with their bias toward demonstrating control and command by active manipulation of organizational features and processes, runs the risk of disrupting smooth-running routines, stirring up antagonism, and generating anxiety without producing enough benefits to justify the turmoil. Indeed, the net result may be merely to exchange one set of problems for another. Sometimes all these costs are worth incurring, but leaders need the self-restraint to hold back until the reasons to believe this is the case are quite strong.

Some schools of business administration warn their graduates not to yield to the temptation to try to remake organizations the instant they arrive on the scene. Such self-control could well be added to the attributes recommended for high government executives.

Interrogatory Skills

Proficiency in conducting interrogations might also be added. A bureau chief, it will be remembered, spends most of his time receiving and reviewing information. To do so effectively calls for adroitness in putting questions, assessing replies, discerning gaps and inconsistencies, distinguishing soft from hard evidence, and sensing what has been withheld or designed to deflect a line of inquiry. It takes a solid foundation of knowledge to interrogate well. It also requires skill and sensitivity. Few other talents stand a chief in better stead.

This is not to say that chiefs are typically in adversary situations when they seek or receive intelligence. But those who provide them

2. The word for it is "iatrogenic" disorders, ailments (often imaginary) induced by a physician. See also Lewis Thomas, *The Lives of a Cell* (Viking, 1974), pp. 81–86.

with information do not share the perspectives of the chiefs and may therefore furnish less balanced or complete pictures than the chiefs require. Much of the information supplied by specialists takes for granted premises about the subjects and about the world generally with which a chief might not agree if the assumptions were made explicit. And "vested interest in an idea" can bias a well-intentioned presentation. Some subordinates, mindful of the fabled fate of messengers who brought bad tidings to the king or hoping to curry favor by telling their superiors what they think they want to hear, report only cheerful, encouraging news no matter what the facts are. It is up to an executive to detect such deficiencies if he wants information he can depend on. For this, he must be able to question sharply.

Sharp questioning demands personal security because a chief who engages in it frequently exposes his limitations. Leaders might understandably worry, after all, about undermining their authority if they revealed themselves to be less informed and sophisticated than those they examine. Yet specialized subordinates, from whom so much intelligence comes to the chiefs, inevitably know more about their areas of expertise than the chiefs do. In interrogating the experts, the chiefs often disclose gaps in their own knowledge, unfamiliarity with basics, and difficulty with technical language. At times, they have to put naive queries or ask for simpler explanations of matters the specialists seem to take it for granted they understand. A chief may sometimes be the only one in a room having difficulty with a concept or an argument or a position that the technicians seem to grasp easily and agree on. Social psychologists have demonstrated how hard it is for many individuals to stand up to such pressure.[3] But if a chief is inclined to forgo challenging interrogation to avoid exposing his shortcomings, the information on which he spends so much of his time becomes unreliable. He pays a high cost for his insecurity.

Skill at interrogation, self-restraint, patience, and aptitude for quick changeover from task to task are not the only qualities from which a bureau chief benefits. Even if they could be identified before appointments are made, they should not be the exclusive criteria of judgment. But they are so pertinent to what bureau chiefs do from day to day that the character of the chiefs' work can hardly be appreciated without recognizing them. Many of the commonly recom-

3. Gardner Lindzey and Elliot Aronson, *The Handbook of Social Psychology,* 2d ed. (Addison-Wesley, 1969), vol. 3, pp. 608–09.

mended qualities, of both the Boy Scout and the Machiavellian varieties, would be helpful anywhere. These four, however, are of special value to high government executives—if the case of the bureau chiefs is typical of those officials.

IMPLICATIONS FOR RESTRUCTURING
THE FEDERAL ADMINISTRATIVE SYSTEM

The behavior of the bureau chiefs in this study also points, at another level of generalization, to reasons for the intractability of some managerial problems afflicting the executive branch generally and the departments in particular that organizational and procedural manipulation has been unable to solve. Certain problems have been remarkably persistent despite generations of experimentation with remedies. In the light of the predicament and activities of the bureau chiefs, it is clear why the problems have resisted correction.

The War for Control of Administration

In the preceding chapter, I observed that the congressional set of influences on the bureaus and the bureau chiefs is the strongest single set and that this helps make unattainable the hierarchical ideal, which envisions a neat administrative pyramid dominated by the president. Congress's constitutional power by itself, however, would not nullify the hierarchical goals of putting the chief executive, through his cabinet, in undisputed charge. Congress's determination to *use* its power to contest the assumption that the administrative machinery of the government belongs to the president via the secretaries is as important as the constitutional provisions. Without the constitutional provisions, it is true, Congress might have a more difficult time asserting its power. But without its resolute will to control administration, the constitutional provisions would be empty rhetoric.

The struggle between the branches of government over the administrative agencies has probably been more intense in recent generations than in the early years of the republic because the size, cost, and powers of the agencies have reached massive proportions. But it is nothing new: it can be traced to the battles between the king and

Parliament in England. For a time kings built up Parliament to free themselves from dependence on feudal barons for the wherewithal to govern, but Parliament eventually turned the king's ministers into its own agents, serving at its pleasure. Its victory over the king was complete. In this country, the independently elected chief executive has not only remained an autonomous political force, but has even expanded his political role. Nevertheless, his efforts to assert mastery over the machinery of administration encountered the same sort of legislative aggressiveness that Parliament exhibited, so the war goes on unabated.

In this century Congress made some notable concessions to the doctrines of executive leadership. The adoption of executive budgeting, the expansion of the Executive Office of the President, the grant to the president of authority to reorganize (even thought it is subject to veto by Congress and to other restrictions), and the broadening of the powers of the secretaries over their departments were all steps toward increased presidential or secretarial control of administration. But the chiefs still seem to find Congress more important for their own and their bureaus' survival and success. The concessions by Congress did not diminish its influence (which may be why it was willing to make them).

Congress has vigorously reasserted its power over administration in recent years. "The trend toward executive branch dominance in the budgetary process was arrested with the passage of the Congressional Budget and Impoundment Control Act of 1974, which restored to Congress some of the power over budget making it had lost and provided it with better means and greater responsibility for controlling the budget."[4] New emphasis on legislative oversight is an expression of its firmness, and it has also applied the legislative veto to more and more areas of administration. Agitation for sweeping "sunset" legislation, providing for the automatic termination of agencies unless continued by positive action by Congress, is another symptom of its sentiments. Congress obviously is not inclined to yield an inch and, in fact, seems ready to expand its authority wherever it can. Under these conditions, reorganizing the executive branch does little to change the orientation of the bureaus and their leaders.

One authority on public administration, Harold Seidman, there-

4. David J. Ott and Attiat F. Ott, *Federal Budget Policy*, 3d ed. (Brookings Institution, 1977), p. 24.

fore concluded that rationalizing the executive branch and executive departments can be achieved only if legislative and administrative organization are brought into line with each other. He did not mean that they should be identical. But, he declared, "congressional organization and executive branch organization are interrelated and constitute two halves of a single system. . . . If the government is to function effectively, congressional organization . . . must be compatible with that of the executive branch."[5]

Perhaps such mutual realignments would have beneficial results. If so, enhancing the influence of the president and the secretaries on the bureaus would not necessarily be among them. On the contrary, a closer fit between the branches might further strengthen the links between agencies and their legislative counterparts. Parallel structures would not help *executive* leadership.

One thing that might strengthen the vertical channels of influence relative to the lateral ones would be renunciation by Congress of its lines to subdivisions of the departments. If Congress dealt with the bureaus only through the departments, the departments would enjoy much greater authority over the bureaus than they now have. Bureau chiefs are spared some of the frustration of the department heads partly because Congress does not establish ties with the chiefs' subordinates the way it does with the secretaries' subordinates. Comparable legislative self-denial at the department level would alter relationships inside the executive branch far more than any reorganization could.

There is little reason to expect such self-restraint from Congress. Its institutional rivalry with the president is enough to discourage voluntary relinquishment of any implement of power. It would also be under pressure from other participants in the governmental system to hold its ground; since interest groups exert influence on agencies because of their leverage on Congress, they would doubtless perceive a diminution of congressional activism as a reduction in their own influence. Groups and individuals who get a more sympathetic hearing from Congress than they think they do from the executive branch would be especially upset. Even people with no immediate stake in the situation might be uneasy about the possible effects on the traditional checks and balances in the American sys-

5. Harold Seidman, *Politics, Position, and Power: The Dynamics of Federal Organization*, 3d ed. (Oxford University Press, 1980), pp. 40, 71.

tem. So Congress would be pushed to preserve its role in administration even if its institutional position did not motivate it to do so.

Yet congressional self-restraint would do much more than structural reform to relieve many of the ailments afflicting the administrative system. As Seidman cogently argued, most structural attacks on administrative problems do not get far because they do not apply to congressional behavior. The correctives have been focused on the wrong factor.

Missing Links

Structural rearrangements do not seem to touch another of the factors shaping the behavior of the bureau chiefs: the meagerness of direction from above. I referred to this in the preceding chapter as a reason to doubt the allegation that chiefs are deliberately recalcitrant, reasoning that nobody can properly be accused of deviousness and disobedience if he gets few orders to evade and resist. On the same grounds, putting great faith in administrative reorganization as a means to better administration is a mistake; if commanders do not command, changing structure will make little difference in the behavior of subordinates.

If I am right in thinking that the secretaries and their aides, with some exceptions,[6] do not ride close herd on the bureau chiefs, this state of affairs demands explanation. Students and practitioners of public administration have been calling for more aggressive departmental leadership for years and have secured increases in the secretaries' formal authority and in the size of their staffs to produce it. Why, then, does it remain so rare?

One possible answer is that the powers of secretaries, despite their growth over the years, remain inadequate. The secretary of the treasury at the time this study was undertaken, W. Michael Blumenthal, contrasted the tools he had as a corporation president with those at his disposal as cabinet officer, and concluded that in the latter capac-

6. Joseph A. Califano, Jr., secretary of health, education, and welfare at the time of this study, was one of the exceptions; he paid more attention to the bureaus in his department, and intervened more in their affairs, than secretaries usually do. Commissioners Stanford Ross and Donald Kennedy were apparently reminded of his interest and concern relatively frequently. Nevertheless, even his supervision was intermittent and, what is more, resulted partly from their conscientiousness in keeping him informed about their operations and clearing actions with him.

ity, "even though I'm technically the chief executive of the Treasury, I have little real power, effective power, to influence how the thing functions."[7] The constraints on his office left him feeling helpless and exasperated.[8]

Another common hypothesis is that the secretaries' span of control has been exceeded by the accretion of programs and bureaus in the departments as the role of government in American society grows. There certainly is reason to believe that the secretaries' attention is more splintered now than it was only a few generations ago.[9] Attempts to relieve their burdens by multiplying assistance evidently have not succeeded; according to Seidman, there is still "a vacuum within the departmental management systems which has never been satisfactorily filled."[10] Creating more staff aides and offices may have added to the fragmentation of the secretaries' energies instead of relieving it. The office of under secretary does not seem to have solved the problem, either. And even introducing new layers of line assistant secretaries between the secretaries and the bureau chiefs[11] has not necessarily improved the situation; "steepening" the administrative "pyramid" has increased the distance between the department heads and their agency executives, reducing the unity and sense of common purpose in the departments. Overtaxed span of control must therefore be regarded as a highly plausible contributory factor to the feebleness of secretarial influence on the bureau chiefs.

Others have been suggested, too. Personal weakness of department heads is one of these. Seidman thinks many secretaries are unqualified for their posts. They "rarely bring to their jobs the unique combination of political insight, administrative skill, leadership, intelligence, and creativity required for the successful management of heterogeneous institutions with multiple and sometimes conflicting

7. W. Michael Blumenthal, "Candid Reflections of a Businessman in Washington," *Fortune* (January 29, 1979), p. 39.

8. The growth of the Office of Management and Budget's power over the last twenty years, commented one of the chiefs, is a factor in this frustration. He declared that the OMB's authority over "(1) programs through line-item decisions on budgets, (2) the administration's positions on pending legislation, and (3) personnel ceilings for individual agencies has given OMB more control over individual agencies than either the secretary or any of his assistants."

9. Herbert Kaufman, *Are Government Organizations Immortal?* (Brookings Institution, 1976), pp. 34–41.

10. *Politics, Position, and Power*, p. 323.

11. Ibid.

purposes," he contends.[12] Similarly, a task force on departmental management working for the first Hoover Commission felt obliged to warn: "Department heads must have the courage to assert their leadership. No amount of staff assistance, and no increase in legal authority, can be a complete substitute for personal courage and determination on the part of the Secretary himself."[13] Presumably the task force took the trouble to point out this need because it was not always met. In this, it echoed the judgment of one of Woodrow Wilson's cabinet officers that "the average head of a department is not highly competent and has not first-rate executive ability."[14] "His conclusion," added a foremost student of the cabinet, Richard F. Fenno, "is a common one."[15] It was certainly consistent with the opinion of Leonard D. White, author of the first textbook on public administration, who said in the fourth edition of that book three decades later, "The previous experience of federal Secretaries does not usually prepare them to exercise quick and effective leadership."[16] This is not to say that department leaders have no impact whatsoever; they could and did affect the bureaus in this study by both formal and informal means. Nevertheless, taking their overall performance into account, informed observers have repeatedly put on them much of the onus for the asserted deficiencies in departmental coordination and cohesiveness.

But sometimes noninterference is a deliberate decision of a secretary rather than a result of external factors governing his behavior; he may choose to keep his distance from an agency in his department. Thus, Commissioner Jerome Kurtz reported, Treasury Secretary Blumenthal elected to stay out of the work of the Internal Revenue Service on the grounds that his involvement would have adversely affected both him and the bureau. It would have damaged him by exposing him to innumerable political demands by individual and corporate taxpayers for favorable tax rulings, and it would have damaged the agency by injecting inappropriate political pressure

12. Ibid., p. 322.

13. U.S. Commission on Organization of the Executive Branch, Task Force on Departmental Management, *Departmental Management in Federal Administration,* prepared for the commission (Government Printing Office, 1949), p. 18.

14. David F. Houston, who was secretary of agriculture from 1913 to 1920 and secretary of the treasury from 1920 to 1921, quoted in Richard F. Fenno, Jr., *The President's Cabinet* (Harvard University Press, 1959), p. 221.

15. Ibid.

16. *Introduction to the Study of Public Administration,* 4th ed. (Macmillan, 1955), p. 80.

into a traditionally professional, nonpartisan operation. The secretary's policy was made explicit before Kurtz accepted the appointment to the IRS and constituted an understanding between the two officials. Blumenthal's nonintervention was a calculated strategy, not an accident of circumstance, an unplanned side effect of other decisions, or a concession extracted from him.

The hiatus between departments and bureaus has also been attributed to Congress. A former secretary of health, education, and welfare lamented that "some elements in Congress . . . have never really wanted the departmental secretaries to be strong," and have therefore resisted efforts to strengthen them.[17] Seidman agrees: "Congress does not concede . . . that a secretary's right to reign over a department necessarily carries with it the power to rule."[18] "Anything other than a passive approach is likely to encounter opposition from the Congress, which believes that major bureaus should be allowed to run themselves without undue secretarial interference."[19]

Finally, the priority of presidential demands and national policy issues over departmental administration has been offered as an explanation for the weakness of secretarial direction of bureaus. For example, a recent secretary of the treasury observed:

> I remember asking a former Secretary of the Treasury years ago, when I never dreamed that I would be in his job: Why don't you do something about the U.S. Customs Service? Why don't you do something about what I saw as the excessive number of customs agents going through bags, on the grounds that they're unlikely to catch much that way? If you want to catch people who smuggle in drugs or dangerous weapons, you have to do it a different way, perhaps with spot checks and not by going through people's individual bags. And he shrugged his shoulders and said, I have no time for that. And I thought to myself, if I were ever in a position of authority, I really would want to do something about that, because as a citizen coming through the U.S. Customs, I always resented that kind of thing, comparing it to Europe.
>
> Now that I'm the Secretary, I realize what he meant, and I haven't done anything about it, because I've spent my time working with the President and my Cabinet colleagues on things that are more important, like economic policy.[20]

17. John W. Gardner, testifying before the Senate Committee on Government Operations in 1971, as quoted in James W. Fesler, *Public Administration: Theory and Practice* (Prentice-Hall, 1980), p. 71.

18. *Politics, Position, and Power,* p. 62.

19. Ibid., p. 322.

20. Blumenthal, "Candid Reflections," p. 40.

He was not alone in his frustration. Fenno reported that cabinet officer after cabinet officer voiced similar sentiments about the competing demands of departmental management and participation in presidential policy councils. "If he wishes to help the President by rendering him good departmental administration, he must focus his energies downward into the department. But as he provides this kind of . . . assistance . . . he cannot lift up his head often enough to look at things from a government-wide, i.e., presidential, standpoint."[21] Most decide it is more important to keep their heads lifted. Similarly, the Hoover Commission task force, after proclaiming that "department heads can provide the vital elements of both political and administrative leadership for Government operations" and that "the administrative duties of the department head are today possibly more important than his political duties," admitted that no secretary could perform both functions himself: "The external demands upon a Secretary are such that he needs a strong person to give continuing attention to internal problems."[22] For the secretaries, policy comes first, and those who decide otherwise regretfully discover that they have "become sucked in and submerged by routine or detail or immediacy."[23]

The choice by the secretaries is easy to understand. Taking part in presidential decisions is exciting and gratifying. It is also an obligation to the chief executive and a social responsibility. It must be much more rewarding than running a department.

Anyway, the element of choice may be very small. Secretaries can hardly decline a summons by the president. Congress, other departments, interest groups, and the communications media pull relentlessly at their time. Their own staffs make claims on them. They are torn by innumerable demands. Giving direction to individual bureaus and bureau chiefs is seldom at the head of the secretaries' lists of things needing attention.

Nor do their aides and lieutenants redress the balance. Explaining why would require an empirical study of administrative behavior at the departmental level. One proposed reason is that the aides and lieutenants are drawn into formulating and promoting legislative

21. Fenno, *The President's Cabinet*, p. 230.
22. *Departmental Management in Federal Administration*, pp. 1, 2, 11.
23. Fenno, *The President's Cabinet*, p. 230.

proposals and into other high-level negotiations that distract them from overseeing their bureaus just as such duties distract their bosses:

Some had thought that their chief function would be to supervise their subordinate units and were amazed to find that they were expected to operate at the highest policy-making levels, involving not only the top staff of their own department or agency but also White House officials and representatives of foreign governments. One Eisenhower Assistant Secretary of Commerce, for example, found that . . . he was deeply involved in international negotiations which brought him into contact with officials in the State Department, the Department of Agriculture, and the White House.[24]

Another hypothesis offers the opposite explanation—the assistant secretaries are so divorced from the secretaries that they feel isolated and useless, without philosophical or policy guidance, and therefore unable properly to lead the segments of their respective departments under their jurisdiction.[25]

Still another hypothesis is that the short tenure of assistant secretaries renders them hesitant, even if they have had government experience in other positions before taking their current posts, to second-guess career experts in the bureaus.[26]

Whatever the reasons, however, the secretaries' assistants tend to behave in much the same fashion as the secretaries themselves, so that oversight of the bureaus remains far from the top priority of the departmental level.[27]

Since I saw the secretarial level only from the perspective of the bureaus, I am in no position to judge whether overextended spans of control, lack of managerial talent among cabinet officers, congres-

24. Dean E. Mann and Jameson W. Doig, *The Assistant Secretaries: Problems and Processes of Appointment* (Brookings Institution, 1965), p. 211.

25. Ibid., p. 212.

26. Ibid., pp. 6–7, 227–31; and Hugh Heclo, *A Government of Strangers: Executive Politics in Washington* (Brookings Institution, 1977), pp. 103–05, 170–80, 187–92.

27. Only one of the chiefs took exception to this description of the relations between the departments and the bureaus, contending that, in his case, "the Department has exercised detailed direction and control over agency functions," especially as the number of assistant secretaries and of departmental staff officers increased. Peculiarly, however, his bureau was frequently identified as one of the more highly autonomous bureaus in the federal government. I was not in a position to judge conclusively whether the department in this case was tightening supervision, giving rise to his feeling that his organization was severely reined in, or whether his tolerance for departmental intervention was narrower than average. My impression was that departmental supervision of his agency was no tighter than that of any other.

sional hostility toward departmental control of bureaus, or pressure on the secretaries and their aides to concentrate on responsibilities other than departmental administration constitutes the best explanation of the insubstantiality of departmental direction of the bureaus. Probably all of them contribute. For that reason, reorganizing the executive branch or the department does not by itself result in any striking changes in administrative behavior.

IMPLICATIONS FOR THEORY

All in all, the administrative system of the federal government, seen in its entirety from the standpoint of bureau headquarters, is something of an enigma. On the one hand, it is strikingly decentralized. The familiar triadic clusters of congressional committees, bureaus, and interest groups in each program area jointly enjoy great influence over the programs with which they are connected.[28] Congress as a whole defers to the committees; the administrative superiors of the bureaus exercise light supervision of their charges; the interest groups are free agents. Thus only weak forces pull the parts together, but strong forces pull them apart. One would expect little unity or consistency.

On the other hand, no part of the system can act without the cooperation, or at least the acquiescence, of other parts, and this forms an intricate network of relationships confining all the constituent elements. Programs intersect at innumerable points, and staff functions cut across each other and all line operations in comparable profusion. Hardly anything can be done anywhere that does not quickly involve other agencies, committees, and interest groups in sister triadic clusters, giving rise to the familiar lament that the business of the government is much more interdepartmental than departmental, and generating the innumerable interagency committees that continue to spring up despite everybody's condemnation of them. Crosscutting jurisdictions keep the self-containment of the individual administrative organizations, and even of the triadic clusters of which they are components, at a low level.

These two aspects of the federal administrative system are not

28. J. Leiper Freeman, *The Political Process: Executive Bureau–Legislative Committee Relations,* rev. ed. (Random House, 1965), pp. 22–30.

easily reconciled. How can it be flying apart if its parts are extensively interrelated?

Unfortunately, this study does not resolve the apparent contradiction. Advocates of either position can find here evidence supporting their views. What is interesting, however, is that a common theme runs through both views: the implication that the administrative system is not fully under control. Those who emphasize centrifugal tendencies ascribe the lack of control to the inability of central governmental leadership to rein in the powerful agencies and their allies. Those who stress the interdependencies of the system attribute the lack of control to rigidities resulting from the web of relationships binding each of the components and therefore the system as a whole; they see the system as resistant, if not impervious, to manipulation by its nominal masters. Thus the complaint from both schools of thought is the same, but the diagnoses, prognoses, and remedies are inevitably quite different.

The centrifugal-tendencies position dictates that central restraints on the components of the system be multiplied and intensified to overcome its disintegrative thrusts. In this view, if present trends continue unchecked, the result will be a plethora of unruly unifunctional governments with no central arena in which differences among the parts can be mediated and directed, leading to incessant conflict, confusion, ineffectiveness, and waste. The only solution, consequently, would be more controls from the center.

The systemic-stasis position suggests that there are already so many fetters on executives and their agencies that they lack the flexibility to do their jobs properly and to respond to changes in the political climate. Logically, the indicated correction would be to loosen the system a little, not to add more shackles from the top; to give agency administrators a little more leeway, not to confine them further.[29] The result allegedly would be more efficiency, effectiveness, and responsiveness to political leadership.

Fear of centrifugal tendencies had the upper hand for many years in the federal government, giving rise to the increase in the size of the

29. See, for example, Commission on Organization of the Executive Branch, *General Management of the Executive Branch,* a report to the Congress (GPO, 1949), recommendations 15, 18, and 20; and *Personnel Management,* a report to the Congress (GPO, 1949), p. 3, recommendation 2, and pp. 48–50. See also *Departmental Management in Federal Administration,* pp. 5–11.

Executive Office of the President (which did not even exist before 1939), the growth of the departmental establishments above the bureau level, the creation of new congressional organs, the agitation for sunset legislation, the elaboration of laws on administrative procedure, the extension of the congressional veto of administrative actions, and the requirement of more and more "impact" statements as a prerequisite for many different kinds of agency actions. That is, the trend has been toward expanding central checks and reviews, not toward reducing them, and toward increasing the number of signatures and approvals for every administrative measure, not toward diminishing them. Occasionally a step is taken in the other direction, as in the decentralization of certain personnel-management powers to agencies in recent years. But these are cyclical departures from a trend line headed the other way. The secular tendency in the federal administrative system has been consistent for a long time[30]—which may explain how the conditions disturbing the systemic-stasis school developed.

The trend could be a deliberate policy choice despite the alleged hazards it entails. Having assessed the risks of autonomous power centers in the system, government leaders apparently concluded they were more to be feared than paralysis. They chose the paths implied by this conclusion, producing the multiplication of controls.

According to the opposing school of thought, however, once you start on this path, you create conditions that drive the trend line up exponentially. As more constraints are imposed, rigidities fixing agencies in their established ways intensify. As a result, complaints that they do not respond to controls also intensify. Further controls, checkpoints, and clearances are therefore introduced. But these only make things worse. So more controls are developed, and the whole process spirals upward.

Moreover, vested interests develop around each new requirement, procedure, and control. The people who administer the new specifi-

---

30. Herbert A. Simon, Donald W. Smithburg, and Victor A. Thompson, *Public Administration* (Knopf, 1950), p. 272, called it "one of the most characteristic administrative trends of our age"; and a quarter of a century later, Francis E. Rourke, in *Bureaucracy, Politics, and Public Policy*, 2d ed. (Little, Brown, 1976), observed that it had continued unabated until the Watergate scandal shook faith in the formulas of an earlier era (pp. 67–68, 143–49). See also Herbert Kaufman, "Administrative Decentralization and Political Power," *Public Administration Review*, vol. 29 (January–February 1969), pp. 3–15.

cations, and people and organizations with commitments and investments based on the premise that the constraints will be maintained, vigorously resist efforts to abolish them. It is easier to go forward than to back up. A ratchet effect thus sets in and keeps the trend line from turning downward.

Logically, of course, the program of the systemic-stasis school could set off an exponential decentralizing trend. To alleviate the problems of control, theorists concerned about tendencies toward paralysis would loosen the system by lifting central controls. According to centrifugal-tendencies doctrine, this would merely aggravate control problems, whereupon the systemic-stasis people would try to improve the situation by yet another application of their standard remedy—further reduction of constraints. Meanwhile, vested interests would assemble around the decentralized processes and prevent reimposition of controls. So the trend line would head down and grow increasingly difficult to reverse.

But that has not happened in the federal administrative system. The secular trend has been continuously upward. Perhaps it was by accident that it started in this direction. Or perhaps the trend started when the cumulative effects of fragmentation created in the nineteenth century engendered a widespread consensus that greater central direction was needed, so that even Congress agreed to strengthen the president and the heads of the executive departments. Whatever started it, its self-reinforcing character kept it going; it gained momentum all through the middle quarters of the twentieth century.

Conceivably it could continue until administrative officers of the future are so enmeshed in centrally imposed constraints that they are virtually helpless. But a trend of this kind is not likely to proceed to a disastrous conclusion. If the multiplication and strengthening of central controls fail to solve the problems that give rise to them, chances are that the advocates of the opposite solution will begin to prevail long before the cataclysm occurs. The hypothesis that control can be improved by broadening administrative discretion instead of narrowing it may thus have its day in practice.

In a sense, then, an internal dynamics seems to be at work in the federal administrative system. That is, at any given time, its state engenders behavior on the part of the people in and associated with it that moves it almost irresistibly toward another state—not inevitably, perhaps, but with a high degree of probability. The inner logic apparently driving the system is, I admit, expressed through the actions, and through the wills and values, of the participants. At the same time, the actions of the participants are determined to a large degree by what they can and cannot do in their organizational context, and even their wills and values are shaped by the organizational situation in which they are immersed. The two sets of factors together help propel and steer the system. Consequently, organizations and the organizational trends and tendencies described here are not simply artifacts of the people who compose and nominally conduct them. They are governed also by their own organizational imperatives.

The idea that a system could have a life of its own, as it were, rather than merely serving human purposes and calculations clashes with many assumptions about intelligence, leadership, management, and democracy. How can anyone believe organizations are other than creations of the human mind and therefore totally subject to human direction? How can anyone lead or manage or hold them accountable if they are impelled by a dynamics inherent in their form and structure? How can anyone control them if they are partly immune to conscious manipulation and influence? The model does not sit well with some cherished beliefs.

But these do not in themselves refute the model, which is consistent with large segments of social science and organization theory. The concept of "role,"[31] for example, rests in part on evidence that the behavior of individuals conforms to the organizational situation in which they find themselves. Dramatic alterations of behavior have taken place when the location of a person in a system was changed,[32] and organization members are often said to give greater weight to organizational goals proclaimed by leaders than to their own personal goals.[33] Highly cohesive organizations may be said to implant behavioral templates, as it were, in their members—organizational perspectives and values instilled so deeply in each individual that the individuals spontaneously wish and voluntarily choose to do what

31. See Bruce J. Biddle and Edwin J. Thomas, eds., *Role Theory: Concepts and Research* (Wiley, 1966), especially chap. 1. But also see the cautionary note in Herbert A. Simon, *Administrative Behavior: A Study of Decision-Making Processes in Administrative Organization*, 3d ed. (Free Press, 1976), pp. xxxvi–xxxvii.

32. Simon, *Administrative Behavior*, p. 214, n. 20.

33. Ibid., pp. 115 and 117–18, and chaps. 10 and 12.

their organizations want of them.[34] That may be one explanation of the remarkable power of nationalism, which often induces people to risk and even sacrifice their lives for a collectivity. Leaders and followers alike are governed by these forces.

The idea that organizations are not simply implements of human intentions is consistent also with homeostatic and cybernetic models of organization behavior. If organizations are self-regulating mechanisms that tend to maintain a steady state by suppressing disturbing factors, every proponent of change—which is to say every complainer about the prevailing state of affairs—would encounter formidable resistance that few could overcome. Not even those inside the organizations could redirect things easily or extensively. That is exactly what this study found. Some theorists reason that the self-regulating character of complex organizations is precisely what makes them controllable, for it frees the controllers to concentrate on what they consider critical.[35] This is doubtless true, but it also circumscribes what they can do in the areas they consider critical. In this sense, the internal dynamics of the organizations, not the efforts of the people in, or interested in, the organizations, could be said to be determining.

This interpretation of organizations could also explain why so many people, with such a wide diversity of interests, regard government agencies—and perhaps all large organizations whether public or private—as "out of control."[36] If the organizations are truly ruled largely by their internal logic, then most people would indeed be unable to make the organizations do their bidding—perhaps only because the rate of response is inevitably too low to satisfy them, but possibly because there is frequently no response to them at all. That is, they would feel inefficacious because they are, in this sense, inefficacious. Of course, other explanations of the broad consensus on the

34. Herbert Kaufman, *The Forest Ranger: A Study in Administrative Behavior* (Johns Hopkins Press, 1960), chap. 6.

35. "If managerial systems were not basically self-regulating, it would never be possible to control them. They would generate too much variety for us to cope with"; Stafford Beer, *Decision and Control* (Wiley, 1966), pp. 417–18. See also Herbert Kaufman, *The Limits of Organizational Change* (University of Alabama Press, 1971), pp. 35–36.

36. Herbert Kaufman, "Fear of Bureaucracy: A Raging Pandemic," *Public Administration Review*, vol. 41 (January–February 1981), pp. 1–9.

intractability of government agencies are equally plausible. But this one is at least as deserving of consideration as they are.

If such an independent dynamics is at work in all large organizations—or at least in the federal administrative system—it would not justify treating as futile all efforts to influence courses of action, calling democratic control of such organizations in or out of government an idle dream, or concluding that it makes no difference whatsoever who the leaders are. Without knowing more about the dynamics, leaping to such conclusions is unwarranted. Conceivably, for instance, the organizational world could be Darwinian, with relatively fixed structural and behavioral patterns competing to survive, and with small differences in the patterns determining which ones flourish and which ones decline.[37] In that case, small effects could prove important in the long run, and maybe sooner. When so little is known, to call striving futile is presumptuous.

At the same time, we should not overestimate what we can achieve. Even if there is a dynamics at work, and even if we figure out how it works, the knowledge may not increase our control over the course of events in the foreseeable future. Improved understanding of the dynamics of evolution did not promptly allow us to manipulate its unfolding. Better knowledge of astronomy did not enable us to make the heavens do our bidding. Modern meteorology does not let us produce weather to order. Knowledge does not guarantee immediate mastery, perhaps not even eventual mastery.

But it can facilitate optimal accommodation to forces we cannot control. It helps us identify patterns in those forces, to predict their effects, and to adjust our tactics and strategies to make the best use of those patterns.

In human experience, understanding of the world we dwell in and our capacity to discover its patterns have often been linked to our willingness to acknowledge the limits of our power over that world. Knowledge may be positively associated with humility. Yet management doctrine seems to me to lean toward the position that managers can and should achieve command of their organizations and that any who do not are simply uninstructed in the "scientific principles" of the field. One of the ironies of life is that people may perform better

37. Herbert Kaufman, "The Natural History of Human Organizations," *Administration and Society*, vol. 7 (August 1975), pp. 131–49, corrected in vol. 7 (November 1975), p. 365.

if they recognize how little they can do than if they approach their tasks believing the myth that they can impose their will on the world. And correspondingly, our theories, our advice, and our research may improve when we admit how much we still have to learn instead of putting great faith in the little we already know,[38] and when we are willing to explore possibilities that at first blush seem unconventional, even bizarre.

38. For example, "the real revolution in medicine, which set the stage for antibiotics and whatever else we have in the way of effective therapy today, had already occurred one hundred years before penicillin. It did not begin with the introduction of science into medicine. That came years later. Like a good many revolutions, this one began with the destruction of dogma. It was discovered, sometime in the 1830s, that the greater part of medicine was nonsense." Lewis Thomas, *The Medusa and the Snail* (Viking, 1979), p. 159.

The Bureaus from Which the Six Were Chosen

APPLYING the definition of "bureau" set forth in chapter 1 to the domestic, civil departments of the federal executive branch as these were described in the *United States Government Manual* for 1977–78, I came up with the following list of agencies constituting the universe from which my "specimens" would be picked.

Department of Agriculture

Agricultural Marketing Service
Agricultural Research Service
Agricultural Stabilization and Conservation Service
Animal and Plant Health Inspection Service
Economic Research Service
Extension Service
Farmer Cooperative Service
Farmers Home Administration
Federal Crop Insurance Corporation
Federal Grain Inspection Service
Food and Nutrition Service
Food Safety and Quality Service
Foreign Agricultural Service
Forest Service
Packers and Stockyards Administration
Soil Conservation Service
Statistical Reporting Service

Department of Commerce

Bureau of the Census
Domestic and International Business Administration*
Economic Development Administration*
Maritime Administration*
National Bureau of Standards
National Oceanic and Atmospheric Administration
Office of Minority Business Enterprise
Patent and Trademark Office
United States Travel Service*

Department of Energy

Energy Information Administration
Energy Regulatory Administration

Department of Health, Education, and Welfare

Center for Disease Control
Food and Drug Administration
Health Care Financing Administration
Health Services Administration
Office of Education
Social Security Administration

Department of Housing and Urban Development

Because HUD's line organization was territorial, all its functional
units were essentially staff arms of the secretary. The only possible
exception would have been the federal insurance administrator,
since there were separate insuring offices in each region. But even
this exception was doubtful because the insuring offices, like the
area offices that handle all other programs, were under the jurisdiction of the regional administrators. For the purposes of this
study, therefore, HUD was regarded as having no true line bureau
chiefs comparable to the others in the project universe.

* Leader designated head *and* assistant secretary.

Department of the Interior

Alaska Power Administration
Bonneville Power Administration
Bureau of Indian Affairs
Bureau of Land Management
Bureau of Mines
Bureau of Outdoor Recreation
Bureau of Reclamation
Fish and Wildlife Service
Geological Survey
Mining Enforcement and Safety Administration
National Park Service
Southeastern Power Administration
Southwestern Power Administration

Department of Justice

Bureau of Prisons
Drug Enforcement Administration
Federal Bureau of Investigation
Federal Prisons Industries, Inc.
Immigration and Naturalization Service
Law Enforcement Assistance Administration
United States Marshals Service

Department of Labor

Bureau of Apprenticeship and Training
Bureau of Labor Statistics
Labor-Management Services Administration†
Office of Federal Contract Compliance Programs‡
Wage and Hour Division
Women's Bureau‡

Department of Transportation

Federal Aviation Administration
Federal Highway Administration

† Leader designated administrator *and* assistant secretary.
‡ Director *and* deputy assistant secretary.

Federal Railroad Administration
Materials Transportation Bureau
National Highway Traffic Safety Administration
St. Lawrence Seaway Development Corporation
United States Coast Guard
Urban Mass Transportation Administration

Department of the Treasury

Bureau of Alcohol, Tobacco, and Firearms
Bureau of Engraving and Printing[§]
Bureau of Government Financial Operations
Bureau of the Mint
Bureau of the Public Debt
Comptroller of the Currency
Federal Law Enforcement Training Center[§]
Internal Revenue Service
United States Customs Service
United States Savings Bond Division
United States Secret Service

§ May not meet field-service criterion.

Profiles of the Bureaus

THE major function of the *Social Security Administration* has always been the distribution of money to individuals made eligible by
law for specified benefits. Its responsibilities have changed during its
history; at various times, for example, it was in charge of unemployment insurance, a range of social services, and medicare, but these
were in other agencies by the time this study began. On the other
hand, federal matching grants to state and local governments for aid
to families with dependent children and some smaller maintenance
assistance programs, which had been removed from the SSA, were
returned to it in 1977. Thus at the time of this study the principal
programs under SSA jurisdiction were old age, survivors, and disability insurance ($82 billion to 33 million people in fiscal year 1977,
by far the dominant program in its charge), supplemental security
income payments to the aged, blind, and disabled ($5.3 billion to
more than 4 million people), and matching grants to state and local
governments for maintenance assistance ($6.2 billion, federal share,
for help to over 11 million people). The SSA was also involved in
administering nearly a billion dollars in benefits to victims of black
lung disease and their survivors (14,000 claims anticipated in fiscal
1978). It was therefore one of the largest agencies in the federal government, and was staffed by well over half of all the employees of
the Department of Health, Education, and Welfare.

Its largest responsibilities were handling millions of benefit claims
each year and mailing tens of millions of checks each month. Thousands of appeals from these administrative actions had to be heard
and decided. Individual records for every eligible person had to be
maintained. Applications for admission to various programs had to
be handled, requests for information, advice, and assistance satisfied,

and federally aided state-administered programs monitored. These massive operations, and all the administrative direction and support they demand, required the services of 86,000 employees at headquarters in Baltimore and in 10 regional offices, 6 service centers, and 1,300 local offices spread over the entire country, with an administrative budget of over $2 billion a year.

From 1935 to 1939 social security was administered by an independent, three-person Social Security Board. In 1939 the board was moved to the Federal Security Agency, and in 1946 it was abolished and its functions transferred to the federal security administrator. The administrator, however, promptly established the Social Security Administration under a commissioner, to whom he delegated most of the functions of the former board. These arrangements continued when the Federal Security Agency was abolished in 1953 and most of its functions and units were taken over by the newly created Department of Health, Education, and Welfare; after that, the SSA had only the powers delegated to it by the secretary of HEW, which were legally (but probably not politically) revocable in toto.

While the SSA had to manage the distribution of funds in proper amounts to qualified recipients, the *Internal Revenue Service* was engaged in bringing money into the Treasury. Besides the obvious differences in the character of the tax-collection and benefits-payment programs, the SSA was run largely as an insurance operation, and an individual account had to be maintained for each insured worker from the day he or she opened one to the day the insured and the last eligible survivors of the insured were gone; but most tax liabilities were incurred for individual years rather than cumulatively over a lifetime and therefore did not require such protracted, continuous records for each person. On the other hand, the IRS processed over 130 million primary and supplemental tax returns in 1977, including 25 million employment tax returns largely for social security old age, survivors, and disability insurance, as well as income, gift, estate, and other returns. More than $358 billion in collections passed through the agency that year. The task was certainly as enormous as the SSA's.

Forms had to be printed and distributed. Taxpayers needed interpretation of the rules, advice, and assistance in filling out the forms. Returns had to be processed. Compliance was increased by audits and investigations and legal action. Appellate procedures were provided for challenges and protests. Special arrangements were made for taxpayers residing abroad. Within the agency, the confidentiality of returns and the integrity of receipts had to be assured, and staff services furnished for the entire agency. In 1977 the IRS had over 84,000 employees—5,000 in national headquarters, the rest in seven regions (each under a regional commissioner) divided into fifty-eight districts (each under a district director) and served by ten service centers, seven regional inspectors, and seven regional counsels. It was a huge, dispersed organization with an annual operating budget in excess of $1.8 billion.

The direct ancestor of the present IRS was the Office of the Commissioner of Internal Revenue, set up in the Department of the Treasury in 1862 to collect the revenues needed to help meet the cost of the Civil War. It remained relatively small until the adoption of the Sixteenth Amendment to the Constitution in 1913 and the subsequent financial requirements of World War I. But it was World War II that introduced the modern scale of internal revenue collection and the modern agency, from which there was to be no major retreat. In 1952, following revelations of corruption in high places, a reorganization plan submitted by President Truman thoroughly reorganized the old Bureau of Internal Revenue, giving it a new name, a new structure, and new financial controls, and extending merit practices to higher levels. The separation of its Division of Alcohol, Tobacco, and Firearms, which became a bureau in the Treasury Department in 1972, was the only diminution of its responsibilities in this period. With this one noteworthy exception, the scale of its activities increased steadily from World War II on.

The *Customs Service,* like the IRS, was a revenue collector for the government but, to an even larger extent than the IRS and the other agencies in the sample, had heavy law enforcement duties, being guardian of the nation's borders against the entry and export of goods not in conformity with a number of statutes and regulations. It was responsible for enforcing hundreds of statutory provisions and thousands of Tariff Schedule requirements, both on its own behalf and on behalf of forty other federal agencies. In 1977 this meant clearing 154,000 ships, 370,000 aircraft, 77 million vehicles, and 263 million people at about 300 ports of entry; processing $150 billion worth of imported goods; collecting $6 billion in duty and taxes; and seizing $1.2 billion worth of illicit drugs, prohibited articles, and undeclared merchandise.

Doing this job required verification of 6.7 million items on 3.6 million entries, a check on more than 43 million individual factors. As in the SSA and the IRS, this called for the preparation, distribution, and processing of millions of forms; a highly dispersed staff (more than 15,000), most of whom worked in nine Customs regions divided into forty-five district offices in which are located the 300 ports of entry; some foreign field offices; a system for handling appeals from administrative decisions; and appropriate overhead and support offices. In 1977 the Customs Service's budget authority came to just under $600 million.

Although the First Congress, in 1789, provided for customs officers and collections, it was not until 1875 that a Division of Customs was set up in the Treasury Department. Organizationally and functionally, this body was the beginning of the later agency. It became the Bureau of Customs in 1927 and was redesignated the Customs Service in 1973.

Like the Customs Service, the *Food and Drug Administration* had a heavy law-enforcement component in its mission. In the broad sense, it was a regulatory agency, whose job was to protect people from unsafe and impure drugs, foods, and cosmetics, and from dangerous radiation, hazardous medical devices, environmental toxins, and similar risks. The scope of its mission varied over the years; between 1970 and 1977, for example, two functions were removed (household product safety, which went to the Consumer Product Safety Commission, and pesticides surveillance, transferred to the Environmental Protection Agency), and five (radiological health, biologics, toxicological research, medical devices and diagnostic products, and monitoring of bioresearch in nonclinical laboratories) were added. In all fields under its jurisdiction, however, it both set standards and tried to see that the standards were observed.

It performed these tasks in fiscal 1977 by conducting 32,000 inspections of establishments where regulated products are made or grown; 94,000 wharf examinations; 680,000 examinations of about 48,000 product samples; 50,000 actions on premarket review of food additives, medical devices, drugs, and biological products; 2,000 compliance and enforcement actions; and 10,000 detentions of imported product-lots. At FDA headquarters, 13,000 inquiries were received and answered, and 9,000 consumer complaints were investigated. And of course it had to assure fair procedures for affected parties, including opportunities to be heard and to challenge and to appeal. For these purposes it had a staff of 7,300, a majority of whom were in 10 regional offices, 22 district offices, 121 resident inspection posts, and the National Center for Toxicological Research. Expenditures in fiscal 1977 came to just over $250 million.

Although there had been research and some federal legislation on food and drugs before the enactment of the Food and Drug Act of 1906, regulation began in earnest when that statute took effect in 1907. The responsibility fell mainly to the Bureau of Chemistry in the Department of Agriculture, whose chief had been a driving force behind the law. In 1927 the research functions of the bureau were separated from the regulatory and enforcement activities. These, along with the regulatory and enforcement responsibilities of some other units of the department, were lodged in a newly created Food, Drug, and Insecticide Administration (renamed the Food and Drug Administration in 1931), which was set up as a separate bureau in the Department of Agriculture. It was transferred to the Federal Security Agency in 1940 and then to HEW when that department was created in 1953.

The *Animal and Plant Health Inspection Service* and the FDA were tangent to one another in several respects. The FDA had a program on animal drugs and feeds and also inspected the areas in which certain animal and human foods were grown—the former to prevent the development of antibiotic-resistant disease-causing bacteria in the course of feeding antibiotic drugs to food animals, the latter to guard against certain forms of contamination. APHIS led the battle to control or eradicate pests and diseases afflicting plants, livestock, and poultry, which often meant promoting the use of selected antibiotics and pesticides. The agencies resembled each other also in that APHIS regulated biologics used for the diagnosis, prevention, and treatment of animal diseases much as the FDA regulated biologics for use on people. Also, the responsibility of APHIS for administering laws on the humane treatment of animals could impinge on the FDA because the laws affected animals used in research as well as pet, performing, and display animals. At its inception APHIS was tangent to the FDA at other points, too, for it was charged with inspecting meat and poultry and their products to assure clean, unadulterated, accurately labeled food for consumers. In 1977, however, this duty was transferred to the newly established Food Safety and Quality Service of the Department of Agriculture.

To discharge its obligations under law, APHIS in fiscal 1978 (the first year after meat and poultry inspection was shifted) had personnel at borders and ports of entry, in every state and possession, and in several foreign countries. They treated hundreds of thousands of acres against pests, bred and released millions of sterile insects and parasites to control pest populations, and inspected 400,000 airplanes and vessels, 43 million vehicles, 110 million pieces of baggage, and 65 million mail packages. They tested 15 million samples as part of the brucellosis eradication program, which was only one of fourteen animal disease and pest control programs; there were also seventeen plant disease and pest control programs, and more than 14,000 animal-care inspections were conducted. The agency was empowered to bar or limit imports and exports and interstate transport of plants and animals not up to established standards or originating in quarantined areas, to attack pests with chemicals, to destroy animals infected with specified diseases (and to compensate the owners), to revoke or suspend licenses and accreditations where these instruments were authorized, to request the Department of Justice to institute suit against violators, and in similar ways to implement and enforce the laws within its province. Like other agencies, APHIS also had to handle appeals from and objections to its decisions and actions. It had a work force of about 4,900 in fiscal 1978 to perform these tasks; they were organized into 10 regions, 38 area offices, and 137 field offices, under which were the numerous field stations and operations. The estimated outlays for that year were just under $219 million.

APHIS was established by order of the secretary of agriculture in 1972 and reaffirmed by another order in 1977, when meat and poultry inspection was removed from it. Its functions, however, had a long history, and the programs assigned to it had been vested in a variety of other components of Agriculture before APHIS was created.

Although the *Forest Service* fought plant and tree pests and diseases as APHIS did, it was different in important respects from its sister agency in the Department of Agriculture and, indeed, from the other agencies in this sample. Its major assignment was the management of more than 187 million acres of land in the national forest system. That meant the protection and use of timber, grazing, wild-life, recreational, wilderness, water, mineral, and scenic resources. From these resources, the service brought in over $700 million to the federal treasury. It also cooperated with state and local governments and private woodlot owners to improve forestry practices beyond na-tional forest boundaries. It conducted a major forestry and forest products research program, both in its own facilities and in coopera-tion with state agricultural colleges. And it participated in human resources programs, such as the Youth Conservation Corps, the Job Corps, the Volunteers in the National Forests, the Senior Community Service Employment Program, and the Young Adult Conservation Corps.

Running such a diversity of programs in fiscal 1977 entailed 154,000 timber sales, 11.4 million animal unit-months of livestock grazing, 54,000 special-use permits, accommodating 200 million visitor-days of recreational visits, and fighting some 13,000 forest fires, not to mention maintaining roads and trails, running camps for the human resources undertakings, battling plant and tree pests and diseases as APHIS did, deterring timber and grazing trespass, and a profusion of other activities. They were carried on by over 20,000 permanent employees and almost as many part-time and temporary ones organized into 9 regional offices, 154 national forest headquar-ters, 662 ranger districts, 8 forest and range experiment stations, 81 research work locations, 17 Job Corps camps, 2 state and private forestry areas, a laboratory, and an institute of tropical forestry. The budget outlays for fiscal 1977 were almost $1.2 billion.

The Forest Service was set up in the Department of Agriculture by statute in 1905. Until then, the forest reserves had been under the Department of the Interior, but the new agency was placed in Agri-culture, to which the reserves were then transferred. Intermittently thereafter, secretaries of the interior demanded that the Forest Ser-vice and the land in its charge be returned to their department but to no avail; the name and location of the bureau has remained un-changed from the day of its creation.

APPENDIX C

Profiles of the Chiefs

STANFORD G. ROSS, forty-seven when sworn in as the seventh commissioner of social security in October 1978, came to office from nine years of private practice as a partner in a Washington law firm. He was a native of St. Louis and a graduate of Washington University in St. Louis and of Harvard Law School, where he had been editor of the law review. From 1956 to 1961 he was associated with law firms in New York and California and held a teaching fellowship at Harvard Law School. Two years as assistant tax legislative counsel in the Treasury Department followed, and then four years as professor at New York University Law School. In 1967–68 he was a White House assistant to President Lyndon B. Johnson, after which he was general counsel of the Department of Transportation. He had written, lectured on taxation, and testified as an expert witness before various congressional committees, and at the time of his nomination by President Carter in August 1978, he was chairman of the Advisory Council on Social Security. He was confirmed by the Senate in September 1978. At the end of 1979 he resigned to return to the private practice of law in Washington.

The commissioner of internal revenue at the time of this study, and the thirty-ninth in the line of succession, was Jerome Kurtz. A lawyer specializing in taxation and a certified public accountant, he was a Philadelphian with degrees from Temple University and from Harvard Law School, where he had been an editor of the law review. In June 1977, at the age of forty-six, he was sworn in by Secretary of the Treasury W. Michael Blumenthal after nomination by President Carter and confirmation by the Senate, having come from a Philadelphia law firm in which he was a partner. He had been associated with the firm for more than twenty years, with interruptions for military service in 1956–57 and for a period as the tax legislative counsel for the Department of the Treasury from 1966 to 1968, which earned him the department's Exceptional Services Award. He had also taught tax law at the Villanova and University of Pennsylvania Law Schools and was a visiting professor at Harvard University, had published articles on taxation, was chairman of the tax section of the Philadelphia Bar Association, and had testified as an expert witness on tax matters before congressional committees.

Robert E. Chasen, sixty when he was appointed U.S. commissioner of customs by Secretary of the Treasury Blumenthal in July 1977, was the eleventh to serve in that post since the Customs Service became a separate bureau in 1927. A graduate of Benjamin Franklin University in Washington, D.C., with postgraduate work at New York University and Columbia University, he started his career in 1940 as a fingerprint specialist for the Federal Bureau of Investigation, where he soon rose to special agent and where he remained until 1952. In that year he joined the International Telephone and Telegraph Corporation as coordinator of plant security and assistant to the vice-president for industrial relations, from which he advanced through a series of positions to the post of vice-president of ITT and general manager of the government and commercial services group. In those capacities, he was board chairman, president, and general manager of various companies and divisions of ITT with responsibility for operations in over thirty countries before returning to government service as commissioner.

Donald Kennedy, the ninth commissioner of food and drugs, was forty-six when appointed by Secretary of Health, Education, and Welfare Joseph A. Califano, Jr., in April 1977. A neurophysiologist with undergraduate and graduate degrees from Harvard and more than sixty articles in major scientific journals to his credit, he was the first nonphysician to occupy the position in over ten years. His career had been largely academic; he taught biology at Syracuse University from 1956 to 1960 and at Stanford University thereafter. At Stanford he was chairman of the department of biological sciences from 1965 to 1972, and both Benjamin Crocker Professor of Human Biology and chairman of the program in human biology (an interdisciplinary program focused on the institutional and scientific basis of selected public policies) from 1974 on. He was chairman of a group making a four-year study of pest control in agriculture for the National

Academy of Sciences/National Research Council, chairman of the academy's division of biology in its assembly of life sciences, and also a member of its steering committee for a world food and nutrition study and of its Institute of Medicine. In 1976 he served as senior consultant to the Office of Science and Technology Policy in the Executive Office of the President. In July 1979 he resigned to return to Stanford University as vice-president and provost, and became president the following year.

Francis J. Mulhern, at fifty-three, became the first administrator of the Animal and Plant Health Inspection Service when it was created by Secretary of Agriculture Earl L. Butz in 1972. But he had already had twenty-seven years of service in the Department of Agriculture. After military service, he earned a doctorate in veterinary medicine from Auburn University in 1945, became a field veterinarian in the old Bureau of Animal Industry, and rose steadily. He held several positions in the Mexico–United States Foot-and-Mouth Disease Eradication Program in Mexico between 1947 and 1952, and in the latter year, after brief assignments in Arizona and Canada, came to Washington to head an animal disease control program. In 1959 he was appointed assistant director of the department's Animal Disease Eradication Division, was made director two years later, became deputy administrator of the Agricultural Research Service in 1967, and associate administrator in 1970. In 1971 he was appointed acting administrator of the Animal and Plant Health Service, which, after a reassignment of functions in 1972, became the Animal and Plant Health Inspection Service with Dr. Mulhern as administrator. He served until he retired in February 1980 to become director of animal health of the Inter-American Institute for Cooperation in Agriculture.

John R. McGuire, tenth chief of the Forest Service when this study began, was a native of Milwaukee. After getting his undergraduate degree at the University of Minnesota, he received a master's degree in forestry at the Yale School of Forestry, and then served five years in the army. He joined the Forest Service in 1949, specializing in forest economics at the Northeastern Forest Experiment Station in Pennsylvania; in 1954 he earned a master's degree in economics at the University of Pennsylvania, and in 1955 became chief of the station's division of forest economic research. In 1957 he took a corresponding position in the Pacific Southwest Forest and Range Experiment Station in California, in which he served until 1962. In 1962–63 he was assigned as a staff assistant to the deputy chief for research in Washington, D.C., and then returned to the experiment station as director. In 1967 he came back to Washington as deputy chief for program planning and legislation, became associate chief in 1971, and was named chief by Secretary of Agriculture Butz on April 30, 1972, at the age of fifty-six. He retired in June 1979.

The day after McGuire retired, on July 1, 1979, R. Max Peterson, fifty-one, was appointed by Secretary of Agriculture Bob Bergland. He was a Missourian, with a civil engineering degree from the University of Missouri, who began his career in the Forest Service in 1949, working on three national forests in California in the course of the next nine years. In 1958, awarded a Rockefeller Foundation fellowship, he spent a year with the Water Resource and Land Use Planning Program at Harvard University and earned a master's degree in public administration in 1959. That was followed by a two-year assignment to the Northern Regional Office in Missoula, Montana, a five-year stint on the Administrative Management and Engineering Staffs in Washington, D.C., and, in 1966, a return to California as regional engineer. In 1971 he was made deputy regional forester for the Southern Region headquarters in Atlanta, and became regional forester in 1972. He returned to Washington as deputy chief for programs and legislation in 1974 and remained in that post until his elevation to the top job.

Bibliography

Appleby, Paul H. *Big Democracy.* New York: Knopf, 1945.

Barnard, Chester I. *The Functions of the Executive.* Cambridge: Harvard University Press, 1938.

Bendix, Reinhard. *Higher Civil Servants in American Society.* Boulder: University of Colorado Press, 1949; reprinted, Westport, Conn.: Greenwood Press, 1974.

Bernstein, Marver H. *The Job of the Federal Executive.* Washington, D.C.: Brookings Institution, 1958.

Blumenthal, W. Michael. "Candid Reflections of a Businessman in Washington," *Fortune,* January 29, 1979.

Boyer, William W. *Bureaucracy on Trial: Policy Making by Government Agencies.* Indianapolis: Bobbs-Merrill, 1964.

Carlson, Sune. *Executive Behaviour: A Study of the Work Load and the Working Methods of Managing Directors.* Stockholm: Strombergs, 1951.

Caro, Robert A. *The Power Broker: Robert Moses and the Fall of New York.* New York: Knopf, 1974.

Corson, John J. *Executives for the Federal Service.* New York: Columbia University Press, 1952.

———, and R. Shale Paul. *Men Near the Top.* Baltimore: Johns Hopkins Press, 1966.

David, Paul T., and Ross Pollock. *Executives for Government.* Washington, D.C.: Brookings Institution, 1957.

Davis, Kenneth Culp. *Administrative Law of the Seventies.* Rochester, N.Y.: Lawyers Cooperative Publishing Company, 1976.

———. *Administrative Law Treatise.* 2d ed. San Diego: K. C. Davis Publishing Company, University of San Diego, 1979.

Derthick, Martha. *Policymaking for Social Security.* Washington, D.C.: Brookings Institution, 1979.

Downs, Anthony. *Inside Bureaucracy.* Boston: Little, Brown, 1967.

Fenno, Richard F., Jr. *The President's Cabinet.* Cambridge: Harvard University Press, 1959.

Fesler, James W. *Public Administration: Theory and Practice.* Englewood Cliffs, N.J.: Prentice-Hall, 1980.

213

Fox, Harrison W., Jr., and Susan Webb Hammond. *Congressional Staffs: The Invisible Force in American Lawmaking.* New York: Free Press, 1977.

Freeman, J. Leiper. *The Political Process: Executive Bureau–Legislative Committee Relations.* Rev. ed. New York: Random House, 1965.

Gulick, Luther, and L. Urwick, eds. *Papers on the Science of Administration.* New York: Institute of Public Administration, 1937.

Halperin, Morton H. *Bureaucratic Politics and Foreign Policy.* Washington, D.C.: Brookings Institution, 1974.

Harris, Joseph P. *Congressional Control of Administration.* Washington, D.C.: Brookings Institution, 1964.

Heclo, Hugh. *A Government of Strangers: Executive Politics in Washington.* Washington, D.C.: Brookings Institution, 1977.

Held, Walter G. *Decisionmaking in the Federal Government: The Wallace S. Sayre Model.* Washington, D.C.: Brookings Institution, 1979.

Kaufman, Herbert. *Administrative Feedback: Monitoring Subordinates' Behavior.* Washington, D.C.: Brookings Institution, 1973.

———. *The Forest Ranger: A Study in Administrative Behavior.* Baltimore: Johns Hopkins Press, 1960.

———. *The Limits of Organizational Change.* University, Ala.: University of Alabama Press, 1971.

———. *Red Tape: Its Origins, Uses, and Abuses.* Washington, D.C.: Brookings Institution, 1977.

Kilpatrick, Franklin P., Milton C. Cummings, Jr., and M. Kent Jennings. *The Image of the Federal Service.* Washington, D.C.: Brookings Institution, 1964.

Kirst, Michael W. *Government Without Passing Laws.* Chapel Hill: University of North Carolina Press, 1969.

Kofmehl, Kenneth. *Professional Staffs of Congress.* 3d ed. West Lafayette, Ind.: Purdue University Press, 1977.

Kornblum, Allan N. *The Moral Hazards: Police Strategies for Honesty and Ethical Behavior.* Lexington, Mass.: Lexington Books, 1976.

Lau, Alan W., Arthur R. Newman, and Laurie A. Broedling, "The Nature of Managerial Work in the Public Sector," *Public Administration Review,* vol. 40 (September–October 1980).

Lewis, Eugene. *Public Entrepreneurship: Toward a Theory of Bureaucratic Political Power: The Organizational Lives of Hyman Rickover, J. Edgar Hoover, and Robert Moses.* Bloomington: Indiana University Press, 1980.

Maass, Arthur A. *Muddy Waters: The Army Engineers and the Nation's Rivers.* Cambridge: Harvard University Press, 1951.

McGeary, M. Nelson. *Gifford Pinchot.* Princeton: Princeton University Press, 1960.

McKinley, Charles. "Federal Administrative Pathology and the Separation of Powers," *Public Administration Review,* vol. 11 (Winter 1951).

Macmahon, Arthur W., and John D. Millett. *Federal Administrators: A Biographical Approach to the Problem of Departmental Management.* New York: Columbia University Press, 1939.

Malbin, Michael J. *Unelected Representatives: Congressional Staff and the Future of Representative Government.* New York: Basic Books, 1979.

Mann, Dean E. "The Selection of Federal Political Executives," *American Political Science Review,* vol. 58 (March 1964).

————, and Jameson W. Doig, *The Assistant Secretaries: Problems and Processes of Appointment.* Washington, D.C.: Brookings Institution, 1965.

Mintzberg, Henry. *The Nature of Managerial Work.* New York: Harper and Row, 1973.

Morgan, Robert J. *Governing Soil Conservation: Thirty Years of the New Decentralization.* Baltimore: Johns Hopkins Press, 1965.

Nienaber, Jeanne, and Aaron Wildavsky. *The Budgeting and Evaluation of Federal Recreation Programs.* New York: Basic Books, 1973.

Parnell, Archie. *Congress and the IRS: Improving the Relationship.* Washington, D.C.: Fund for Public Policy Research, 1980.

Pinchot, Gifford. *Breaking New Ground.* New York: Harcourt, Brace, 1947.

Pressman, Jeffrey L., and Aaron Wildavsky. *Implementation.* Berkeley: University of California Press, 1973.

Price, David E. *Who Makes the Laws? Creativity and Power in Senate Committees.* Cambridge: Schenkman, 1972.

Robinson, Glen O. *The Forest Service: A Study in Public Land Management.* Baltimore: Johns Hopkins University Press, 1975.

Rourke, Francis E. *Bureaucracy, Politics, and Public Policy.* 2d ed. Boston: Little, Brown, 1976.

Saxon, O. Glenn. "Tenure of Secretaries, Under Secretaries, Assistant Secretaries, and Bureau Chiefs," in U.S. Commission on Organization of the Executive Branch of the Government, *Appendices to Study of Departmental Management,* no. 1. U.S. Commission on Organization of the Executive Branch of the Government, no date.

Seidman, Harold. *Politics, Position, and Power: The Dynamics of Federal Organization.* 3d ed. New York: Oxford University Press, 1980.

Simon, Herbert A. *Administrative Behavior: A Study of Decision-Making Processes in Administrative Organization.* 3d ed. New York: Free Press, 1976.

————, Donald W. Smithburg, and Victor A. Thompson. *Public Administration.* New York: Knopf, 1950.

Smith, Michael E. "Bureau Chiefs in the Federal Government, 1958," *Public Policy, 1960.* Harvard University, Graduate School of Public Administration, 1960.

Sproull, Lee Sonastine. "Managerial Attention in New Education Programs: A Micro-Behavioral Study of Program Implementation." Ph.D. dissertation, Stanford University, 1977.

Stanley, David T. *The Higher Civil Service: An Evaluation of Federal Personnel Practices.* Washington, D.C.: Brookings Institution, 1964.

————. "The Quality of Senior Management in Governments in the United States." Working Paper for the National Academy of Public Administration. Washington, D.C.: NAPA, 1979.

————, Dean E. Mann, and Jameson W. Doig. *Men Who Govern: A Biographical Profile of Federal Political Executives.* Washington, D.C.: Brookings Institution, 1967.

Stewart, Rosemary. *Managers and Their Jobs: A Study of the Similarities and Differences in the Ways Managers Spend Their Time.* London: Macmillan, 1967.

Terrell, John Upton. *The Man Who Rediscovered America: A Biography of John Wesley Powell.* New York: Weybright and Talley, 1969.

Thomas, William C., Jr. "Generalist versus Specialist: Careers in a Municipal Bureaucracy," *Public Administration Review,* vol. 21 (Winter 1961).

U.S. Commission on Organization of the Executive Branch of the Government. *General Management of the Executive Branch.* A Report to the Congress. Washington, D.C.: Government Printing Office, 1949.

————. Task Force on Departmental Management. *Management in Federal Administration.* Prepared for the commission. Washington, D.C.: Government Printing Office, 1949.

U.S. Customs Service. Department of the Treasury. *Customs U.S.A.* A special edition of *Customs Today* on the activities of the U.S. Customs Service for fiscal year 1978. Washington, D.C.: 1978.

U.S. Department of Health, Education, and Welfare. Review Panel on New Drug Regulation. *Investigation of Allegations Relating to the Bureau of Drugs, Food and Drug Administration.* Washington, D.C.: Department of Health, Education, and Welfare, 1977.

Warner, W. Lloyd, Paul P. Van Riper, Norman H. Martin, and Orvis F. Collins. *The American Federal Executive.* New Haven: Yale University Press, 1963.

White, Leonard D. *Introduction to the Study of Public Administration.* 4th ed. New York: Macmillan, 1955.

Wildavsky, Aaron. *The Politics of the Budgetary Process.* 3d ed. Boston: Little, Brown, 1979.

Wilson, James Q. *The Investigators: Managing FBI and Narcotics Agents.* New York: Basic Books, 1978.

Index

Administrative Procedure Act, 96
Administrative regulations: governmentwide, 98–102; departmental and bureau, 108–12
Agendas. *See* Bureau agendas
Agriculture, Department of, 7, 63
Altmeyer, Arthur, 123n
American Federation of Government Employees, 112
Animal and Plant Health Inspection Service (APHIS), 7, 8; and Congress, 50, 104; emergency situations, 130, 131; and foreign governments, 74, 75; information dissemination, 67; and interest groups, 70; labor-management contract, 112; laws affecting, 94; line of appeal, 39; and Office of Technology Assessment, 55; personnel, 118; policy continuity, 159, 160; published regulations, 110, 111; relations with sister agencies, 63; and state governments, 73; training programs, 120
Anton, Thomas J., 116n
Aronson, Elliott, 83n, 180n
Autonomy, bureau, 9, 161–72

Ball, Robert M., 123n, 151, 152
Baucus, Max, 80n
Beer, Stafford, 195n
Bernstein, Marver H., 3n
Biddle, Bruce J., 194n
Blumenthal, W. Michael, 184–85, 186–87
Boffey, Philip M., 3n
Boyer, William W., 47n
Briefings of bureau chiefs, 33–39; for congressional testimony, 37, 51
Budget, federal: constraints on bureaus, 124–25; OMB guidelines, 58, 101; zero-based, 101
Bureau agendas, 124–33

Bureau chiefs: allocation of time, 19, 45, 77–78, 86, 87–89; and bureau prestige, 144–49; command, 86–87; and communications media, 26, 27, 35, 71–72; constraints on, 91; coordination by, 86–87; department heads and, 3, 59–62, 184–88; and equal employment opportunity, 156; factors influencing, 134–38; functions, 17, 86, 88–90; importance, 1, 2; job satisfaction, 173–74; length of service, 9, 122–23, 133–34; limitations of data on, 13–15; organizational tone set by, 140–44; personal qualities, 175–81; policy decisions, 149–56; research observations on, 10–12; sample for study, 4–5, 7–10
Bureau of Land Management, 63
Bureaus: defined, 5–7; selection of, 7–10. *See also* Bureau agendas; Bureau chiefs; External relations, bureau; Personnel, bureau; Programmed work behavior; specific bureaus

Califano, Joseph A., Jr., 167n, 184n
Campbell, Rita Ricardo, 141n
Cardwell, James B., 150, 152n
Carlson, Sune, 33n
Cartwright, Dorwin, 83n
Centrifugal tendencies in administrative system, 190, 191–92, 193
Chasen, Robert E., 13, 22, 148, 154
Church, Frank, 106
Clientele, bureau, 66–71
Cohen, Wilbur J., 151
Cohn, Victor, 142n
Command, 86–87
Commission on Organization of the Executive Branch of the Government. *See* Hoover Commission